Vagrants and Vagabonds

Early American Places is a collaborative project of the University of Georgia Press, New York University Press, Northern Illinois University Press, and the University of Nebraska Press. The series is supported by the Andrew W. Mellon Foundation. For more information, please visit www.earlyamericanplaces.org.

ADVISORY BOARD
Vincent Brown, *Duke University*
Andrew Cayton, *Miami University*
Cornelia Hughes Dayton, *University of Connecticut*
Nicole Eustace, *New York University*
Amy S. Greenberg, *Pennsylvania State University*
Ramón A. Gutiérrez, *University of Chicago*
Peter Charles Hoffer, *University of Georgia*
Karen Ordahl Kupperman, *New York University*
Joshua Piker, *College of William & Mary*
Mark M. Smith, *University of South Carolina*
Rosemarie Zagarri, *George Mason University*

Vagrants and Vagabonds
Poverty and Mobility in the
Early American Republic

KRISTIN O'BRASSILL-KULFAN

New York University Press
NEW YORK

NEW YORK UNIVERSITY PRESS
New York
www.nyupress.org

© 2019 by New York University

All rights reserved

References to Internet websites (URLs) were accurate at the time of writing. Neither the author nor New York University Press is responsible for URLs that may have expired or changed since the manuscript was prepared.

Library of Congress Cataloging-in-Publication Data

Names: O'Brassill-Kulfan, Kristin, author.
Title: Vagrants and vagabonds : poverty and mobility in the early American republic / Kristin O'Brassill-Kulfan.
Other titles: Poverty and mobility in the early American republic
Description: New York : New York University Press, [2018] | Series: Early American places | Includes bibliographical references and index.
Identifiers: LCCN 2017060989 | ISBN 9781479845255 (hbk. : alk. paper)
Subjects: LCSH: Rogues and vagabonds—United States—History—19th century. | Vagrancy—United States—History—19th century. | Poor—United States—History—19th century. | United States—Social conditions—19th century.
Classification: LCC HV4505 .O24 2018 | DDC 305.5/692097309034—dc23
LC record available at https://lccn.loc.gov/2017060989

New York University Press books are printed on acid-free paper, and their binding materials are chosen for strength and durability. We strive to use environmentally responsible suppliers and materials to the greatest extent possible in publishing our books.

Manufactured in the United States of America

10 9 8 7 6 5 4 3 2 1

Also available as an ebook

Contents

	Introduction	1
1	"She Is Doubtless a Very Vagrant": Poverty and Mobility on the Legal Landscape	13
2	"A Wandering Life": The Physical Landscape of Indigent Transiency	36
3	"The Removal of So Many Human Beings ... Like Felons": Forced Migration of the Poor	58
4	"Since He Was Free": Vagabondage, Race, and Emancipation	84
5	"Punishment for Their Misfortunes": Discretion, Incarceration, and Resistance	112
6	"It Was amongst the Vagrant Class ... That Cholera Was Most Fatal": Mobility, Poverty, and Disease	134
	Conclusion	157
	Acknowledgments	161
	List of Abbreviations	165
	Appendix	167
	Notes	173
	Index	221
	About the Author	227

Introduction

In 1841, a young Scottish woman named Isabella Stewart donned an outfit of men's clothing, walked to Liverpool, and hired on to a ship's crew under the name of "Billy Stewart." She passed "as a sailor boy . . . dressed in the habiliments, neatly rigged from top to toe" and "actually performed the duty of a lad on board . . . for several days" before the crew's suspicions led to the revealing of her identity as "a healthy, stout female, 16 years of age." Stewart was punished for her deception by the captain, A. Turley, with passing the rest of the voyage in steerage wearing "female apparel." Newspapers throughout the antebellum United States reported on Stewart's escapades. But underpinning the interest stimulated by the thought of a dainty young woman performing the hard labor of seafaring was a question of the relationship between subsistence and travel: according to the *National Gazette*, Stewart was "a destitute girl, who had taken this method to get a passage to America."[1] Participation in the Atlantic world's economy of makeshifts sometimes required going to great lengths, and often, as it did for Stewart, great distances.[2]

Stewart's illicit mobility involved a complete revamping of her identity for the sake of cobbling together a living for herself, like so many others traveling to and residing within the antebellum United States. Unlike many single-paragraph nineteenth-century newspaper sensations, however, Stewart's notoriety was not limited to this one dramatic episode. Over a year after her arrival in the United States, she graced headlines in Philadelphia as "The Sailor Girl" about "whose adventures . . . a pretty romantic story" had been told by the press, when the city police reported committing her as a vagrant.[3] While similar romantic stories may have appealed to early nineteenth-century readers, the names of people like Stewart are more likely to appear on prison dockets than in travelogues.[4] Arrests for vagrancy—a category reserved for the poor, wanderers, beggars, and those lacking "legal settlement"—were the ubiquitous result of a complex system of bureaucracy and policing of the poor and transient in the early American republic.[5]

The vagrants, poor migrants, and homeless people targeted by this system comprised a subaltern class that prompted frequent and often punitive legislation, inciting both the pity and scorn of the public. The identities and personal narratives of these peripatetic individuals provide insight into the material realities of poverty experienced by huge swaths of the lower classes in the early republic, from sailors to laundresses to canal builders to hucksters to rag pickers and bone collectors. This combination of poverty and mobility, which is referred to here as "indigent transiency," was among the most significant factors in determining how the poor lived, interacted with, and were viewed by local and state governments and their representatives, both under the law and by law enforcement. Despite important differences in their identities and how they worked and moved, these groups occupied a distinct legal category, sharing a level of poverty and instability that placed them at odds with authorities, under constant scrutiny, and vulnerable to frequent attempts by the state to control their movements.[6]

The policing of vagrancy and poor people's mobility were key functions of local and state authority in the early American republic. Indeed, the state's desire to curb indigent transiency through careful policing drove the evolution of the modern police force, as criminal justice historians have documented.[7] This book examines the interrelated legal constructions, experiences, and management of indigent transiency, seeking to determine what new information can be gleaned about poverty and class in this period by paying careful attention to mobility. It follows the vagrants and pauper migrants whose geographical movements contravened settlement laws, penal codes, and welfare policies. It charts why and how the itinerant poor were forcibly transported to places deemed by the state to be their legal settlements through the process of pauper removal long after most historians acknowledge removal to have ended. It also considers the ways in which fugitive slaves and runaway servants experienced a transition from the oppression of unfree labor status to the oppression of poverty after participating in illicit forms of mobility, through mechanisms designed to curtail movement, punish vagrancy, and both facilitate and stanch manumissions. Indigent transiency, in its many shapes and through the varied forms of its management, was central to legally defining and shaping the role of the state and contemporary conceptions of community, class and labor status, the spread of disease, and the transformation of state-sanctioned punishment in the early American republic.[8]

In the first half of the nineteenth century, poverty was foremost among the nation's challenges.[9] The expansion of capitalism and industrialization in this period caused a financial calamity for the poor, which worsened during the depression that began in 1816, with the most detrimental effects being felt in the 1820s and 1830s. Widespread poverty resulting from even longer-lasting economic crises that began in 1819 and 1837 led to mass unemployment, prompting many thousands in the United States to take to the road in search of work and economic stability.[10] Regular employment was hard to come by for workers, especially for unskilled day and wage laborers. As an 1820 report issued by the Society for the Prevention of Pauperism in New York lamented, "There are so many to labor, and so little labor to be done, that many must be idle; or if employed, it is for wages that will not enable them to provide the necessaries of life."[11] Many indigent transients lamented this situation, reporting an ongoing search for sufficiently remunerative work.[12]

This satiated northern labor market forced many workers to move from job to job at a quick pace. When options dwindled in one location, workers and their families were left to either request relief or move on. For those who had already moved in search of work at least once in recent months or years, that often left only the latter option, as their mobility would have likely rendered them ineligible for public welfare, which was in most cases limited to those with legal settlement, which could take a long time to earn and be difficult to acquire.[13] These circumstances resulted in making these decades the peak of nineteenth-century working Americans' mobility, which in turn led authorities to create new and update old methods for managing the poor and itinerant.[14] The more Americans moved, the more important stasis and residency became to officials. Legal settlement was essentially rendered as a commodity and those who lacked it could be forced out. The strain placed on the poor relief system and the shift toward intensified punitive policies against the itinerant poor were partially the result of the inadequacy of colonial and early national poor law systems for dealing with the crisis brought on by the gradual transition to capitalism by the 1820s.[15]

In the early decades of the nineteenth century, many thousands of people in the United States were hungry, cold, and placeless. Their experiences were part and parcel of the shift toward the commodification, wage labor, and economic contingency that defined early capitalism. Their stories narrate the mobility and poverty that challenged the reciprocal relationships on which early republic market economies and communities were based, reminding us that the history of American poverty is also the history of capitalism and of labor. In this socioeconomic environment, the three were inextricably linked.[16] Across the board, as Seth Rockman explains, the poor were constrained by limited "opportunities to pursue subsistence outside wage labor," by the deterrence of "geographical mobility through residency requirements for the franchise or access to public welfare," and by the enforcement of "vagrancy statutes that [made] it illegal not to labor," policing people's activities "for the needs of a capitalist market system," as tools to force individuals to labor to the standard of the law.[17] Such legislation and policing led to the criminalization of the exercise of economic and social agency by the poor, by punishing their movements and subsistence activities. In these ways, economic pressures led to social control disproportionately impacting the lower classes, particularly through the regular and systematic enforcement of vagrancy laws.[18]

Vagrants were defined by the law as idlers and nonlaborers, presumed to be withholding their labor, thereby robbing the community of its fullest potential for economic viability. As a result, the policing of vagrancy can be viewed as an expression of capitalistic morality, through which the state defined community in economic terms, through participation in the market. This class-oriented and economically charged definition of community and society precluded assimilation into new communities for wage laborers who could not earn enough to subsist and were thus forcibly removed, either through incarceration or forced migration.[19] Exploring the mechanics of the poor laws, removal policies, and vagrancy statutes that intervened in the lives of the poor can expand our understanding of state authority and its use of welfare and penal systems to exercise social, economic, behavioral, and spatial control over the lower classes.[20]

There was a shared transatlantic culture linked to indigent transiency, and most of the relevant laws addressing indigent transiency in the United States have a root in early English jurisprudence. But the implementation of these laws and imposition of these categories on the population of the United States were influenced by factors unique to the nation, especially on points where race and labor distribution were key.[21] The nature of the founding of the United States—gradual expansion across vast swaths of land—has meant that mobility has been construed as central to not only the formation of the nation but also to the formation of the identities of Americans.[22] Although there were many similarities across the Mid-Atlantic in authorities' approaches to dealing with poverty, mobility, and vagrancy, a completely unified stance did not exist. This was a result of the weakness of the federal apparatus in the early American republic, which generally left management of poor relief and geographical movement to local governments and occasionally to the states.[23] This led to a variety of different management approaches and lent significant discretionary power to local authorities who interacted directly with indigent transients.[24]

Because of poor people's frequent and extended mobility, indigent transiency became a central factor in meting out poor relief, drawing boundaries around communities, defining the function of policing, and shaping the penal system in the early American republic. These processes occurred in a dynamic space that connected diverse communities and crossed state lines.[25] This is not to suggest that there existed uniformity of laws or experience across the whole region but rather that there was a shared conception of indigent transiency—as well as efforts to diminish and control it—across these states in the early republic. Indigent transiency provides a lens through which to examine the ways in which gender, race, ethnicity, and labor status affected how the state defined and interacted with varying groups among the poor and mobile lower classes in this period.

What follows here is a study that utilizes both qualitative analysis and some quantitative analysis to investigate the lives of indigent transients and the nature of poor relief policies, vagrancy laws, and incarceration in the early nineteenth century. By analyzing applicable laws, discourse, and quantitative data, this book considers the following questions: What new information can we learn about poverty in this period by foregrounding mobility? What does it say about the nature of poverty and class division in the early American republic that settlement and removal systems were the primary vehicles used to relieve and manage the poor? To whom were these laws applied, and upon whom were these systems imposed? How were lives of vagrants and indigent transients affected by settlement, vagrancy, poor laws, and law enforcement? What can the details of their lives, choices, and experiences reveal about the nature of vagrancy and the understandings of class and geographical movement in the early

American republic? So many of the members of this subaltern class were far from rooted, and it was their mobility that defined the law. In turn, then, this book asks: What defined their mobility? And what can it tell us about the experience of poverty and subsistence in the early republic?[26]

Indigent transiency offers a useful framework within which to investigate the systems at work in the lives of the lower classes in the early republic.[27] It acts as an epistemologically inclusive term to encompass the actions and identities that have variously been used to describe, in the early modern period, vagabonds and idlers; in the eighteenth and nineteenth centuries, vagrants; and in the nineteenth and twentieth centuries, tramps and hoboes.[28] These terms reflect the diverse social contexts in which they were used, as well as the changing cultural interpretations of the actions they described.[29] Analyzing indigent transiency as it was experienced by early Americans illustrates key aspects of how communities were shaped and defined by the emergence of capitalism, evolving class divisions, stasis, and municipal-level management of the poor. In turn, this study reveals how indigent transiency defined community membership and, by extension, American citizenship at the street level.[30]

This book examines limitations on certain forms of mobility and punishment of indigent transiency as manifestations of the state's largely reactionary efforts to exert social, spatial, behavioral, and economic control on the lower and working classes in response to the social and economic instability that defined the period. Indigent transiency is especially salient when considering the impact that settlement, removal, and vagrancy laws had across demographic lines. In many ways, in the early nineteenth-century Mid-Atlantic, women and men, enslaved and free laborers, and white and black people subject to the legal system that governed indigent transients were considered, because of their impoverishment or mobility, equally threatening and deserving of punishment before the law. In other important ways, however, these laws were racialized and gendered, drawing deeply unequal and punitive reactions from authorities. Legislators, law enforcement officers, and some contemporaries saw people of color, immigrants, and itinerants as drains on community coffers, unlikely to contribute to the community welfare.[31] Authorities combatted this perceived problem by punishing transients as "vagrants" and restricting the availability of poor relief. This had a significant impact on the lower classes who used poor relief to sustain themselves between crises as a survival mechanism as well as an integral component of regular subsistence for those with limited employment opportunities or other financial or material provisions.[32] Laws and prosecution related to legal settlements and residency governed how poor relief was administered throughout American history.

Mobility and the control of movement were central facets of life in the early American republic.[33] From the implied interstate freedom of movement written into the Articles of Confederation, to the exclusion from that legal movement of the poor and criminal, voluntary and forced migration have defined American history. Scholars such as Ruth Wallis Herndon, Cornelia H. Dayton, and Sharon V. Salinger have charted early practices of warning individuals to leave a given residential district to prevent them from becoming a drain on public relief budgets (an important touchstone for understanding early New England communities, in particular).[34] In general, historians have agreed that by the 1770s, warning no longer served as a legal mechanism by which to extricate an individual from a district but rather as a means to protect the limited available funds of public relief, allowing the wandering poor to be present in a district but not to receive public aid.[35] On this point, the distinction between the regions in the New England states and farther south, in the Mid-Atlantic states, is clear. In the latter, removal was a key component in the management of indigent transients, and poor people were forcibly and physically removed to their place of legal settlement with regularity into the 1830s, with this practice occurring as recently as the 1930s.[36] Pauper removal was far from the only forced migration scheme explored in the early nineteenth century to regulate demographic distribution, control population size and makeup, and establish homogeneous financially stable white communities. While distinct because it predated many of these efforts and established one of the largest bureaucratic enterprises of the early American republic, it will be argued here that it was part of a larger trend in politics and governance in this period that generated efforts toward African recolonization and laid the groundwork for the fugitive slave laws that instigated the Civil War. The goals, functions, and consequences of pauper removal will be discussed in detail in chapter 3.

When discussing poverty and welfare in this period, an apparent dichotomy between the deserving and undeserving poor has predominated in historians' mid-twentieth-century efforts to document the reformist impulse in the Jacksonian era.[37] Michael Katz has argued that this was a result of the "redefinition of poverty as a moral condition" across social categories which "accompanied the transition to capitalism . . . in early nineteenth-century America."[38] Most studies of poverty and poor relief in the nineteenth-century United States have focused on this dichotomy as of the utmost importance in determining how the poor moved through the relief system and how they were viewed by administrators. Indeed, the very term "pauper" when used to describe a poor person implied unworthiness of aid, and thus, as an administrative category, historians have argued, offered relief officials a line in the sand that could be used to justify declining aid.[39] Historians have argued that the undeserving poor were usually sent to workhouses, whereas the deserving poor tended to be eligible for relief in institutions that did not necessarily have work requirements, such as traditional almshouses. Yet of course it was not so clear-cut because most almshouses used the labor of their inmates to offset operation costs, even if hard labor was not a condition of entry for everyone housed within their walls. Causes of commitment to almshouses and workhouses show that many were in serious need of relief, and there was little distinction made between those who might be considered undeserving or deserving.[40] Even where such determinations of worthiness did play an important role, distinctions between those being classified by officials were often so opaque as to be nearly useless.[41] Relief providers' assessments of the moral worthiness of an individual to receive welfare were not as central to the operations of public welfare officials as other administrative concerns. For poor relief officials who followed the laws that governed their activities, this determination was not based on moral grounds, as many historians have suggested—at least for public assistance. Rather, their day-to-day administrative functions centered on determinations of legal eligibility of an individual to receive relief in a specific district, in accordance with settlement and removal laws. Thus, for poor relief recipients, one's previous mobility and residency status was of greater importance to those meting out relief than was one's morality or worthiness. One's place of legal settlement was far more likely to determine where someone was incarcerated—in a jail, almshouse, or workhouse—or if one was to be relieved, ignored, or removed. Identifying the role which mobility and residency played in the lives of the poor allows for a fresh look at the system that both aided and penalized a large portion of the population of the early United States, revealing a complicated legal, social, and economic landscape of poverty, relief, bureaucracy, and policing. It also adds dimension to our understanding of local government functions in this period, which often preempted or took precedence over state or federal operations.

Most studies of vagrancy and mobility among the poor in the United States focus on the late nineteenth-century tramp scare and early twentieth-century hobohemia, with a few exceptions covering the post-Revolutionary period.[42] The literature on postbellum labor contracts and laws against beggars acknowledges American vagrancy laws as an "inheritance" from early modern England but moves from this colonial legacy directly into the Civil War and Reconstruction.[43] Historians have argued that in the tumultuous Reconstruction period, vagrancy laws were devised as transitional measures for the transformation of labor and society following the abolition of slavery.[44] The evidence discussed here suggests that the same can be said of the "first emancipation" in the era of gradual manumission.[45] Then, as recurred in the postbellum period, fear and the desire to "protect" communities from mobile black laborers incapable of providing for themselves in the absence of the so-called provisions of bondage drove the use of vagrancy statutes and laws limiting the geographical movement of free and recently emancipated blacks, as well as others whose industrious labor was viewed as a safeguard against beggary and the need for poor relief.[46] At the end of the eighteenth century, gradual abolition laws were introduced that contained provisions for the control of the labor and assessment of the personal industry of manumitted slaves, and during the antebellum era, laws that had governed the movements of the poor and facilitated forced migration were deployed against fugitive slaves and free people of color. After emancipation, these laws were selectively transformed into what we know as the black codes. This book argues that the transition to white authorities' reliance on vagrancy laws and codified limitations of movement and residence based on race and class, which has usually been pointed to in the aftermath of slave emancipation at the close of the Civil War, began across the North, where piecemeal and gradual emancipations instigated huge shifts in populations and policies in the early nineteenth century.[47]

In this study, the roads and footpaths of the early republic are cast as loci for interrogating the relationship between poverty, labor, and control in the lives of the poor.[48] It charts the narratives of transients' lives with a view to reconstructing their geographical mobility. Testimonies such as those of convicted vagrant Samuel Gantdron, who "walked the whole distance from the Bay to the Keystone State . . . in search of employment" in 1837, and of Rachel Johnson, whose husband had traveled from Philadelphia "to the state of New York, whence he came on a raft" in 1830, make it possible to explore the material realities of indigent transiency and vagrancy in the early republic.[49] Due to its position as a border region and its function as a transitional zone for transatlantic immigrants, regional migrants, and fugitives from slavery, the Mid-Atlantic region provides an especially useful framework within which to locate itinerant individuals who passed between almshouses and jails in multiple states, finding employment and temporary shelter along the way, on the most frequently traveled paths and roads in early nineteenth-century America. Fluidity of geographical focus is an essential component to studying the fluidity of movement undertaken by the indigent transients with whom this study is concerned, but naturally some areas receive more coverage based on source availability and analytical significance. Certainly, one city cannot stand in for an entire region, nor can several cities; wherever possible, legal and practical differences between cities, counties, and states within the Mid-Atlantic are noted, while acknowledging the analytical value of looking at trends across and circulations throughout the region.

This book draws from sources that document the experiences and perspectives of indigent transients as closely as possible to their own perspectives. Largely, these are biographies and cartographies that were generated by the recording of interviews to determine the legal settlements of the poor, referred to as "examinations of paupers" or "settlement examinations," a discussion of which will follow here. These examinations have their limitations as windows into transients' experiences, as many if not most of these interviews were coerced, having generally been recorded with participants exhibiting varying degrees of willingness to recount their life's experiences to a stranger acting as an ear of the state.[50] Conducted most often by guardians of the poor and justices of the peace, these interviews were the legal depositions of indigent transients asked to justify their presence in a given locality by listing their birthplace, employment history, travels, and former residences.[51] While coercion was an operative component of the examination process, transients also often used the opportunity to represent their life's travels, choices, and their status in a way that they felt reflected well on them, endeavoring to provide information that might sway the outcome of the interview in their favor.[52] Settlement examinations, along with vagrancy dockets, prison registers, and a variety of almshouse system-generated documents, point to relationships between poverty, labor, and control that profoundly affected the lives of the poor in this period.[53] These records point to an overlap between vagrant and pauper populations that reflects the relationship between the two in life as well as in law, and suggests that the demographics of indigent transients in this period were starkly different than later in the nineteenth century. These examinations depict an interconnected geographical region, wherein the stateless, unsettled, and poor—as well as institutional knowledge relevant to them—traveled in swirls and eddies.[54]

From the lines of these trajectories and the nature of their intersections with the state and its subsidiaries, it is possible to chart both personal efforts at subsistence and the impact of the state on the individual.[55] Chapter 1 provides an overview of the laws that governed the mobility of the lower classes, especially in their most potent form: the regulation of vagrancy, management of the poor, and provision of poor relief. Residence, transiency, and poverty shaped the construction of citizenship in the United States, establishing the legal landscape in which the poor and mobile lived. The experiences of indigent transients, especially vagrants, and authorities' responses to them, were central to the formulation of citizenship in the early republic. These experiences and movements are explored in chapter 2, which charts the geographical landscape of indigent transiency in the nineteenth century, utilizing examinations of paupers to reconstruct the life stories shared by these individuals. The data extracted from these narratives reveal that women and people of color comprised a much larger proportion of the indigent transient population in the early nineteenth century than they did by the middle and later nineteenth century.[56] The paths taken by these individuals preoccupied poor relief officials, who speculated about the directions of paupers' travels and aimed to limit the mobility of the poor.

This limitation often took the form of pauper removal, which is discussed in detail in chapter 3. Pauper removal, the forced migration of poor transients, was a method of carrying out legal proscription of mobility by the poor through linking class status with legality of presence, as an adjunct to the policing of vagrancy. Thousands of paupers were transported by poor relief and law enforcement authorities to their state-recognized places of legal settlement every year in the early nineteenth century. Many paupers' lives were punctuated by these experiences of forced transportation, most of which were preceded by passage through the revolving doors of the almshouse or the prison. The system that facilitated the provision of relief, the punishment of vagrancy, and the relocation of itinerants was both gendered and racialized in important ways. Chapter 4 explores transiency and vagrancy as by-products of emancipation and discusses the associated legal protections against vagrancy that were included in emancipation law. By incorporating the experiences of fugitive slaves, as participation in a form of illicit mobility, into the historiography of vagrancy, the definition of indigent transiency is broadened. Early nineteenth-century lawmakers and slaveholders used vagrancy laws to, in some cases, prevent manumissions and, in others, to limit the mobility of recently freed people and ensure that their labor could be maintained. Authorities' efforts to prevent slaves from running away through punitive capture and return laws were built on the legal precedents found in poor relief, vagrancy, and pauper removal laws.

Chapter 5 explores the function of the policing of vagrancy in the early nineteenth-century Mid-Atlantic by charting the experiences of convicted vagrants from arrest to incarceration to release. Authorities exercised significant discretion in their policing and sentencing of indigent transients, leading many vagrants to the almshouse and many paupers to the jail. What they experienced inside and outside of those institutions' walls reveals that there was extensive overlap between these populations, whose physical conditions were even more vulnerable than their social and legal conditions. These corporeal experiences are discussed in chapter 6, which proposes that vagrants were central to societal understandings of the dissemination of disease, as well as an especial public health concern in their own right, as a population suffering from exposure, hunger, and a profound lack of the most basic human necessities, as a direct result of not just their poverty but also their mobility. Vagrants were popularly vilified as carriers of disease, and particularly associated with the spread of cholera during the 1832 epidemic. Poverty was pathologized by authorities in ways that played out in the punishment and incarceration of vagrants, clearly demonstrated in a case study at Philadelphia's vagrant prison, Arch Street.

By considering the stories of vagrants and paupers alongside the laws that governed them and the processes by which they came into contact with those laws, a complicated system of social, economic, and behavioral control comes into focus. Alongside poverty, the extent of an individual's mobility determined their worthiness to be present in a community, their likelihood of being arrested, their ability to receive subsistence relief, and their vulnerability to state control. Mobility was, in the early American republic, a dominant feature in the lives of the poor as well as the metric by which they were assessed by law enforcement, relief authorities, and many people passing them on the road. The particular ways in which this mobility was curbed, punished, and sometimes reversed elucidates important aspects of the lives of the poor in this period, as well as the evolution of laws aiming to manage them—from vagrancy to relief to removal to incarceration—which remain relevant in the twenty-first century.

1 / "She Is Doubtless a Very Vagrant": Poverty and Mobility on the Legal Landscape

"What constitutes a vagrant?" asked a headline above a sarcastic anecdote that was reprinted in numerous nineteenth-century publications. The story described a vagabond who was met on the street by a magistrate, who accused him of being a vagrant who did not possess visible means of subsistence. When asked to give an account of himself, as was customary, the man extracted from the pocket of "his tattered coat a loaf of bread, and half of a dried codfish. Holding them up, with a triumphant look and gesture to the magistrate, exclaimed . . . I'm no vagrant! An't them visible means o' support, I should like to know?"[1] The clause in most vagrancy statutes that rendered the largest number of individuals vulnerable to arrest was the one requiring individuals to have "visible means of support," that is, the obvious ability to provide for oneself or one's family the basic necessities of life—food, shelter, clothing. Those who could not do so were vulnerable to punishment under vagrancy law, exactly what the man with the bread and codfish in his pocket was symbolically trying to avoid.

Vagrancy has been defined in many ways across centuries and national borders. Vagrants have, in an Anglo-American tradition, been viewed as a group of individuals linked by law whose bodily movements were in some way threatening to the state, writ large.[2] But this definition stretched beyond convicted vagrants and encompassed the more widely defined population of itinerant workers and the wandering poor—essentially, indigent transients. These persons, on whom this study focuses, traversed not only a physical landscape but one marked by policies and bounded by laws. Since its inception, the United States was a society that embodied a contradiction consisting of two sides of a coin; the one enshrining a right to freedom of movement and the other suspicious of any who might exercise it.[3] To early Americans, strangers, those without a personal or professional connection to a community—whether born in the United States or abroad—were regarded as suspect.[4]

This chapter will explore the laws that governed the mobility of the lower classes in the Mid-Atlantic region in the early nineteenth century, namely poor laws and vagrancy statutes, as well as the impact they had on individuals subject to them. It argues that vagrancy and settlement laws ought to be viewed in concert with each other in order to evaluate the significance of mobility in the lives of the poor in this period. It also discusses the ways in which residence, transiency, and poverty shaped the construction of citizenship in the United States and established a legal and social landscape in which the actions of the poor, and especially the mobile poor, were criminalized.

Distrust of strangers, and especially poor strangers, was embodied in Anglo-American legal traditions. To the English settlers in North America, as Christopher Tomlins has explained, "law was the conceptual structure, the organizational discourse, by which their moves were enabled, the bridge that bore them across the ocean and planted them on the other side." It "established the context for migrants' liberty to be mobile by prescribing its extent; that is, the extent of their freedom to depart one place and move and set down elsewhere," and in so doing, "established the actual conditions and effects of mobility and settlement, influencing who might go where" in this newly constructed legal territory. Most importantly, as Tomlins argues, this conceptualization of law "organized mobile migrating masses into discrete socioeconomic segments with very distinct legal-relational profiles: freemen; households . . . landowners and the landless; the settled and the wanderers; vagrants and runaways; slaves." The transplantation of these social relationships onto the landscape that would become the United States essentially transferred the power of the English monarch to control the mobility or immobility of the population within its jurisdiction "according to the best interests of the state," which was so often utilized to maintain the boundaries of the socioeconomic categories laid out in law.[5]

This transplantation led to limitations on the physical movements of the poor being written into the founding documents of the United States.[6] The Articles of Confederation, the proto-constitutional document that comprised the first attempt to unite the states under a centralized government, banned interstate travel by vagrants and the poor. Article 4 granted that "the free inhabitants of each of these states, *paupers, vagabonds, and fugitives from justice excepted* . . . shall have free ingress and regress to and from any other state."[7] As historians of travel have recognized, in the early republic, the act, circumstances, and process of travel were integral to how Americans conceived of the privileges of citizenship.[8] At the moment of the founding of the United States, the revocable right to be mobile was tied to class status. By curtailing freedom of travel for certain groups within the United States, lawmakers sent a clear message about citizenship, delineating the classes who were worthy of participating in its privileges.[9] As the transportation revolution in the early nineteenth century gradually allowed greater segments of the population the ability to move more easily and at greater speeds, efforts to curtail undesirable mobility increased. States that had not already done so went on to legislate their own limits on the ingress of paupers, as Pennsylvania did in 1821, out of a proprietary effort to "prevent the increase of pauperism in this Commonwealth."[10]

People who traveled too much or participated in any form of mobility deemed inappropriate or excessive were stripped of their right to be mobile.[11] In this legal climate, then, any discussion of indigent transients is a discussion of an illicit form of mobility. Such a categorization could include one pauper's journey on foot across a bridge from New Jersey to Philadelphia, or from New York to Pittsburgh to Ohio via boat and stagecoach. It could describe the clandestine movement northward of a fugitive slave under cover of night out of Virginia, facilitated by the Underground Railroad, or the relocation of a Marylander following his imprisonment for vagrancy. All these actions were viewed as disorderly occupations of space. The policing of vagrancy was meant to reorder that space.[12]

States used vagrancy statutes and settlement laws to uphold this ban on indigent transiency. In these laws, the distinction between resident and nonresident poor was of utmost importance because vagrants and other transients were subject to harsher punishments and less likely to be eligible for subsistence aid.[13] Vagrancy statutes functioned as forms of antimigratory policing that contravened the rights of free ingress and regress afforded to residents of the United States. But the pauper and vagabond provision in the Articles of Confederation provided a window through which law creators and law enforcers were able to control the movements of the unemployed and destitute classes that was not declared unconstitutional until 1940. Even then, the ruling came only after states had mobilized border patrols to keep migrants from entering their territory during the Great Depression.[14] These efforts were slightly more modern versions of settlement and removal laws.[15]

Regulation of legal settlements was bound up in state poor laws. Possessing legal settlement usually entitled one to receive poor relief in that location, as a privilege of municipal citizenship. In Pennsylvania after 1803, one could gain a legal settlement in a number of ways: by holding public office for one year, paying public poor taxes for two years, leasing a residence valued at over ten pounds for at least one year, serving at least a one-year term as an unmarried, childless indentured servant, or being a woman married to a man or widowed by a man with a legal settlement. Delaware and Maryland's provisions for gaining legal settlement rights were very similar, stipulating a year's residence, property ownership, payment of poor taxes, or service as an indentured servant. In Delaware, an individual also gained a legal settlement in a district by being born there.[16] New Jersey required only a year's continuous residence by a property holder, migrant, or indentured servant in order to gain a legal settlement.[17] In New York after 1801, one could gain a legal settlement by holding public office for one year, renting and occupying a residence valued at a minimum of thirty dollars for two years, paying public poor tax for two years, or being an indentured servant in a New York district for at least two years.[18] After 1812, Pennsylvania held transients to the standards for gaining a legal settlement in whatever state they held one, as opposed to the standards in the state they'd entered. This suggests an expectation of awareness of law and process for one's home or place of official residence, but not necessarily the same level of knowledge for anywhere else one resided.[19]

By the early twentieth century, states had introduced many amendments to settlement statutes resulting from "the increased volume of migration" that began during the Great Depression. These were primarily designed to make it more challenging to gain settlement in a given district, discouraging migration by the poor to prevent increased welfare costs. The intervening century appears to have had little effect on lawmakers' perspectives; the mobility of the underclasses continued to be viewed as a threat, and it was the indigent who suffered the consequences of stagnant opportunities, lack of relief, and involuntary removal.[20]

Just as early nineteenth-century poor laws did not account for the exponentially increasing mobility of the poor, as they were rooted in colonial and even Elizabethan expectations, so too, in the early twentieth century, laws were not adjusted to reflect the changes the previous century had brought but rather drew on earlier iterations of poor laws.[21] Legislation managing mobile poor populations throughout much of United States history addressed two forms of indigent transiency: physical homelessness and legal homelessness. Individuals who experienced one or both fell under the purview of vagrancy law as individuals who "lodg[ed] . . . in the open air" or who did not possess any legal settlement.[22] Mobility and work shaped not only the prosecution of vagrancy but also the distribution of food and fuel to the poor, qualifications for suffrage, and social constructions of morality in general. Debates over the rights of indigent transients to participate in either form of so-called membership—territorial or civic—generally concluded that citizenship was a laurel to be earned rather than a recognition of participation. In order for lawmakers, police, and guardians of the poor to ward off the admission of unworthy individuals to this imagined community, they sought to regulate the physical locations of indigent transients' bodies.[23]

Antimigratory Policies

American lawmakers did not invent new policies from whole cloth in the nineteenth century. During the colonial period, settlement and removal laws, poor laws, and, often under the purview of poor laws, vagrancy statutes were imported wholesale from England. These laws had been used to curb the movements of—and enforce punishments against—the mobile poor, beggars, and the homeless since the fourteenth century. When the anticipated prosperity in Massachusetts and Virginia did not meet the needs of all those colonies' inhabitants, a class of wandering beggars emerged, leading colonial authorities to implement English poor laws in their own territories, many of which matched very closely the Vagabond Code of 1531 and the Vagrancy Act of 1824. Poor laws provided financial relief for the needy while simultaneously punishing expressions of said neediness deemed inappropriate.[24] The Revolutionary War plunged the new nation into an economic crisis, with formerly lucrative British commerce cut off, rampant inflation, and large debts from the war effort.[25] As a result, the 1780s saw the first dramatic upturn in the numbers of the homeless and mobile poor in the new nation, individuals who came to comprise a new and more transient lower class that filled the roads and cities.[26]

It was at the tail end of the eighteenth century that many state legislatures began to revise the colonial poor laws that had governed the needy and disorderly classes up to that point. Thereafter, most states did not amend these laws or pass new legislation until after the Panic of 1819, when a deep economic recession took hold.[27] In New York and Pennsylvania, the changes that were made in the 1780s were similar and substantive. Both states (Pennsylvania in 1782 and New York in 1784 and 1785), whose poor laws were dominated by the needs of their large cities, restructured the authoritative bodies that administered poor relief to increase efficiency across their jurisdictions. In 1784, New York also passed a new law requiring legal settlement for poor relief, which effectively reimplemented colonial settlement law. New York's revisions also granted local municipalities the ability to manage the disorderly or burdensome poor as they saw fit, which led to a rise in the auctioning of pauper labor "to the highest bidder" and the forced indenturing of children, all in an effort to recoup the costs of welfare provision and to prevent idleness among the poor.[28] Pennsylvania's 1782 poor law revision similarly provided for forced indenture of poor people who might "become chargeable" to the public welfare as a result of "their own lewdness, drunkenness, or other evil practices," in order to alleviate the financial burden incurred by providing for their maintenance and to prevent the congregation of vagrants and other unwanted indigents in Philadelphia.[29] The swelling poor population in these years also prompted the creation of a system of almshouse administration in Delaware in 1791, which previously had only a limited de facto provision in place to house the homeless indigent among local citizens.[30]

Poor laws and statutes regulating relief administration were inextricably linked to vagrancy statutes, and provisions for the management of vagrants and the disorderly were often written into states' welfare laws. This was the case, for example, in New Jersey, where the vagrancy provisions of colonial welfare statutes survived well into the nineteenth century.[31] In Maryland, law enforcement officers were instructed to observe the movements of the poor in order to, as an 1811 law stipulated, "restrain poor people from going . . . from one county to another."[32] Any poor person who attempted to travel outside of their district was subject to vagrancy arrest, in punishment for their withdrawal of their labor. The availability and stability of their labor was viewed as so essential as to warrant the policing of their movement for economic purposes.[33]

Towns, cities, counties, and states expended huge portions of their municipal budgets in providing for the emergency and maintenance needs of the indigent. Payment into these budgets was considered an obligation of taxable citizens, and, generally, only residents were eligible for poor relief. Some estimates suggest that in Philadelphia, "roughly one-quarter of the population" was classified as laboring poor, paying only "the minimum amount of taxes."[34] Transients often paid no taxes: one of the common rules in the complex settlement qualification process was the payment of poor taxes, which were seen as a way for paupers to balance out the use of resources for their care. This provided the basis for the pauper removal system: individuals who had not paid poor tax to a town or earned residence by some other means that contributed to the local economy, such as labor or indenture, were sent back to the last place where they had done so.

Economic downturn has generally been the most common impetus for widespread geographical movement, especially by white Americans. This was especially true in the years following the War of 1812, when estimates suggest that more than a quarter of the labor force in Philadelphia was unemployed. Time brought little relief. In the midst of the fallout from the Panic of 1819, members of the Society for the Prevention of Pauperism in New York wrote in 1820 that "public attention has been awakened: the sources of poverty and crime are becoming subjects of daily inquiry, and plans of productive industry among the needy and idle, a desideratum of general interest."[35] It is estimated that around one-tenth of the population of New York City received poor relief in 1820, prompting grave concerns over provisions for the poor and the sustainability of offering aid to such large numbers of the needy. In this period, the streets of New York were filled with destitute vagrants and paupers.[36] With greater unemployment came greater transiency, as more people moved in pursuit of work. Unemployment remained high through the 1820s, at roughly one-fifth of the city's residents, about twenty thousand in a population of one hundred thousand, peaking after the Panic of 1837 at nearly forty percent of the labor force.[37] Well into the 1840s, New York City authorities estimated that about one in seven persons who were in the city on a given day were part of the "floating" population of vagrants and transients, totaling about fifty thousand individuals.[38] Even counting only those who were actually convicted of vagrancy or incarcerated in the vagrant cellars of the almshouse yields a figure of nearly 2 percent of the entire city population in Philadelphia in the 1820s.[39]

Laws regulating the settlement, movement, and punishment of the poor shared broad similarities throughout the Mid-Atlantic region. Here, nearly all perceived the primary threat of a vagrant's presence to be their class status, as opposed to their race, ethnicity, or gender, though these laws and their implementation were affected by these categories to varying degrees.[40] But there were some local and state-specific qualities in the writing and implementation of vagrancy laws. New York's vagrancy laws were descriptively enumerated, as were those of most states: a vagrant was an idle, unemployed person or beggar of alms, but also any person "wandering abroad and lodging in taverns, groceries, beer-houses, out-houses, market-places, sheds or barns, or in the open air, and not giving a good account of themselves."[41] In Kingston, New York, in 1839, for example, Ann Elmendorff was committed to jail as a vagrant for being "found . . . an idle person, not having visable [sic] lawful means to maintain herself, and living without employment, and a vagrant within the intent and meaning of the . . . statute."[42] Convictions commonly ran in these fashions, with vagrants serving between a few days and two full months in county jails. Punishments for vagrants in New York were slightly harsher than in the other Mid-Atlantic states: the latter stipulated that justices could incarcerate vagrants for up to thirty days, whereas the former allowed for sixty days, providing justices with the option to determine whether further punishment to ward against recidivism, by sentencing vagrants to serve part of their term on a diet of bread and water, was warranted.[43] These tougher punishments for vagrants in New York may have been prompted by the growing number of poor immigrants who came through the state and traveled onward, especially following the American Revolution and the War of 1812, who were viewed as potentially dangerous to the economic health of the state.

In New York as well as Pennsylvania, justices were authorized to determine whether a convicted vagrant was better suited to incarceration in the prison or in the almshouse, and in both, justices exercised their personal discretion in making this call. For example, when Joseph Ruland was convicted of vagrancy in Kingston, New York, in 1839, he was charged with having been "found without any visable [sic] means of support and sleeping in barns and in the open air," and was deemed by the justice of the peace to be "an improper person to be sent to the poor-house," and was committed to the county jail.[44] This was common phrasing for vagrancy convictions in New York and reflected authorities' efforts to distinguish between the needy poor and the criminal poor.

Pennsylvania's vagrancy laws, which originated in the colonial period, were more direct than New York's, enumerating fewer categories of people. These laws targeted beggars, nonresidents, destitute persons, and others considered to be vagabonds, stipulating that if an individual was perceived by a law enforcement officer to occupy one of these categories, they were to be arrested as a vagrant and incarcerated. Penal records associated with vagrancy convictions provide a raw articulation of exactly which aspects of an individual's mobility, poverty, or appearance were being identified as threatening enough to warrant arrest. For a woman named Unis Maria Quin, arrested on 7 March 1832, it was because she had been found "wandering about the streets without a house," a common offense recorded by watchmen in early Philadelphia.[45]

Throughout the Mid-Atlantic, members of municipal government and police forces apprehended, arrested, and meted out punishments to vagrants and indigent transients. These included justices of the peace, guardians of the poor, magistrates, constables, and city watchmen. In Philadelphia, night watchmen were singled out for the task by the mayor's office. Since 1771, the legislature had tasked this force with apprehending "all night walkers," "vagabonds," and anyone found "disturbing the peace."[46] Nightly patrols were not only "authorized to challenge all persons whom they may find loitering about the streets, and if such persons cannot give a satisfactory account of themselves, they may arrest and hold them in custody," but in fact were "required to arrest all night strollers, malefactors, vagrants, and disorderly persons" they encountered on their beats.[47]

Pennsylvania's poor laws were revised in 1836, after a series of other laws curbing the mobility of the poor had taken effect. The state's laws applying to vagrants up until this point had been in place since 1767, expanded somewhat by the 1782 law previously mentioned, and were reinforced by the consolidation of power resulting from the constitution of 1790. The 1767 law had granted constables the right to arrest disorderly persons and vagrants and to incarcerate them for up to thirty days; it applied to vagrants, vagabonds, and other disorderly persons but did not explicitly define who, or what actions, would qualify as such. The murky nature of the late eighteenth-century vagrancy statute was clarified by the Pennsylvania legislature with the 1836 revision to the poor law. These changes included the introduction of a detailed, five-part definition of *persons* who would be deemed "liable to the penalties imposed by law upon vagrants." Rather than listing the actions that would have warranted a criminal conviction as a vagrant, the law described vagrant persons as those "who shall unlawfully return into any district, whence they have been legally removed." The law also identified individuals who did not "have the wherewith to maintain themselves and their families, live idly and without employment," those who refused employment offered to them, or who "wander[ed] abroad and begged." Finally, itinerant strangers were targeted directly, under the final category of "persons who shall come from any place without this commonwealth to any place within it . . . and shall follow no labor, trade, occupation, or business, and have no visible means of subsistence, and can give no reasonable account of themselves."[48] These statutory constructions are notable for their recognition that vagrancy was viewed not as an act committed in a given moment (in the manner of similarly punished offenses such as petit larceny or swearing) but as an identity-based and perhaps lifelong characteristic of an individual.[49]

New York, Pennsylvania, Maryland, and New Jersey all had clear laws providing for the apprehension and punishment of vagrants. Delaware, on the other hand, followed a different model, without writing explicit vagrancy punishments into state law. Some citizens were outraged by this seeming oversight when, by the late 1830s, as gradual manumission was beginning to take effect, free black mobility blossomed. Concerned white residents circulated dozens of petitions decrying the geographical freedom of people of color, which led to the introduction of punitive racialized vagrancy laws in Delaware at a much later date than in neighboring states.[50]

Of the Mid-Atlantic states, Maryland's vagrancy laws provided for the harshest punishments. A city-specific 1812 law stipulated that anyone convicted of vagrancy in Baltimore was to be sentenced to incarceration in the penitentiary for a full year. It is difficult to determine whether these laws functioned as a deterrent in any way, though it might be speculated that the subsistence-based nature of actions that most commonly led to vagrancy convictions (sleeping outdoors or begging for food) would have decreased the likelihood of that outcome. At least one contemporary argued that Baltimore's "rigid" treatment of paupers and vagrants had "the effect . . . of driving the idle, dissolute, vagrant class to other places." This assertion may have had some truth to it. However, in looking at the birthplaces and former residences of Philadelphia's nonresident paupers in the 1820s and 1830s, more hailed from New York, Delaware, and New Jersey than from Maryland (between 1822 and 1831).[51]

In Maryland, between 1812 and 1819, 186 individuals spent a year incarcerated in the penitentiary on vagrancy charges.[52] Vagrants incarcerated in the city almshouse in the 1820s were held for shorter sentences, but recidivists and elopers were punished severely: according to one report, if any pauper left the almshouse without permission and was "returned as a vagrant within twelve months," he would be "kept one week in solitary confinement on bread and water, and detained one month in addition to the time he was adjudged to serve on his first admission." And if the situation warranted, at the discretion of the overseer, the vagrant might be "showered," that is, placed in a "small apartment or case, to the back of which slats are nailed in such a manner as to form nearly a semi-circle, and a corresponding semi-circular frame is attached to the inside of the door; so, as when shut, to completely inclose the sufferer, and keep him in a perpendicular position. Above, a barrel is fixed, with small holes in the bottom of it, and is so managed, that either the whole quantity of water may descend at once, or drip very slowly. This last is considered the most effectual mode of punishing, and is quite severe."[53] Between whipping, forced removal, hard labor, food restrictions, and "showering," many vagrants and paupers were subject to corporal punishment for their actions and identities.

Pass systems were used to facilitate local authorities' efforts to manage indigent transients in the early nineteenth century.[54] New Jersey's was instituted under the colonial government in 1774 and remained on the books as part of the state's vagrancy statute well into the nineteenth century.[55] Justices were required to issue individuals who did possess a legal settlement within the colony a document that served as evidence of their legal settlement. This would be used to instigate their forced removal, from the hands of one town's constable to the next, on the route from the site of their apprehension via "the readiest way to his, her or their place of settlement." For transients who did *not* have legal settlement within the colony, justices would use this "pass warrant" to see that "he, she, or they ... be conveyed back by every city ... through which they have been suffered to stroll and wander unapprehended, and so to be transported out of this colony, and to be set on shore in that province from which he, she or they strolled and wandered first." If, after this forced process of removal, a transient returned to the colony, constables were required "to carry him, her or them to the whipping post, and to strip him her or them to the bare back, and to give them a number of lashes, not exceeding twenty." Once this was done, the removal process would be repeated, constable by constable.[56] Systems like this, for the removal of poor people and vagrants who did not reside in a given location, were in place throughout the Northeast well into the twentieth century and will be discussed in greater detail in chapter 3. In practice, they required justices of the peace and overseers of the poor to identify individuals who were not legally settled in their jurisdiction and have them physically removed to the place where they did possess a legal settlement. These laws protected local residents, all but ensuring that they could receive relief if they needed it, but for those lacking residency, they effectively withdrew the volition of mobility from the paupers and vagrants to whom they were applied.

New York's poor laws provide an excellent vantage point for looking not only at the ways in which high transiency among the poor shaped settlement laws but also vice versa. These laws are an important starting point in considering the connections between poverty and mobility, and particularly the joint functions of poor laws and vagrancy statutes in the late eighteenth and early nineteenth centuries.[57] In New York, significant changes to the poor law were made between 1784 and 1824. The state's early poor laws established the system that allocated poor relief on the basis of residence. Each city, town, or other district was responsible for its own poor, leaving statewide provision piecemeal.[58] This system was effective in that it provided a clear legal precedent against which all requests for assistance could be checked, giving local officials, responsible for judging whether an individual was eligible for relief by formal examination, a direct line to the legal intent of the law. But early penalties for paupers who returned to a location from which they had been formally removed were serious: women could receive up to twenty-five lashes, while men could receive up to thirty-nine at public whippings. Corporal punishments of removed paupers and other violations by the disorderly poor were largely replaced by arrest under vagrancy statutes by the 1820s.[59]

The amendments made between 1784 and 1824 point to the challenges endured by the institutionalized poor and the bureaucratic issues faced by those charged with their care. One important conversation lawmakers and philanthropists were having was whether overseers of the poor ought to provide aid to sick nonresident paupers regardless of settlement status, instead of removing them to their place of legal settlement on peril of worsening illness or causing death. This question, which was addressed in an 1821 amendment to the state's poor law, was important for determining how to treat indigent immigrants who had no legal settlement in the United States. The amendment allowed for the removal of immigrants who had arrived in the country via the port of New York to be returned to the city, to be carried out in the same manner as would the removal of a pauper to a documented legal settlement.[60] This policy, as well as the general influx of indigent transients into New York City, concerned many residents. One commentator lamented, "Why should we support all the vagabonds in our city? It will ruin us."[61] The overwhelming numbers of indigent transients in New York City defied the use of settlement examinations or pauper-by-pauper removals to stem the tide, as smaller cities were often able to manage. As one concerned citizen claimed, "the whites and blacks are pouring into our city from all quarters, and unless speedily removed, will get such a footing by obtaining what is in law called a settlement, that it will be impossible . . . to get them away."[62] City officials attempted to prevent this by employing the city's vagrancy statute, which was so expansive that it would have made it possible to arrest most of the poor residents within city limits.[63] In 1824, the New York State legislature attempted to address the consequences of the relief system's emphasis on removal as opposed to the provision of welfare in a major revision to the state's poor law. The new law included sections for the management of vagrancy, to some extent, within the welfare system; magistrates were authorized to use their own discretion when making arrests of vagrants, to determine whether they ought to be incarcerated in the prison or the almshouse.[64]

Indigent transiency punctuated the lives of a great number of individuals who populated the almshouses, jails, outdoor relief rolls, and roads of the nation throughout the nineteenth century. But the laws and public response to these individuals in the early decades set the tone both figuratively and legislatively for how migrants, paupers, the unemployed, vagrants, tramps, and hoboes would live in America until well into the twentieth century. These contours in American legal culture reveal that in the United States, the lower class is and historically has been bound by a duty to work or otherwise visibly demonstrate their fiscal responsibility in order to avoid punishment, which harkens back to the Protestant work ethic. This resulted in the development of the two specific civic obligations shared by all inhabitants of the United States, resident or alien, as outlined by Linda Kerber: the obligations to pay taxes and to "avoid vagrancy."[65] As Amy Dru Stanley has argued, vagrancy laws were perceived to have "rescued beggars" who would otherwise be seen as pathetic withholders of their labor "from the abject status of taking favors without rendering an equivalent." In the increasingly capitalistic nation, a term of incarceration settled the proverbial bill incurred by a vagrant's criminality.[66] This obligation to avoid vagrancy was central to conversations about citizenship in the early American republic because vagrancy was viewed as an action that voided civic privileges, as demonstrated by the exclusions in Article 4 of the Articles of Confederation. But this perspective amounted to more than de facto perception and prosecution; it was codified in settlement laws and suffrage exclusions.[67]

Vagrants, Citizenship, and Voting Rights

Settlement laws governed the movements of the poor, their access to welfare, and in some cases even the jobs that they could work. This was for primarily economic reasons: to protect districts from paying to care for or paying to punish individuals who did not have a legal claim in their territory. But there were social and ideological reasons as well, and many states and individual districts prohibited nonresidents from participating in political life. For many, especially among the lower classes, the combined forces of rootlessness and residency restrictions for voting limited the impact of migrants on political life in the nineteenth-century United States.[68]

Yet, the social role of transients was central to Pennsylvania's debates over suffrage in the antebellum era. These discussions illustrated the relationship between citizenship and vagrancy, and the impact of vagrants' presence in the public sphere and on policy. In the late 1830s, Pennsylvania revised its poor laws and its state constitution, redefining participation and exclusion from state citizenship. These amendments were largely in response to the growing population of free blacks in the commonwealth, which expanded exponentially during the antebellum era, whom many lawmakers wanted to prevent from gaining a voice in the state's political and civic business.[69] The legacy of Pennsylvania's revised 1838 constitution was the disenfranchisement of African American males who had technically possessed legal suffrage rights prior to that point, though in practice very few had been able to exercise them. A closer look at the convention's proceedings reveals that much of the argument surrounding suffrage at the convention was rooted in a discussion of class and mobility, as well as race. At the meetings where the constitutional amendments were discussed, "vagrants" and "wandering" paupers were described as the antithesis of the informed voter and held up as examples in arguments that favored limiting the voting rights of Pennsylvanians. The manner in which vagrants were discussed by the commonwealth's representative body elucidates many contemporary perceptions of the homeless and transient, as well as "appropriate" political engagement of the populace. That in the first few months of the meetings, conveners were issuing detailed descriptions of vagrants as unfit for the franchise points to a larger conversation that had been going on in the region since around 1820, as the poor population began to grow substantially. The dialogue that ensued in the state legislators' attempts at constructing a new constitution to better reflect the commonwealth's population and the contemporary zeitgeist reveals what is often only an implicit process.⁷⁰ By casting the actions of vagrants as actions that contravene the privileges of citizens, the poor were further alienated from not only public discourse but also civic rights.

In 1836, Pennsylvania legislators had revised the commonwealth's existing poor laws in an effort to increase effectiveness by enumerating the types of persons chargeable as vagrants and clarifying various welfare provisions.⁷¹ In the course of the debates over the changes to the constitution, lawmakers used strident rhetoric to discuss the dangers of these individuals and to make the case for excluding the poor from civic life. Representative Benjamin Martin asserted that he "would never consent to bring down the standard of the laboring classes to the standard of the vagrant or of the black man" by allowing either of them to vote.⁷² This assertion directly linked the issues of suffrage and race: legislators wished to bar vagrants and African Americans from both voting and, by extension, citizenship.

The call for race-based exclusion from the franchise that historians have discussed extensively was, in these proceedings, predicated upon class-based perceptions of the would-be electorate.⁷³ This was discussed mainly in relation to the most visibly impoverished, those most vulnerable to accusations of vagrancy. Officials and upper-class citizens were outraged that the poor were often found sleeping in public places or along thoroughfares. In the proceedings of the 1837–38 Constitutional Convention, the infractions detailed by the legislators were primarily sanitary or sartorial violations. Vagrants were described by delegate William Darlington as those who "slept in the market house" and by delegate John Cummin as "those who lie in barns."⁷⁴ Phrases like these, repeatedly used in the proceedings, were especially relevant in the debate over residency clauses in suffrage legislation. Members of the assembly argued that poor vagrants could be prevented from voting by requiring, for example, ten days' residence in the locality prior to an election in order to have one's vote accepted. The grounds on which the conveners opposed voting rights of the mobile poor were not solely transience but rather associations of virtue and hygiene with the transient. These statements give insight into how these legislators perceived vagrancy to exist: as such constant mobility that even a ten-day residency requirement could prohibit their meeting suffrage standards.

It is important to note that, though vagrancy has tended to imply a lack of steady income, there was little to no official conception of unemployment in this period.⁷⁵ Nonworking able-bodied men were nearly always considered voluntarily vagrant and thus depraved; women, the ill or elderly, and children were only occasionally considered above that same level. The mere physical appearance of vagrants was sufficient to arrest and prosecute lower-class individuals who looked similar or could be found in the same locations. The language used to describe these "paupers, vagrants, and convicts" places vagrants as potential electors as a danger to respectable society at large: as pestilence itself, or bringers of pestilence. These terms have generally been considered figurative, employed by reformers dedicated to "civic sanitation." One representative warned, "It would be better to get rid of this . . . before the plague reached the city."[76] Part of the danger of allowing vagrants to engage in civic life, lawmakers reasoned, was that they may vote against the interests of the ruling elite. Legislators voiced concerns that opening suffrage to more of the population would degrade the more "industrious" citizens among them and "confound the honest poor man with the vagabond"; it would, one representative argued, redefine the word "freemen" to "mean . . . the vile, the vagabond, the idle."[77]

The vagrancy acts and poor laws in antebellum Pennsylvania took sleeping in public or wearing dirty clothing as constitutive of vagrancy itself.[78] Representatives at the convention soliloquized on the bodies and physical habits of the vagrants they wished to exclude from civic participation. These bodies, they claimed, wore clothing that had been run through "mudholes"; vagrants adorned themselves with cravats that had been "wash[ed] in hog trough."[79] Statements like these reflect the early nineteenth-century belief espoused by most of the middle and upper classes that "vicious habits" and inherent dirtiness were the causes of poor health.[80] Physicians published studies finding that "dirt, debauchery, and idleness led to increased mortality"; thus, the idle vagrant embodied both the political and social threat of poverty, withdrawal from the economy, and opposition to the ruling elite, as well as the physical danger of illness.[81] As contemporary judges and lawyers deemed an accusation of vagrancy as actionable, this defined the wearing of visibly dirty clothing as an arrestable offense, adding levels of meaning to their references of the visual impact of these mobile and poor individuals.

By the close of the constitutional convention in 1838, Pennsylvania's requirement that an individual be resident for two years before becoming eligible to vote had been decreased to one year, but a ten-day minimum residency requirement to vote in a given district had also been introduced.[82] The conflation of citizen participation, stasis, and socioeconomic status that can be read in the debates of the convention held up the vagrant as one of the ultimate threats to society. By using "idle vagrants" as the metric for being undeserving of suffrage, Pennsylvania's legislators placed the vagrant at the center of the antebellum debate regarding citizenship.[83] Pennsylvania's 1838 constitution makes it quite clear whom a majority of the elected officials viewed as unworthy of citizenship rights: "the vagrant and the black man," the "pauper," and the "convict."

Vagrancy as Defined and Connoted

Vagrancy statutes contained implications of mobility that were rooted in the reality of transiency and instability so closely linked with poverty in the eighteenth- and nineteenth-century Mid-Atlantic. Mobility and, for some among the static indigent population, homelessness could and did result in vagrancy convictions. Such was the case for a Philadelphia woman named Charlotte Palmer, who served a month's sentence for vagrancy in 1823 for being "in the street having no home." Not quite two weeks after her release, she was arrested again, this time not for completely static poverty but for being a "strolling vagrant."[84] Vagrancy has historically included an implied element of mobility, but antebellum uses of the term encompass a pantheon of actions within the category of vagrant activity, including homelessness, working as a huckster, begging, or scavenging.[85] For some, vagrancy involved local itinerancy as a result of homelessness, while for others it involved traversing numerous states in search of subsistence, or squatting illegally.

For twenty-five-year-old Margaret Caster, arrested as a vagrant in Philadelphia on 17 March 1823, on the oaths of two citizens, it was the crime of "having no legal residence."[86] Caster was apprehended and sentenced to thirty days in the county prison. She served the full length of her sentence, but her situation did not change upon release, nor was this conviction a deviation from her previous lot in life. Almost exactly one year earlier, Caster had entered the Philadelphia Almshouse, homeless and illiterate, unable to sign her own name. She testified to having not lived for a year in "any one place, nor kept house."[87] By February 1828, little about her circumstances had improved, and she had returned to the almshouse, lacking even wage work to fall back on, or any residence to shield her from the vagaries of being jobless and homeless in winter. Caster's story is that of the local pauper vagrant: she did not travel far throughout her life, her residence having been determined as a young child by her parents' location and then, as an indentured servant from the age of ten, by her master, until she reached adulthood, at which time she relocated to Philadelphia to try her luck in the city.[88] As her conviction record states, it appears that her vagrancy was more a diagnosis of poverty than of movement. This was true for thousands among the populations of convicted vagrants in the nineteenth-century United States.

For many others, both class status and movement influenced their sentencing. For Samuel Gantdron, it was a combination of destitution and substantial movement that led to his arrest as a vagrant in the summer of 1837. He was described in the *Philadelphia Public Ledger*, a newspaper notorious for printing colorful depictions of wanderers, criminals, and disorderly persons, as "a loafer and vagrant from Boston . . . picked up by one of the city watch." But his description of his own affairs included no loafing: he reported having "walked the whole distance from the Bay to the Keystone State . . . in search of employment." His appearance and unfamiliar face had been grounds enough to "induct" him "into the watch house," regardless of his claim to be pursuing legitimate means of subsistence.[89]

But of course punishment for mobility was not the only motive governing the policing of vagrancy; enforcing the value of personal industry by penalizing that which authorities considered to be "idleness" was also an important factor. Vagrancy statutes targeted individuals lacking visible means of subsistence, which could be signified by proof of employment or by evidence that one had food, clothing, and/or shelter for themselves or their families. Those who did not were viewed as idle or lacking an industrious character, and thus subject to punishment for vagrancy. As the legal structures necessary to prop up the inherent imbalance of power in wage labor took firmer shape in this period, legal pressure and economic pressure joined forces to limit the options of the poor to provide for themselves.[90] The daily reality faced by many individuals who lacked private means and were not eligible for or willing to request public relief in some form was an attempt at striking a balance between achieving a legal subsistence and committing crimes for subsistence. Begging—whether for food, shelter, or money—was illegal in every state. For both the persistent and the transient poor, this posed a serious quandary: requesting the means to access subsistence goods or services (food, clothing, shelter) could warrant a vagrancy charge for begging, whereas illegally obtaining the goods could warrant a charge for theft. The result of this conundrum was an environment where these two paths often converged in the policing of the poor. Settlement and subsistence were the driving concepts behind poor relief, meaning that individuals who actively sought to reach subsistence for themselves in acceptable ways (generally through consistent work in the same location) were typically afforded aid in their place of legal settlement. Those who were not able to do so, and pursued unacceptable means of reaching subsistence, were subject to arrest for unlawful activities such as vagrancy, begging, and petit larceny.

The discretionary nature of vagrancy policing in this period meant that the responses of constables, watchmen, justices, and other versions of early police officers were based on the actions of vagrants, which were classified and defined in terms of their economic and moral implications. The records documenting arrest and incarceration for vagrancy lend themselves to a more human-centered analysis of the policing of the transient and homeless in the antebellum Mid-Atlantic. These cases validate historians' assessments that nineteenth-century vagrants were "quintessentially . . . the wandering poor."[91] Their proliferation in this period was blamed on a variety of factors, many of which have been delineated here. But when asked directly, in a survey conducted by the Pennsylvania Society for the Promotion of Public Economy, what the "alleged cause . . . of their poverty was," poor Philadelphians blamed the market factors that have perennially affected working families the most deeply: namely, "the great disproportion which exists between the prices of labor of men and women" and "the high prices of provisions" that were, of necessity, "generally purchased . . . in small quantities, from the grocery and liquor stores, at a very exorbitant advance upon the prime cost."[92] And even these considerations, of course, applied only to those who were able to find work, and to afford even marked-up groceries: those who could not do either of these things often resorted to illegal procuring methods often construed as vagrancy (including begging, and rag and bone collecting).[93]

In New York City in 1832, a man named James Rogers stole a bag of oats from a market stand. He was convicted of petit larceny, but he did not serve the punishment for theft; rather, he was committed as a vagrant to spend sixty days in the penitentiary.[94] Rogers had participated in an illicit economy of subsistence, as did hundreds of others across the city and thousands across the country that day. Rogers had committed, by his act of food theft, one of the actions of vagrancy: lacking visible means of subsistence. His infraction was cast as a violation of a vagrancy law instead of as a property crime. This reflects the connection between poverty and criminality clearly seen by the arresting justice, which reflected the legal structure that placed codes for the punishment of vagrancy under states' poor laws.[95]

In Esopus, New York, a small town near the Hudson River, on 7 October 1844, a local justice of the peace created a nonfiction Jean Valjean when he arrested a man named John Cox for "stealing one loaf a [sic] bread of Patrick McDermot." McDermot lived in Eddyville, about nine miles up the river, and his stolen bread had a "value of ten cents."[96] Cox was convicted five days after committing the act of petit larceny for which he was charged and sentenced to "be imprisoned in the Common Jail" of Ulster County for "fifteen days." Lengths of sentencing for petit larceny were not necessarily proportionate to the value of the stolen item. A sample of food thefts committed in Ulster County, New York, in the 1830s and 1840s shows that while Cox's loaf of bread was only valued at ten cents and deserving of fifteen days in jail, Lucius Sands's theft of "ten fowls" valued at $3.75 warranted ninety days in jail. Meanwhile, Benjamin York's theft of a half bushel of corn, valued at five dollars, sent him to jail for thirty days. Small thefts of food like the ones listed above showcase the range of efforts used by the poor to meet the physical needs of themselves and their families.[97]

As the conviction of James Rogers illustrates, acts of subsistence crime could take many forms: theft of food, necessary winter clothing, or fishing supplies. In looking at even a small sample of petit larceny convictions in the Mid-Atlantic, the material circumstances of food theft cases points to the systematic criminalization of subsistence efforts.[98] In Kingston, New York, during the five-year period between 1839 and 1844, 114 convictions for minor crimes were recorded by the justices of the peace. Of those records, eighty-eight—about 77 percent of the convictions—were for criminal acts of subsistence, including theft of food, firewood, or basic clothing items, lodging in the open air, and begging for food or shelter. The prosecution of the petty theft of food as vagrancy tells us that, at least occasionally, an individual's inability to legally procure food was construed as a lack of visible means of subsistence. This is a glimpse into the ways in which justices of the peace and city watchmen used the discretion of their position to police the activities of the poor and mobile, a de facto exhibition of the prosecutable subsistence activities of the poor falling under vagrancy law. Law enforcement officials had ample room to interpret poor laws in such a way as to expand their role to include the policing of other crimes under the purview of vagrancy law, which points to the importance of discretion and the readability of class and criminality on the street.

Many of the actions listed in vagrancy statutes can be classified as subsistence crimes. The convictions of individuals like James Rogers suggest that for many, vagrancy was not necessarily a voluntary commission of a minor offense but rather a necessary act of subsistence. The means used by the poor to meet subsistence level, and the discretion employed by authorities in policing the use of these means, is often revealed in the descriptions included in some convictions for vagrancy. Chief among these was vagrants' choices, or lack of choices, for sleeping quarters. For example, in Philadelphia in the winter of 1823, a woman named Sarah Godfrey reported to police a man named Thomas Cane after she "found him in her closet this night being destitute of a home."[99] Many indigent transients, like Cane, were led by desperation to find creative solutions to improve their chances at some small comforts. These improvised subsistence efforts often resulted in arrest. For example, a group of men who found quiet places to pass the night on a Philadelphia wharf in 1838 were arrested as vagrants because they had been "found sleeping on a bed of coal ashes" or with their heads "pillowed . . . on a cordwood stack."[100]

The local and long-distance mobility of individuals like Margaret Caster and Samuel Gantdron led poor relief institutions and law enforcement to work together to maintain a network of communication and transportation that often stretched beyond the boundaries of their jurisdictions. Guardians, overseers of the poor, justices of the peace, and other individuals who carried out the business of poor relief and pauper management in the nineteenth century were, as a rule, well-versed in the applicable laws and their roles in applying them. Significantly, they were also aware of individuals at other institutions, possibly quite distant from their own, who undertook similar tasks. By communicating in writing and, when possible or necessary, in person, about procedures for almshouse admittance, offering relief to paupers, and validating paupers' residency claims, officials used the channels available to them in their professional and interpersonal networks to carry out their duties establishing connections that facilitated the minutiae of the poor relief process. These connections were complemented by the necessary communications with penal institutions and law enforcers when almshouse residency included an element of punishment.

Authorities' attempts to regulate movement by and aid offered to indigent transients offer glimpses of the reality of the lives of the poor during the era of reform that shaped almshouse and magisterial policies toward indigents. It meant that vagrants and paupers were discussed, treated, and transported across town, county, and state lines.[101] This complicated further the already circuitous definitions of vagrants both in legal terminology and in actual identity. The case of Mary Nelson is an intriguing example of this. On 11 March 1828, Philadelphia Almshouse steward Jeremiah Peirsol responded to a letter describing her circumstances that he had received from Staats Van Deursen in New Brunswick, New Jersey, one of the town's poor relief authorities, who had just encountered Nelson.[102] She had apparently been "brought" there in December "much intoxicated" along with her child, who "was in good health and clean" while "*she* was filthy" (emphasis in original).[103] According to the almshouse officials who admitted her, "the impression was, that she could not be the mother of the child; but in the absence of evidence, we could not determine." The officials did not trust Nelson's claims that the child was her own because the disparity in their level of cleanliness was too great.[104] In their efforts to determine whether she was the rightful parent to the child, Nelson was interrogated. According to Peirsol, "The history the woman gave of herself was . . . that for several years, she had been living in the Southern States, and had been to St. Augustine, Florida." The combination of her travels, her destitution, and her filthiness led the managers to determine that she was "doubtless, a very vagrant, whose residence cannot easily be ascertained."

Lacking clear recourse as to where to send Nelson—which determining her legal residence would have provided—she, along with the child who was presumed not to be her own—were both discharged. Legal guardian or not, Nelson had given the appearance of providing sufficient care for the child, at least prior to their presumed arrival in New Brunswick, for Peirsol to assert that if they "had witnessed any ill-usage of the child, it is not probable that she would have been permitted to take it hence. Ill treatment, would, most certainly, justify any civil authority in providing for an abused and helpless infant." Still, Nelson and the child had been allowed to leave the institution together, despite the almshouse managers' clear impression that the child had been kidnapped. To make amends, Peirsol asserted that "nothing could be more gratifying than to return the child to its parents, if [Nelson] is not the mother" and prompted Van Deursen to consider "whether describing both in an advertisement, with a request for its republication in all newspapers, would be advisable."[105] The thought process of guardians of the poor in determining eligibility for aid and assignment of status as a vagrant is illustrated in Mary Nelson's case. While individual watchmen and magistrates had their own definitions of perceived vagrancy, and states' statutory definitions were not all identical, a sufficiently pervasive concept remained. It was so great that a disparity in cleanliness, coupled with any history of migration, between a self-identified mother and her child was sufficient grounds for the assignation of vagrancy.

Conclusion

Stories like Nelson's showcase vagrancy's place at the nexus of legal and lived homelessness, shaped by transatlantic social and cultural understandings of vagrancy. Because one of the keys to an individual being perceived as a vagrant was the extent of their mobility, the independent sojourn of a woman such as Mary Nelson in Florida was suspicious to authorities.[106] The importance of mobility as a factor in vagrancy convictions, as well as a determinant of poor relief eligibility, necessitates looking more closely at the physical movements that constituted that mobility, which will be considered in chapter 2.

The poor laws and vagrancy statutes that have been discussed up to this point generate more questions than they answer about the behaviors that they were designed to regulate and resolve. By investigating the individuals to whom these laws were applied, both de jure and de facto, as will be done in the following chapter, the circumstances that most often led to their creation become clear. The results offer a perspective on the early American republic wherein geographical mobility was often the only choice for an individual to maintain their livelihood, and was simultaneously the primary barrier to fulfilling their economic need.

2 / "A Wandering Life": The Physical Landscape of Indigent Transiency

In 1833, Lucy Ann Griffin did not know where her husband had lived and worked prior to meeting her, and she was uncertain whether he "had a settlement in any part" of Pennsylvania, where she currently resided. Following his criminal conviction in 1832 and incarceration in the state penitentiary, he promised to return to her after his release, and did not. "All that she could remember from his conversations," she testified in January 1833, was "that he had led a wandering life."[1] A wandering life, in the early republic Mid-Atlantic, could mean many things. It could describe the choice of a seafarer, going years without spending more than a week at a time in port, or a beggar seeking alms as he or she traveled. It could describe a fugitive slave, seeking refuge in free territory, fearful of staying in one place for too long, or a day laborer traversing from job site to job site. Lifestyles like these became commonplace when, as Douglas Lamar Jones has noted, "patterns of persistence declined more sharply" at the end of the eighteenth century and were replaced by increased mobility and "more volatile rural and urban populations of nineteenth-century America."[2] This mobility was by turns voluntary, coerced, prompted by need and want, and inspired by resistance.[3]

This chapter aims to lay out, to the extent possible, the physical landscape of indigent transiency that accompanied the legal one. States attempted to curb migration of the lower classes by criminalizing transiency and disenfranchising the poor and mobile because geographical mobility by the poor destabilized relief systems and threatened the moral, social, and economic order. Transients' mobility was viewed

FIGURE 2.1. David J. Kennedy, The Bettering House or House of Employment, Philadelphia 1828. This watercolor depicts Philadelphia's almshouse as it stood in 1828. This facility, also known as the "Bettering House" and "House of Employment," housed, incarcerated, and treated the city's poor from 1767 to 1835, when a new almshouse was constructed at Blockley. (Watercolors Collection, The Historical Society of Pennsylvania, Philadelphia)

as a tool for undermining established expectations for labor distribution, charity, and moral conduct.[4] Under this view, geographical fixity constituted a prerequisite for citizenship, which was codified repeatedly in the regulation of settlement, poor relief, and suffrage. Welfare officials often conflated pauper migration with vagrancy and were thus suspicious of indigent transients and reluctant to offer assistance to those lacking settlement.[5] These restrictive and prescriptive laws prompt many questions: In this period, what did illicit mobility look like? How were different forms of transiency experienced? This chapter will examine individual testimony and narratives of transiency as sources of knowledge about the identities and geographical movements of transients. It will consider how authorities viewed indigent transiency in juxtaposition to actual routes traveled by pauper migrants and vagrants. Finally, it will present evidence that significant shifts in the demographic makeup of the population of indigent transients took place throughout the nineteenth century and are indicative of profound socioeconomic changes that affected the lowest and most mobile classes in this period.[6]

This chapter will expand the scope used to analyze these sources in order to consider the population data and narratives of itinerancy in relation to larger historiographical questions about mobility, poverty, labor status, race, and gender. By drawing from settlement interviews and "examinations of paupers" it will chart the geographic movement of the vagrants, pauper migrants, and other indigent transients whose travels are outlined in these documents. These sources narrate the movements and subsistence efforts of people like itinerant pauper and free African American Ebenezer Widdington, who testified in 1834 that he had "been living about—as best he could" across the antebellum Mid-Atlantic.[7]

Cartographies of Transiency

There were some common patterns of migration among the poor. When transient John Devar was interviewed in Philadelphia in 1822, he claimed to have traveled southward from Lower Canada without mentioning a stop in New York. The guardian of the poor examining him singled out what he perceived as an omission, making an especial inquiry to this effect. Devar had landed from Ireland in St. John's in Newfoundland in July of that year, staying for only five days before going to Quebec, and "from there to Boston," where he stayed one week, then sailed to Baltimore.[8] The guardian's incredulity seems to suggest that northern transients arriving in Philadelphia rarely came by sea but instead more commonly traveled overland through New York City. The patterns of movement by the mobile poor during the height of early nineteenth-century pauper transiency were not quite as simple as almshouse authorities may have believed. Indigent transiency generally involved both urban and rural destinations and was predominantly undertaken as a form of subsistence migration. Rather, they reflected the decisions of workers seeking amenable circumstances both in employment and in the availability of assistance, seeking to bridge gaps between seasonal employment, day labor, and often wageless winters. But the perceived danger of the movements of this population led to regionally determined efforts to manage it.

One contemporary statistician, D. B. Warden, claimed that "in the middle states, on the Atlantic coast, the paupers have been estimated at 1 to 230 inhabitants," whereas "in the interior" the figure was only 1 in 350, and "of these a large proportion are foreigners and worn-out

FIGURE 2.2. J. C. Wild, Alms House, 1840. This painting depicts the Philadelphia Almshouse at Blockley, which was constructed to replace the city's previous almshouse in 1835 and remained in operation until it became part of the Philadelphia General Hospital in 1916. (The Library Company of Philadelphia)

negroes."[9] In 1833, Baltimore mayor Jesse Hunt addressed the need for his own city to be in communication with "the Mayors of New York and Philadelphia on the subject of paupers," as all received a constant flow of nationally and internationally migrant paupers every year. Their concerns, Hunt hoped, could be presented to Congress as a request that the federal government offer assistance in the cities' efforts to manage the populations of "foreign Paupers" who arrived in their cities "in the most deplorable condition."[10] Coordinated efforts to manage the pauper population across states were rare, but individual guardians and overseers of the poor did maintain nearly constant communication regarding individual paupers' settlement and relief. In Hunt's case, there does not appear to have been any official response to this request, but he was far from alone in his concerns. New York's Society for the Prevention of Pauperism reported in 1821 that "the foreigners and their children, comprising two-thirds of the whole number of persons in that establishment, do, in general, anticipate and rely on being supported there, before they embark for this country or, at least, during the period requisite to gain a legal residence in this city."[11] Although perceptions of the extent of foreign pauper immigration were generally inflated, their impact was significant in socioculturally linking the populations of the United States and Europe, as just shy of a quarter of nonresident paupers examined in the Philadelphia Almshouse between 1821 and 1844 had been born outside of the United States.[12]

In July 1837, the *Philadelphia Public Ledger* introduced a city police report detailing the arrests of several indigent transients with an explanation of the general population of vagrants' seasonal movements: "The ushering in of this month generally ushers into the Mayorial [sic] office a goodly quantity of loafers, who continue to increase throughout the fall and winter." These migrants tended to "travel South," possibly seeking more temperate weather. For them, that decision would have likely been more than a preference of climate, as it was noted that while some "make up a residence of thirty days ... in Moyamensing prison," following their arrest as vagrants, "by far the greater number take up their quarters in the Blockley palace over the Schuylkill." This tongue-in-cheek explanation of seasonal travel patterns implies that more of these travelers were indigent than criminal, more likely to deserve a stint in the Blockley Almshouse than in prison.[13] But it also may reflect logical choices made by the transient poor who aimed to eke out a few more weeks of outdoor labor options before winter closed in, moving gradually south to finish off autumn agricultural, maritime, and construction labor opportunities.

Overseers and trustees of the poor's perceptions of the source of those admitted to almshouses elsewhere confirm these southward migration patterns: officials and philanthropists in New York were concerned about European migrants becoming homeless or transient paupers after arriving in their port, or crossing into the state from the north, having walked overland from "Lower Canada," often "approach[ing] the city through New-Jersey or Connecticut." One observer claimed that it was at the start of every September that "all the paupers residing in the small towns of the neighboring counties of this state, New-Jersey and Connecticut, will be moving to this city to avail themselves of an early application for rooms in the Alms House."[14] Farther south, the mayor of Philadelphia reputedly interrogated a convicted vagrant, accusing him of having "came here two days ago from N. York" because he had "heard doubtless of the big Alms-house, and comfortable winter quarters, we have here." The vagrant asserted the contrary, but the mayor remained convinced otherwise, using such a possibility to argue in defense of pauper removal, stating that it was "enough to be compelled to support those who are already among us, without having all the vagrants of New York to provide for likewise."[15] But New Yorkers were threatened by northward migration, which one commentator claimed was the result of "a late law of Georgia" that "forced away several hundred free blacks, the greater part of which" migrated to New York. In the summer of 1820, it was feared that those "emigrants from the south [were] now paupers in this city, and will, *no doubt*, in the winter either have to be supported at the public expense, or will support themselves by thieving."[16] Some contemporaries viewed welfare provisions as an incentive to the poor, claiming that it was the availability of relief "which peoples those towns, where the best accommodations and amplest funds exist, with the vagrants and paupers of the surrounding country, and stimulates the march of hundreds from the interior to the city at the approach of winter, and invites the indigent from foreign countries, or determines them to a city residence after their arrival."[17] Of course, larger cities like New York, Philadelphia, and Baltimore were more likely to offer opportunities for winter employment, even if they took the form of unreliable day to day labor, as opportunities in rural areas tended to be more directly tied to the seasonal agricultural calendar.

Members of the Philadelphia Society for the Promotion of Public Economy claimed in 1817 that the city provided so effectively for its poor that it was their "opinion [that] the charitable institutions induce the poor to come here from all quarters."[18] Meanwhile, Baltimore almshouse officials were convinced that poor Pennsylvanians had heard of the apparent spaciousness of the facilities and quality of the food provided in this Maryland city and thus elected to walk "upwards of one hundred miles" in order to enjoy the superior comforts of Baltimore's almshouse."[19] These comments reflect some truths about migration patterns in the early nineteenth-century Mid-Atlantic but are likely more instructive about authorities' fears of overaccommodating the poor and criminal. But with several major metropolitan areas in reasonably close proximity to each other, many paupers may have intentionally chosen to select the option best suited to them – from job opportunities to open almshouses – out of the variety of possibilities available for their subsistence.

While immigrant vagrants were especially alarming to authorities, their foreignness was not necessarily the characteristic of greatest concern. Authorities' prioritizing of inquiries regarding mobility and settlement qualifications meant that native-born transients were also unwelcome and targeted for punishment, as Joseph Gille learned when he was arrested as a vagrant in 1837. He had arrived in Philadelphia from Pittsburgh "but fourteen days" before his arrest for idleness, having "not been able to obtain work for more than half [that] time." Gille's success at finding a full week of wage labor did not prevent the city patrol from viewing him as sufficiently idle to warrant a vagrancy conviction.[20] Levi Holmes, a "Yankee," was a subsistence migrant when he was arrested as a vagrant in 1836. He had evidently "been employed cutting nails in Essex County, and was making an effort to reach his home in Massachusetts, but was without the means of so doing." Having not managed to improve "his fortunes during his sojourn in the Key Stone State," the mayor "adverted to [Holmes's] pedal proportions, hinted their capacity to bear him home."[21] Holmes and Samuel Gantdron, who also claimed to have "walked the whole distance from the Bay to the Keystone State ... in search of employment," covered incredible distances on foot, while others managed to supplement their walking with travel by stagecoach or ship when possible.[22] Many indigent transients traveled from city to city, and the largest and most populous urban port cities with large migrant populations were all within about a hundred-mile radius of Philadelphia: Baltimore, New York City, and New Castle, Delaware. It is also worth noting that these cities were often only the most recent stop in a long line of locations through which migrants passed. And with greater concentration of opportunities for day labor, many transients traveled between these cities repeatedly. The labor market in the Mid-Atlantic in the first decades of the nineteenth century was growing increasingly dependent on a workforce of mobile laborers, and workers responded to this change with as much flexibility as their material circumstances could afford or forced them to accept. While early nineteenth century American capitalism in this case all but required regional movement and the crossing of state and municipal borders, the poor relief administration was an arm of the state operating within completely fixed boundaries, largely due to the municipal taxation system that funded welfare and penal systems. Many indigent transients, especially mobile wage workers, were likely unaware or unconcerned about the borders they crossed, drawn instead by the possibility of work, relief, or proximity to family. Yet their activities were defined by authorities almost exclusively in the terms related to their inability to remain geographically fixed. What transients may have viewed as arbitrary distinctions between locations, administrators bound to local, tax-based systems of poor relief and jail funding viewed as relinquishment of rights resulting from transiency or lack of settlement.

Because of many indigent transients' significant mobility, many of the narratives in the examinations of paupers taken in the Philadelphia Almshouse read like travelogues. In general, they offer minimal knowledge about the place where the narratives were recorded and far more about the places through which the pauper had traveled. One transient, Park Cullen, a widower with three children, was interviewed in Philadelphia, but his settlement interview reports that he had traveled from Ireland to New Brunswick in Lower Canada, to Boston to "various places in the Eastern States," to New York City and Philadelphia, all in the span of two years.[23] Transiency in the Mid-Atlantic was circulatory in this way: all of the states in the region were well-represented by those interviewed in the Philadelphia Almshouse, with individuals who had traveled from New York, Delaware, Maryland, and New Jersey comprising more than a quarter between 1822 and 1844.[24] Work in shipping and fishing especially led many workers to cross state lines in the Mid-Atlantic, which laborers commonly referred to as "following" work along the shore, a phrase used in 1822 by William Gore and Samuel Benton, who were both employed on the wharves, the latter in Baltimore, New Jersey, and Philadelphia.[25]

The travels of Joseph Robinson, who was interviewed as a nonresident pauper in the Philadelphia Almshouse on New Year's Eve of 1822, were also broad and circuitous. He testified to having been born in Ireland and then migrated to the United States four years previous. He landed in New York but only stayed three weeks before traveling onward to Philadelphia, where he resided for three months. He kept moving, living in Ohio for nine months, Union County, Pennsylvania, for six months, Brownsville for four months, and for some time in Bedford before returning to Philadelphia. Because he had arrived in this country at the port of New York and not gained a legal settlement anywhere else in the meantime, New York was the closest he had to a legal residence, and it was to there that he was removed that day.[26]

There were countless methods of eking out subsistence from place to place, both in terms of securing labor and wages and also, of course, physical relocation, much of which involved regional circulation. In describing these relocations, transients offer instructive details about the modes of transportation available to them, and their descriptions of the time spans they spent in each location offer insight into the longevity of casual employment arrangements. A woman named Rachel Johnson, when asked about the whereabouts of her husband, who was not with her in Philadelphia, stated that he had "returned to the state of New York, whence he came on a raft."[27] Jeremiah Mahaney, an Irish immigrant who landed in New York, stayed there for four years before traveling "to the West Indies" where he "lived 8 months, then returned to New York and lived 2 months, then went to Newark and lived one winter" before traveling to Philadelphia, where he gave the interview detailing this trajectory.[28] Theophilus Grew was more general in describing his transiency when he was examined as a pauper in the Philadelphia Almshouse in 1828. He had been born in Montgomery County and "bound an apprentice" to a nearby shoemaker, but "after serving him about six years, he ran away from his master." After absconding, he "wandered about for several years" before settling in Bucks County. There were periods of sustained employment in his life up until he reached the almshouse at the age of thirty-three, but he worked as a day laborer for much of 1828.[29] A Virginia-born man named Willoughby Newton Howell had been bound by indenture to a "sadler" in Bedford County, Pennsylvania. As soon as he was free, at age twenty-one, "He enlisted ... in the United States Army for eighteen years" and was discharged in New Orleans in 1815. After leaving the army, he testified in the Philadelphia Almshouse in the spring of 1829 that he had spent the next fourteen years "wandering about," not earning a legal settlement in any of the states he passed through on his journey north. He had only been in Philadelphia for four days when he was examined by the guardians of the poor there.[30]

For many transients, both the pattern of their behavior as well as their categorization under the law traveled with them across state lines. Basel Dobbins was twenty-three years old when he was sentenced to serve a yearlong punishment for vagrancy in Maryland's penitentiary on 11 March 1812.[31] He was a laborer who had been born in Baltimore County, and after completing his prison sentence in 1813, he remained there for a few more years. Sometime around 1817, Dobbins left Baltimore and ended up in Philadelphia, where he "followed laboring ... about 2½ years." Shortly thereafter, he enlisted in the army and was later discharged at Fort Scott in Georgia. He returned to Baltimore, and for the next year, Dobbins traveled between Baltimore and Philadelphia until he was again arrested as a "vagrant and idle disorderly man" in Philadelphia on 5 August 1822. By February 1823, he was examined as a nonresident pauper in the almshouse, possibly as the result of another vagrancy arrest or for relief.[32] In either case, Dobbins's indigent transiency was recognizable to authorities in both Maryland and Pennsylvania.

Mary O'Neil's trajectory appears to have been similar to Dobbins's path. Born in Ireland, she was forty-five years old when she was arrested for vagrancy in Baltimore on 17 June 1818. O'Neil had been working as a house servant in Baltimore prior to her arrest, suggesting that she had either only recently become unemployed, or the actions that led to her arrest for vagrancy may have fallen under categories other than the pauperism clauses of vagrancy statutes.[33] She served her full year's term in the penitentiary and was released in 1819. In "the fall of 1821," she made her way to Philadelphia. When her testimony was recorded in the almshouse there, it was noted that O'Neil said she did "not know her age (say abt. 50 years)," but had landed in Baltimore when she was about twelve years old.[34] O'Neil and Dobbins both received aid and were punished across state lines as vagrants and paupers, illustrating the salient characteristics and activities associated with indigent transiency.

For many of these individuals, transiency began with the first move, voluntary or involuntary; for some this was the transatlantic journey from Europe, for others, forced migration from Africa or the Caribbean. The Mid-Atlantic was a center for the circulatory spatial movement of the transient population on the Atlantic coast in this period, growing daily as recently arrived immigrants joined their ranks. Far from exclusively traveling between major urban areas, most transients stopped in smaller towns between capitals.[35] Travel times between these cities, even on foot, were generally between a few days and a week in any direction. Testimonies like Samuel Meninger's are representative of this form of migration: he had "no settled place of residence" but had "lived for short periods in the states of New Jersey, New York, and Maryland," followed by Philadelphia.[36] Some transients offered more detailed explanations, like Irish immigrant John China, who had landed in Portland, Maine, staying for eighteen months before moving on to Boston, then to New York, where he "stayed a few days," before traveling to Philadelphia, where he "lived 13 weeks." He "then returned to New York" and stayed about eight weeks, before traveling back to Philadelphia yet again.[37]

"Real Poverty!!!," Spatiality, and Temporality

Under nineteenth-century laws in the Mid-Atlantic, wandering—even in the effort to seek employment—was not only unacceptable when done outside of one's settlement but was also prosecutable. But laws against wandering by beggars and job seekers could hardly act as deterrents against mobility where few if any other options for securing subsistence were available. For unskilled laborers, transience was a repetitious feature of working life; canal-building, road construction, and fishing industries required frequent moves to follow job availability. While this certainly explains some individuals' patterns of mobility, others evidently had greater periods of instability and lack of work or residence than those who, for example, sailed with the United States Navy or merchant marine. Thirty-year-old Isaac Wiley was one such veteran. Born in New York, he began "following the sea" with "the U.S. Service" at age sixteen. He worked on a canal in Columbia, South Carolina, before being "hired by the month for 13 months to various places," followed by a temporary move back to New York. He then relocated to Philadelphia, where he found employment "type pounding" before beginning work on "the canal on Schuylkill."[38] Service in a military capacity or as a private sailor appears to have increased individual likelihood for continued transience long after discharge, with many veterans not only staying on the move but traveling greater distances than much of the civilian population. This may have been one of the results of the relocation often involved with military service, or a consequence of the economic challenges that so many veterans faced.[39]

Much skepticism surrounded narratives of destitution involving military service or time spent at sea. Indeed, several tropes of false misfortune were singled out as tactics used by the belligerent or unworthy poor to beg alms: "playing the old soldier," house fires, widowhood, the destitute sailor, and so on. This tendency not to believe the poor was written into New Jersey's colonial vagrancy and poor laws, which remained in effect in the state well into the nineteenth century, putting constables on guard that "all poor indigent persons strolling ... about this colony, under pretence of losses by fire, or having their goods and effects destroyed ... shall be esteemed vagrants and vagabonds."[40] But some among the homeless and unsettled were able to identify ways in which the punitive system of vagrancy policing might be in itself a tool for subsistence, in the absence of preferable alternatives. An 1839 article in Philadelphia's *Public Ledger* describing the arrest of a veteran as a vagrant and his tales of woe emphasized for readers the veracity of the descriptions to follow with the title "Real Poverty!!!"[41] George Morris was "an old revolutionary soldier, who had fought under Com. McDonough, and left his leg in the battle on Lake Champlain," who was now, almost sixty years later, "poverty stricken." The article takes an incredulous tone in recording that Morris had approached a city watchman and "requested him to commit him to the County Prison for thirty days as a Vagrant!!" His motivation in posing "this singular and strange request" was that he "had not a cent in the world" for shelter or sustenance. He had survived on nothing for some time, but when he injured his wrist, he was no longer able to bear the way he had spent his previous nights "lain on the commons in the rear of . . . Commissioners' Hall, chilled to the bones with cold." Morris had been denied a government pension because he lacked proper identification documents, was physically incapable of work, and had no other access to money for medical care. The watchman granted Morris's request, and he was sent as a vagrant to the county prison.[42]

Requests like Morris's, while uncommon in this period, were not entirely unheard of.[43] A man listed as "H. Bigelow" in a Philadelphia police report from 1836 had encountered a watchman one evening and explained his obvious "destitute condition" to him by the fact that he "had not had his liberty," and when he left prison, "he had not been furnished with one cent, even to obtain a meal of victuals." Furthermore, he "had not yet been able to obtain work." In response, the mayor offered him "a trifle . . . for his immediate relief."[44] Release from the prison or almshouse often left the formerly incarcerated penniless and worse off than they had been upon entry, especially if they had been employed before their arrest. When John Ramsay was arrested for disorderly behavior on 19 March 1836, he was said to have "confused ideas of geography." He had evidently "recently been discharged from the almshouse" when he was taken up for drunkenness. Ramsay averred that he was "entirely guiltless" of being "the worse for liquor" but rather was "subject to epileptic fits." Upon leaving the almshouse, he intended to travel to Lebanon, and notwithstanding his lack of apparent knowledge as to its location, his judgment was suspended. A few days later, however, he had yet to leave the city, and one morning "went up to a watchman" and explained to him "that he was nearly perished with cold and hunger" and hoped for assistance. According to the report from the Mayor's Office, "the Mayor gave him a small amount to get something to stay the cravings of hunger, and to pay his fare over Schuylkill bridge," as he evidently hoped to stop in Chester "for his clothes," and Ramsay was sent on his way.[45]

For indigent transients, stopping in a city for more than a few days in order to seek work increased one's vulnerability to a vagrancy arrest, yet settlement claims required a lengthy term of residence in a given area. Watchmen monitored new arrivals to the city vigilantly, meaning that many indigent transients who were unable to find work quickly enough often found themselves arrested for vagrancy. The overwhelming majority of pauper examinations from the Philadelphia Almshouse conclude with the testimony of the interviewed individual as to the length of time that had passed since they had lived anywhere long enough to have gained a legal settlement. In the case of Charles Hough, interviewed in 1827, he had not "lived more than 6 months with any one person since he left his father in Bucks County." He had, instead, lived in Doylestown until he "went to New York." He "remained there 9 months, then went to various places staid but a short time in each." Hough's trajectory was common, ending with a yearlong stay in Philadelphia but without work or his own home, as he had never "kept house."[46]

The element of temporality in short-term employment and residence lent punctuation to the lives of many transients. Susan Hall, for example, was described by the overseers of the poor as a mulatto when she was examined in the Philadelphia Almshouse as a nonresident on 25 February 1822. There, she testified that she had "lived in Philadelphia and Wilmington by terns [sic] ever since she was 10 years old, without ever living one whole year at any one time" in either location, or in any service job. Her first recorded arrest as a vagrant followed this almshouse interview almost exactly one year later, on 3 March 1823, when she was convicted "with being a disorderly vagrant."[47] Her name appears subsequently on the vagrant docket at this time of year, suggesting that perhaps Hall's journeys between Pennsylvania and Delaware, as the winter weather began to break in early March, drew the suspicion of the city watchmen. Examiners recorded transients' self-reported timescales, as in the case of the free African American woman Loraina Butler, who had "not lived more than 2 months with one person, nor kept a house" in the previous four or so years. She had been born in Shippensburg and raised as an indentured servant until the age of nineteen, when she "went to Pittsburgh," where she "remained about 2 years, but not more than 5 months with one person." She lived, worked, and married in Harrisburg and then moved on to Philadelphia two years later.[48]

Many settlement examinations also reflect the seasonal nature of migration and efforts among transients to secure a job placement to carry through the winter. Margaret Hempstead worked as a domestic servant for various families for several months at a time, at John Abbott's "from the fall to the next April," then in Nathaniel Trimble's family "from August 1827, till the following Spring." In November 1828, having not secured a position for the cold season, she entered the almshouse.[49] Evan Richardson had been bound by indenture to a West Chester farmer, Thomas Hoopes, and upon his release, he alternated by season between Philadelphia, where he "worked a summer for William Lybrand," and

West Chester, to where he returned in winter "and worked for Thomas Hoopes," then spent "the next summer" laboring once again for William Lybrand. Richardson testified in the autumn of 1828 that "last winter he lived in Wilmington, State of Delaware," but by the following November, he had entered the almshouse.[50] Hudson Springer's maritime experience, on the other hand, necessitated seasonal employment. He had "followed shalloping" and also "attended ferry for Jos. Bisban 2 seasons" before he "went to sea and continued to follow the sea" seasonally, out of ports in New Jersey and Pennsylvania.[51]

The testimonies of the most destitute, ill, and disorderly report similar institutional experiences in their examinations. For Richard Mickilravy, this meant that a period traveling between Washington, DC, Virginia, and the West Indies was followed up with a short stay in an almshouse in Green County, New York. Three months and an intervening journey to Philadelphia later, and he was admitted to the latter city's almshouse.[52] It was not uncommon for transients to end up voluntarily or involuntarily held in several different almshouses either in order to receive medical care or as part of a settlement and removal process.[53] Furthermore, cartographies of transiency were created through the management of poor relief itself, because movement was essential for itinerant paupers to obtain relief even within their region of legal settlement. In upstate New York counties, paupers seeking relief in their town of settlement would be, when approved, transported to the county seat, where the almshouse was generally located. Park Cullen, an Irish immigrant who had traveled through "various places in the Eastern States," spent "4½ months in the N. York Hospital" before his time in the Philadelphia Almshouse.[54] Rebecca Benson, an eighteen-year-old African American woman, was born in Delaware and spent her childhood there as an indentured servant, migrating to Philadelphia upon obtaining her freedom. She was removed from the Philadelphia Almshouse back to her legal settlement in New Castle, Delaware, and died in the almshouse there several years later.[55] John Steele "wandered from New York to Ohio working at his trade" and shuttled back and forth between almshouses in Lancaster, Pennsylvania, Philadelphia, and elsewhere in the 1830s.[56]

William Stewart embarked on a similar path as a childhood oyster seller when he either ran away from family or indenture, wandering from Blockley Township to Philadelphia at "about nine years of age." He was found "strolling about the streets" when "Peter Burton, a coulred [sic] man took him for charity." Burton provided him with a set of clothes "and sent him to sell oysters." According to Stewart, almost ten years after the fact, he had had little choice in the matter: "there was no bargain as to what he was to do." When he took ill, Burton was unable to provide him medical care, so he sought admission to the almshouse hospital in the city. He "was sent to the Shugar [sic] House," the separate facility reserved for almshouse patients with contagious diseases. While he was there, "Burton died," and Stewart had "remained in the Alms House ever since."[57]

Edward Campbell, too, was orphaned at a young age. He had been born in New York and relocated to Philadelphia with his parents, where the family lived until both his parents died before he reached the age of thirteen. He then signed on to work for William McKibbons in Westmoreland County, where he remained for nearly four years. He received wages of three dollars per month from McKibbons but, for whatever reason, chose to leave and take a reduction in wages to work for David Cook nearby at two dollars per month. He did not remain in Westmoreland County long after, returning to Philadelphia to pursue independent employment that ended up contributing to his transiency, when he took up "the business of peddling books."[58]

Population Shifts among Nineteenth-Century Indigent Transients

While there are countless similarities across the archive of settlement testimonies, over time, some marked differences become clear. The nineteenth century saw repeated and dramatic changes in the population of vagrants, tramps, and transients that traversed the United States. And though demographic data for indigent transients are often scarce or incomplete, some conclusions can be drawn about the individuals who comprised this group in the early republic. Chief among these are the differences in nativity, gender, and race to be found in geographical and chronological comparisons, which had a profound impact on the options available to individuals and on their perception by authorities.

An example of one early shift can be seen over just a few short years among the poor in Philadelphia. In 1817, a fatally cold winter prompted several prominent Pennsylvania philanthropists to investigate the extent of poverty among Philadelphia's lower classes and propose a solution for their relief, so that the crisis they faced that winter might not be repeated. This effort, led by the Society for the Promotion of Public Economy, involved conducting extensive surveys among the city's population. What they discovered was that almost half (44 percent), 540 of the

1,239 individuals who received poor relief that year, were nonresidents.[59] Among them, the majority were foreign-born, predominantly Irish and English, and only a small number had come from other states in the Union. Poverty worsened over the next decade, owing largely to the fallout of the Panic of 1819, which had completely destabilized the American economy.[60] In the years that followed, the characteristics of the population of indigent transients in the city changed dramatically. The marked differences between this group in 1817 and those represented in settlement interviews of nonresident paupers from ten years later, in 1827, by guardians of the poor stand as a reference point for how the geographic mobility of the poor in this region also changed in those intervening years. Whereas in 1817, most of the nonresident paupers receiving aid in Philadelphia were from Europe (predominantly Ireland), by the 1820s, paupers from other states, especially in the Mid-Atlantic, were found in triple the numbers of European-born paupers.[61] Indeed, the port of Philadelphia, the nation's second-largest city until 1840, welcomed some of the highest numbers of immigrants in the nation each year.[62] This change does not seem to be explained by a shift in foreign immigration into Philadelphia, as the city's port saw a significant increase in the number of migrants entering in this period.[63] Rather, it likely reflects an increase in the overall number of indigent transients traveling through, to, or within the city in this decade. Beyond these considerations, in Philadelphia, the high point of indigent transiency in the entire nineteenth century was 1826, when it is estimated that one in every hundred persons in the city was a convicted vagrant, and the rate of indigent transients was probably even higher once those who went unpunished are considered.[64]

The shift from internationally transient to regionally transient migrants receiving aid in Philadelphia between 1817 and 1827 may provide insight into the nature of this surge in mobility among the poor in the late 1820s. The economic depression that followed the Panic of 1819 led many Americans to take to the roads in search of work in neighboring counties and states, making the 1820s a pivotal decade for the lower classes in the United States.[65] During these years, internal migration within the Northeast increased dramatically, causing the populations of nonresident paupers to swell, and in turn, prompting investigations by state legislatures and local governments into the "increase in pauperism" in their jurisdictions.[66] This could point to one of the impetuses for reform efforts escalating in this period, and most certainly led to New York's poor relief overhaul in 1824, which allowed transients to be relieved in situ rather than only in their place of legal residence.[67] In the 1820s, a number of investigations were conducted to inquire into the "condition of the poor and the administration of relief" through legislative committees and beneficent groups in an effort to diagnose the cause of this dramatic rise in pauperism.[68] Pennsylvania overhauled its poor laws over a decade later in 1836, introducing a new provision to allow for the punishment as vagrants of paupers who had been removed, as nonresidents, from a jurisdiction where they did not possess legal settlement (presumably in response to a larger number of individuals returning after removal).[69]

The dominant image of the indigent transient in American culture is the young, white, male tramp with ragged clothing and a bundle atop his shoulder.[70] This stereotype is fairly accurate for the late nineteenth century: statistical data from New York and Philadelphia, as well as other cities, show that from the 1870s onward, the vast majority of vagrants and tramps fit that description.[71] But these characteristics did not match those of the typical indigent transient of fifty years earlier. Both early and later nineteenth-century indigent transients were characterized by a tendency to, as one contemporary newspaper article phrased it, "sleep nowhere . . . and pay for [their] lodgings with nothing at all." But stark differences are found between the two.[72] By the 1870s, individuals being arrested for vagrancy were more often tramps—that is, voluntary indigent transients—seeking work or following an entrepreneurial spirit. Tramping in this way was less common earlier in the nineteenth century.[73] Rather, many indigent transients in almshouses and jails in the antebellum era were subsistence migrants, including whole families.

One of the largest samples of demographic data for vagrants in the earlier period, from Philadelphia, paints a picture of a distinctly different population. During the 1820s, among vagrants incarcerated in the Philadelphia Prison, half were black, while barely under half were women.[74] Between 1823 and 1899, the overall representation of both groups in the vagrant population of the Philadelphia Prison decreased significantly.[75] In 1826, 46 percent of the vagrants incarcerated there were women, and 46 percent were black. Fifty years later, in 1876, only 20 percent were women, and 3.5 percent were black, marking a dramatic change in the population, with far fewer women and people of color incarcerated for vagrancy.[76]

To hone in more closely on the indigent transients for whom the most information is available, population data can be extracted from the testimonies offered in settlement examinations. Among 1,600 indigent transients interviewed for settlement in the Philadelphia Almshouse between 1822 and 1844, 40 percent were women, and 25 percent were people of color.[77] In a collection of just over one hundred nonresident examinations in Huntington, New York, on Long Island covering the same period, there were fewer women at only 26 percent, but there was similar overall distribution, with 25 percent people of color, only 7 percent foreign-born, and 13 percent not local to Long Island.[78] In Baltimore's Calverton Almshouse in the 1830s, nearly half of the relieved paupers were long-distance migrants, with 36 percent being foreign-born and 10 percent born out of state.[79] The homogeneity of their geographical trajectories and narratives of employment and poverty, however, suggests that the connections between these groups were not just perceived but, at least in some cases, completely tangible.[80] This is especially seen, as will be addressed later, in the testimonies of individuals who crossed these distinctions in their own lives as vagrant paupers.

The racial composition of the indigent transient population circulating throughout the Mid-Atlantic was also significantly different in the earlier decades of the nineteenth century than it was to become as the antebellum era wore on. In Philadelphia, African Americans represented four to five times their proportion in the city population in the prison's vagrant docket between 1823 and 1826, but by 1850 were represented in proportion to their numbers in the overall population.[81] During those same years, African Americans comprised two and a half times their proportion in the city in the nonresident pauper population at the almshouse. Demographic breakdowns from other regional institutions confirm the same: African Americans were overrepresented among the indigent transient population in the 1820s, and almost completely absent by 1850. African Americans comprised 26 percent of the vagrants incarcerated in New York City's Bellevue Penitentiary in 1820—nearly three times their total population in the city (8.8 percent, or 10,886/126,706).[82] In the New Castle County Almshouse in Delaware, the percentages of nonresident African Americans were similar to Philadelphia, at roughly 25 percent, from 1822 to 1827. By 1855, no African Americans were recorded among nonresident paupers in that almshouse.[83] In Huntington, New York, well over a third of the extant settlement examinations taken between 1811 and 1829 were for African Americans, while the records indicate only one African American examined as a transient between 1830 and 1841.[84] This dramatic decline in recorded numbers of African American indigent transients can be attributed to the simultaneous increase in racially motivated violence from the 1830s to the 1850s, especially in border regions. With increasingly open hostility expressed by whites in the Mid-Atlantic and, after 1850, the passage of the Fugitive

Slave Act, the risks of voluntary mobility may have prevented many African Americans from taking to the road.[85]

The gender composition of the indigent transient population circulating throughout the Mid-Atlantic mirrored the decrease in African Americans in the same group, albeit at a slightly slower pace. A variety of factors influenced female transiency and other life choices that were specific to their gender. Catharine Shaw, a twenty-eight-year-old Irish-born married woman with two children testified in 1823 that she "don't know where her husband is, he left her six weeks ago." They had migrated together from Ireland to New York in 1821, and by the end of 1822, he had abandoned Catharine and their two children. She left New York three days after Christmas and traveled to Philadelphia. She was removed on 16 January 1823, likely back to New York. Martha Erwin had been born in Washington, DC, and after marrying, moved with her husband to New York, but "he abandoned her, 6 mos after they got" there, joining the army. Harriott Davis was born in Cape May, New Jersey, and "left there for the first time 3 years ago & came to Philad." after "her husband deserted her at the town of Cape May." Elizabeth Sammons, a "mulatto, married woman," had been born in Camden, Delaware, and lived there with her husband and child until "her husband deserted her" there, and she "came to Philad." with her young son, Joseph.[86] The first steps taken by many younger wives after desertion by their husbands were more inclined toward travel and transiency than immediate seeking of public aid. Some may have taken to the road in search of their husbands or to join other family members. These choices could have been based on the varying material means available to individuals but could also reflect a view of mobility as a means to subsistence that was, perhaps for some, preferable to institutional poor relief. There was also a long-standing tradition of widows relocating to urban areas where, with greater diversity of employment opportunities usually available, they would be more likely to find means of supporting themselves.[87]

There were regional differences in the gender divide of indigent transiency in the early decades of the nineteenth century as well. Vagrants were a common sight in mid-1820s New Orleans, with proportionate rates of conviction: 36 percent of all arrests made in the city were for vagrancy, but almost none of those charged were women.[88] Similar gender distribution is also found among the incarcerated in antebellum Georgia, where very few women were imprisoned in this period. The ones who were, however, were predominantly committed for minor crimes including "vagrancy and disorderly conduct."[89]

In Baltimore in the 1830s, trustees of the poor estimated the number of "strangers," indicating those without legal residency, in the Calverton Almshouse to be just shy of 10 percent of the overall pauper population. Among these indigent transients, an average of just 13 percent were women.[90] The root of disparities like this one may lie in how individual cities policed gendered crime, especially prostitution. It is well-known that prostitutes were routinely arrested as vagrants in New York City, and the same was common in Philadelphia until the early years of the nineteenth century. By then, punishment of prostitution was being processed independently, dramatically decreasing the likelihood that a vagrancy conviction would be the punishment for sexual deviance in that city.[91] This suggests, at least in some contexts, that the prosecution of indigent transients may have been a reflection of the equalizing effects of poor laws and vagrancy statutes regardless of gender.[92] At any rate, the policing of sexual activity in the nineteenth century was in flux and likely affected the representation of women among the vagrant population whose "sexual misconduct" would occasionally be adjudicated as disorderly conduct.[93]

The cause for the dramatic decline in the number of women among the convicted transient poor may have been a gradually growing pool of available work for women throughout the nineteenth century. On the other hand, the general absence of women from the tramp population after the 1870s may have been the result of late nineteenth-century conceptualizations of gender and women's moral status.[94] This raises the question, then, of why the impact of republican mother and "separate spheres" ideologies failed to diminish the population of earlier nineteenth-century homeless women. These sociocultural trends were constructed within a middle-class milieu and likely offered little to women in the lower classes. In general, social historians have understood the role of gender in geographical transiency within the framework of the larger demographic shift that occurred in the nineteenth-century transient population. By the 1890s, indigent transients were predominantly voluntary transients and working-class tramps—a far cry from those in the early republic who were the destitute, wandering poor, comprised proportionately of women and families searching for work and subsistence.[95]

Part of this change may be explained by the dramatic expansion of private relief agencies in the first half of the nineteenth century, a large proportion of which were specifically designed to aid women and children.[96] The provision of support for the poor was under constant scrutiny, and many contemporaries firmly believed that the provision of relief prompted idleness and dissipation. Still, many private and some public organizations provided aid for "deserving" women and men throughout the century.[97] Indigent transients' lives were significantly affected by changes in how public and private welfare was distributed, and a rise in the latter could have precipitated a decline in the likelihood of women to seek opportunities elsewhere when aid existed where they were. For the most part, however, private relief providers exercised greater discretion in providing aid because it was generally believed that "private poor relief should aid the worthy poor" who were willing to conduct themselves in a way that portrayed that they were satisfactorily "industrious" and "deferential."[98] Women were often seen as more suitable recipients of relief than men because of their status as dependents who were potentially vulnerable to the neglect or abandonment of male providers and protectors. For some women, a dedication to reforming their sexual conduct and abandoning prostitution or other licentious activities was a prerequisite for receiving assistance in places like Magdalen asylums, which may have affected a small proportion of female indigent transients.[99]

Conclusion

Examining who experienced indigent transiency in this period helps us understand what is and is not unique about poverty in the early nineteenth-century United States and why the criminalization of poverty emerged so starkly in this period. The social geography of the roads in the nineteenth-century Mid-Atlantic was marked by subsistence migrants circulating between major capital cities and small market towns, traveling as long or as frequently as was necessary to find or keep work or locate public assistance. The demographics of indigent transients changed dramatically near the middle of the century, as the population of white male transients grew and fewer women and African Americans took to the road. Populations of indigent transients in almshouses as relief-seekers and prisons as incarcerated vagrants were reflective of the larger patterns of mobility among a class in which distinctions between these groups were often unclear. The "wandering lives" that many paupers and vagrants led threatened the stability of community boundaries and marked their activities for punishment.

"Too many persons," one guardian of the poor wrote in 1829, arrived in the city "from the country," from a wide variety of regional occupations and locations, "canals . . . railroads, farms, and towns." Cities, he warned, needed to "take some measures of self-defense, or permit" their organizations "to be run down" by indigent transients.[100] Throughout the early decades of the nineteenth century, this concern remained pervasive as economic stability continued to prove elusive, especially following the Panic of 1837, which prompted another period of instability, considered by some scholars to have been the nation's "first great depression."[101] The severity of the economic depressions of the 1820s through 1840s was most pronounced and protracted for the lowest classes, especially the transient. One of the "measures of self-defense" that was available to guardians and overseers was the use of settlement and removal laws to forcibly eject indigent transients from their jurisdictions, which contributed to the dramatic amount of movement being undertaken in the early American republic, as will be discussed in chapter 3.

3 / "The Removal of So Many Human Beings... Like Felons": Forced Migration of the Poor

In the summer of 1809, Sarah Turner was sentenced to be whipped "ten lashes upon her naked back" in the city of Poughkeepsie, New York. This punishment, to be carried out "with a whip suitable for that purpose," was levied upon Turner as a result of her unsanctioned geographical movement. At some point in the previous year or so, Turner had arrived in Poughkeepsie after having traveled through the Hudson River town of Marlborough and spending at least some time in nearby Shawangunk. According to Poughkeepsie's justices of the peace, Turner was a pauper considered "likely to become chargeable" to the city, possibly because she was accompanied by her "infant child" and thus viewed as unlikely to be able to sufficiently provide for herself. As a result, she had been forcibly removed by constables and justices of the peace from Poughkeepsie in February of that year. But Turner did not comply and had illegally returned to the city in the subsequent months.[1] This vagrant activity violated New York State's poor law, the punishment for which was the whipping post: up to twenty-five lashes for women and thirty-nine lashes for men, followed by "retransportation" back toward the indigent transient's place of legal settlement.[2]

Forced transportation of the transient poor, generally referred to as pauper removal, was a ubiquitous and legally sanctioned method by which state and local authorities exerted control over the movements of the poor and limited fiscal liability for the care of poor individuals and families who had no claim on their district through residency or the payment of poor taxes.[3] Toward the end of the nineteenth century, pauper removal became an especially unwieldy option, as general populations, and along with them, the numbers of indigent transients, grew exponentially. But throughout the first half of the nineteenth century, many paupers' physical networks were dramatically altered in this way after penal or other institutional contact was made. This commonly occurred in two ways: as voluntary relocation based on poor relief options or settlement laws, or through forced removal and transportation by police or almshouse officials.[4] It rarely resulted in the kind of corporal punishment that Sarah Turner experienced in Poughkeepsie in 1809—poor laws in New York and New Jersey were the only ones in the Mid-Atlantic to include whipping as a potential punishment for paupers or vagrants, and officials upholding these laws resorted to this punishment infrequently. Many poor people lived in a single district for all or most of their lives, often receiving poor relief over many years. But thousands of paupers, including those lacking legal settlement because of recent movement or despite years of residence, as well as those considered vagrants, were subject to removal and forced migration in this period—in its own way a form of corporal punishment.[5] Pauper removal was a method of carrying out legal proscription of transiency for the poor by linking class status with legality of presence. Many paupers' relationships with the state were shaped by their experiences passing through the revolving doors of the almshouse and the prison, navigating a system that was both gendered and racialized.

The history of pauper removal in the United States, as adopted from English law, began with the warning systems of the eighteenth century, early manifestations of settlement and removal laws that allowed town officials to escort indigent transients outside the boundaries of their jurisdiction in order to prevent them from becoming "chargeable" to the town for poor relief.[6] Most discussions of this practice focus on New England, but most states had settlement and removal laws dating to this period.[7] In Rhode Island, this process was the result of interrogation, coercion, and the overwhelming potential for personal disaster, as transients were forced to leave or were forcibly removed to their place of legal settlement.[8] These efforts were not uniform, however, as a contemporaneous warning system in Boston was primarily a bureaucratic effort to absolve the city of responsibility to care for nonresident indigent transients and did not often result in actual removal. In the Mid-Atlantic states in the early nineteenth century, however, the physical removal of paupers was common and well-regulated.[9]

Settlement and removal processes in the Mid-Atlantic were more similar to Rhode Island's than Massachusetts', utilizing forced migration as an alternative to the provision of in situ welfare for indigent transients.[10] By the 1820s, with the ranks of indigent transients swelling, removal become infeasible for some cities, and many overseers of the poor and justices of the peace turned to incarceration in prisons and almshouses as a simpler alternative until that, too, became unsustainable.[11] In 1824, the state legislature of New York effectively abolished the forced transport of transient paupers between counties, stipulating that relief was to be provided to the mobile poor wherever they happened to require it, request it, or come under police jurisdiction. And the law had teeth: overseers of the poor or justices of the peace who violated the removal policy could be fined or imprisoned for noncompliance.[12] Transportation of paupers continued after 1824, but under less punitive terms.[13] New York was unique in its effort to limit removals through legislation, as other northern states retained the laws that allowed for and regulated the practice throughout the antebellum period.[14] In fact, it was not until 1969 that the United States Supreme Court declared that laws requiring an individual to have residency in a given location in order to receive relief were unconstitutional.[15] Throughout much of the rest of the Northeast in the nineteenth century, settlement and removal laws, coupled with vagrancy statutes, continued their same general function of countering what Tim Cresswell has described as "the threat of an industrial poor gathering ... during economic downturns hoping for relief."[16]

This logic extended to immigration as well: long-standing laws allowing for the removal of paupers shaped immigration laws, making it possible for states to order "the compulsory return, or deportation, of destitute foreigners already in America, to their countries of origin," as Hidetaka Hirota has documented. In this way, the Supreme Court's 1837 ruling in *New York v. Miln* "legitimized immigration control by states."[17] Deportation policies drew on the strength and ubiquity of pauper removal practices to specifically designate poor immigrants, just as they had indigent transients, as excludable or deportable people. The *Miln* ruling reflected and provided a legal, if hyperbolic, basis for antipauper sentiment. In this case, which clearly delineates the functions of the police power of the states, the Supreme Court asserted that it was "as necessary for a state to provide precautionary measures against the moral pestilence of paupers, vagabonds, and possibly convicts as it is to guard against the physical pestilence which may arise from unsound and infectious articles imported or from a ship."[18] By extension, then, according to the court, states were given the power to "prevent [their] citizens from being oppressed by the support of multitudes of poor persons who come from foreign countries without possessing the means of supporting themselves."[19] Poor migrants, then, whether foreign or from another state in the Union, as well as their children, who could "be deemed liable to become chargeable on the city" were subject to the mayor's power to order "the removal of such person ... without delay to the place of his last settlement."[20] In Pennsylvania, passenger laws regulating immigration were instituted under the commonwealth's poor law. The Philadelphia Guardians of the Poor were charged with implementing it by evaluating the socioeconomic status of recent international arrivals and collecting head money from landing ships. They also facilitated removals of foreign paupers, and, of necessity, addressed the many cases of poverty and destitution among recent immigrants who entered the almshouse daily. New York, meanwhile, developed even more punitive policies to allow authorities to manage, exclude, and deport foreign paupers, specifically targeting the Irish.[21]

Beyond simply balancing the relief accounts or shifting fiscal responsibility for the poor, removal undermined the voluntary transiency of the lower classes and replaced it with a state-sanctioned form of mobility. The methods of policing vagrants' and paupers' spatial movements are instructive of cultural understandings of mobility in the early republic Mid-Atlantic, in which rootlessness and transiency among the lower classes were seen as criminal, and pauper removal was configured as a form of vagrancy policing. Examining these two legal categories and the individuals who occupied them together affords a deeper understanding of the experiences of indigent transients as well as cultural and legal conceptions of class in the early republic. Pauper incarceration, relief, and removal were not strictly surveillance schemes that enabled authorities to control the behavior of the poor; they also supported a complicated economic balancing act that relied on social monitoring in order to remain in the black. Removal was viewed as a long-term solution to an ongoing problem: in many cases, relieving the transient poor in situ would have saved districts money, as removal was often more expensive than temporarily providing food or shelter. Removal was intended to offer long-term immunity from any obligation to pay for the relief of indigent transients, and it upheld the law's clear definition of community membership earned by sustained residence and payment of municipal taxes.[22]

Using an archive of sources that document the removal process in Pennsylvania and New York, consisting primarily of almshouse and prison records, this chapter argues that the laws which structured it and their implementation reveal much about the lives of the poor, how authorities viewed them, and the ways in which they experienced poverty and forced transportation. Examining pauper removal emphasizes the particular importance of recognizing how the welfare systems that facilitated this work were complicit in the policing of the geographical movement of the poor. Furthermore, it demonstrates the importance of considering poor laws and vagrancy statutes in the context of state power.[23]

Pauper removal may have been a theoretical fixture on the legal landscape, but indigent transients were also physically moving and being moved on a literal landscape, the experience of which was shaped by their race, gender, and labor status. Although only a small portion of the population experienced pauper removal personally, it represents a significant episode in the evolution of poverty and its management in the United States and documents efforts at state control of mobility for certain groups. The pauper removal process demonstrates the longevity of the impact that incarceration and policing could have on the poor and communities and depicts a network of communication surrounding indigent transiency that crossed state lines and factored into regional perceptions of population and movement. The state-coerced movement of the mobile poor embodied what was essentially a reversal of volition for those who experienced it.

Law and Process in Pauper Removal

In most states, generally from the 1780s into the early twentieth century, an individual was only eligible to receive public aid in their place of legal settlement.[24] This was not the same location as their residence necessarily but, rather, the location where they had worked for the same employer for a given length of time, owned land or paid poor tax, served an indenture, or rented a home for a given length of time. Requirements varied from state to state, and the qualifications were tweaked by legislators throughout the period to control allocation of poor relief and certain privileges, such as suffrage. In the Mid-Atlantic region, New York and Pennsylvania's records on pauper removal are the strongest, though Delaware and New Jersey also enforced pauper removal as a means of managing the population of itinerant poor.[25] Maryland, on the other hand, had an almost completely unenforced colonial settlement law that was neither updated nor repealed in the nineteenth century and contained no provisions for removal.[26] When a study committee appointed by the Philadelphia Guardians of the Poor visited the Baltimore Almshouse in 1827, they reported that the overseers there were not "restricted to sending [to the almshouse] those only who have a legal settlement... but may also send such indigent and distressed persons, as in their opinion the dictates of humanity or peculiar circumstances render proper or necessary. Their service," they reported, was "gratuitous." The provision of aid to nonresidents was often administered through outdoor relief as opposed to almshouse admission but was not restricted on the basis of residence.[27]

The infrastructure and transportation routes into and out of New York City and Philadelphia made the two cities especial hubs for voluntary migration by paupers and made authorities' efforts of forced removal feasible. In general, almshouses were bound by common understanding to provide food and medical care to persons in dire need, regardless of residence. But doing so placed a strain on poor relief budgets and, at least in New York, the practice was a point of contention.[28] Some almshouses provided shelter or medical treatment to nonresidents by using means other than allocated local poor tax funds, such as state appropriations, profits of residents' labor, or charitable donations. Still, for immigrants as well as regional migrants whose place of legal settlement was inaccessible to them, obtaining relief if they became indigent could be a challenge. And if they did gain admission to an almshouse to receive that relief, circumstances could move beyond their control quite quickly.

The most effective method for guardians of the poor to manage the size of their pauper populations—as well as their accounts—was pauper removal: physical relocation of the nonresident indigent by a law enforcement officer.[29] Other options were less reliable. In some cases, the overseers of the poor in the pauper's present location could contact the overseers in the pauper's place of legal settlement in order to request payment for their maintenance. Whether or not payment would be forthcoming was unpredictable at best. If, on the other hand, a pauper's legal residence was easily ascertained, a constable could readily be hired to transfer the pauper directly to the care of the responsible overseers of the poor. These decisions seem to have been made entirely without the input of the pauper, beyond their initial answering of questions during an interview or settlement examination. However, the records of some of the examination and removal processes provide the pauper's perspective on the experience of transportation. The frequency of resistance during the removal process in the records examined here for New York and Pennsylvania suggests that paupers were afforded at most a minimal role in determining the timing or location of their relocation, in providing the requested information about their legal settlement. Much of the transportation of transients that occurred—though it is difficult to quantify exactly how much—was an involuntary result of a criminal conviction. James Gurum, for example, was arrested on 17 March 1819 for being a "vagrant . . . having no legal residence" and was sentenced to spend one month in a Philadelphia prison or however long it took until he could be "removed to Princeton, New Jersey by the Guardians of the Poor." This evidently required some time; he had already served five days beyond his thirty-day sentence when he was sent to the almshouse on 22 April 1819 to await removal to his legal settlement.[30] In both New York and Pennsylvania, individuals could also enter the almshouse via sentencing by magistrates, justices, or city watchmen for vagrancy and other socially disorderly activities or by requesting admission for medical aid or shelter. Vagrants and the nonresident indigent were all vulnerable to removal processes.[31]

In New York, when a district's overseers of the poor determined that a pauper had no legal claim to aid in their district, they contacted two of the local justices of the peace. Justices would issue "a warrant for transporting Paupers to their last legal residence" by completing a fill-in-the-blank form (the very existence of which can perhaps be seen as an indicator of how common the practice was), addressed to "any constable of the town" where the pauper was being relocated. In the 1827 case of a New York pauper woman named Elizabeth Colley, justices of the peace of Huntington in Suffolk County were requesting the attention of constables in Brookhaven in the same county. As Colley was, at the time of the request, "now delivering a child," she was considered "likely to become a charge." The justices "command[ed]" the constables "to convey the said Elizabeth Colley from and out of our said town of Huntington to the town of Brookhaven."[32] These forms, completed by constables and justices, were to accompany the pauper to their destination as evidence that examinations had proven that the individual had a claim to legal settlement in that place.[33]

In Philadelphia, removal of nonresident paupers was a fundamental duty of the guardians of the poor. According to an internal management guide from 1817, a *Manual for the Philadelphia Guardians of the Poor*, "the great object of this incorporation is to provide for the support and relief of such Poor persons as have a legal settlement within its limits, or, may be found therein, having such settlement elsewhere. The latter are to be relieved by the guardians until they can be removed by the agent,

"THE REMOVAL OF SO MANY HUMAN BEINGS ... LIKE FELONS" / 65

to their place of settlement."[34] The manual offered detailed instruction on the implementation of settlement laws and the process for removal. The managers of the almshouse supervised the removal process, while agents and assistant agents conducted actual examination interviews and coordinated the practical components of the removal process. The regulations for the internal government of the almshouse stipulated that assistant agents carry out the physical removal of nonresident paupers, while agents reported to the managers and Board of Guardians regularly on the settlement of those in the almshouse, and the number of individuals lacking settlement who were removed. It was understood that resistance was a likely part of the removal process; the almshouse rules and regulations suggested that "if the pauper refuses to go, or is unable to be removed, the guardian is to report the case to the next meeting of the board for their decision, taking care in the meantime, that such person shall not suffer for want of necessary relief." Despite the clarity of duties laid out for individual almshouse officials and the general management and provision of relief in the city, there was dissatisfaction among officials, legislators, and the public. Related grievances were aired at a town meeting held in 1827, where it was asserted "that part of the existing law which has reference to the removal of paupers, is certainly very defective," but no legislative response appears to have followed.[35]

The geographical movement, in both urban and rural areas, that resulted from pauper removal was not exclusively unidirectional. Incarcerated vagrants and individuals who were subject to forcible transportation often resisted by absconding, frequently to the location from which they had been removed. In the 1830 case of Mary Miller, a justice of the peace arrived at the Philadelphia Almshouse to collect Miller and her young child and escort them to the city docks. The night before, an order of removal had been left with an agent of the almshouse that required Miller and her child to board a boat that would transport them down the Schuylkill River to Reading, Pennsylvania—about seventy-five miles away—the next morning. When the justice attempted to carry out the order, Miller refused to comply. She resisted until it was "too late—the boat was gone." Simply put, as the Guardians of the Poor lamented, she stood firm that she "would not" go. But by the next day, through persuasion, change of heart, or force, the justice of the peace had Miller's compliance, and she and her child were removed from Philadelphia.[36] The laws that shaped the document that authorized their removal stipulated that if she were to return to the city, she would be vulnerable to arrest as a vagrant.[37] Miller was born in Berks County and had lived in

Schuylkill County as a child. She had worked as a domestic servant in Orwigsburg and later in Reading and Philadelphia. She found herself in the almshouse in 1830 as a single mother who had "not worked for any one person for a year since she left Orwigsburg."[38] Having traveled away from her home and not possessing the means to sustain herself, Miller had become an indigent transient, vulnerable to punishments designed to simplify public welfare that had the effect of penalizing the geographical movement of persons like herself.[39]

In 1824, officials representing Rockland County, New York, orchestrated the removal of sixty-two-year-old Benjamin Pierson, who was residing within the county at the time in Clarkstown and deemed likely "to become chargeable" to the town. Pierson was apparently issued an order of removal by local justices of the peace to return to his place of legal residence in Huntington and "refused to comply." Clarkstown constables were alerted that he was to be remanded into custody and that they were held responsible to "convey [him] . . . out of the said town Clarkstown to the city of New York and deliver him in charge of a constable there and so from constable to constable by the nearest and most convenient route to the town of Huntington."[40] When an African American man from Ulster County, New York, named Johnathan Shaylor absconded from the almshouse where he had been incarcerated as a vagrant, the overseers sought him out, traveling eighteen miles before they found him so that he might be "brought back."[41] While most indigent transients had very little, if any, role in determining how they were treated, relieved, or punished by authorities, some clearly found ways to resist. The commonality of resistance to pauper removal such as was used by Pierson and Miller, and by the numerous other paupers who eloped before removal could be undertaken, is illustrative of how at least some indigent transients experienced removal—as involuntary, forced transportation. It was not only indigent transients held in almshouses who were subject to removal processes. Transient vagrants whose residence could be determined during their incarceration in a local jail or prison were also subject to removal. Benjamin Smith, for example, was arrested for vagrancy in 1819 in Philadelphia and sentenced to be held for "one month unless sooner removed to Salem New Jersey where he belongs."[42]

Even when cooperation was not a factor, efforts to find the most appropriate location for needy nonresidents were often ineffectual. In some cases, when almshouse officials were unable to transport a pauper back to their place of legal residence, an intermediate location would be selected, or, in the case of immigrants, individuals might be returned to the port city where they had first arrived in the United States.[43] Twenty-three-year-old white man Edward Armstrong was born in Boston and testified to having lived his whole life there until he reached Philadelphia. Boston remained his legal residence, but when he was removed from the Philadelphia Almshouse on 16 January 1823, he was sent to New York.[44] It may have been intended as a midpoint, whence the overseers of the poor in New York could send him farther north, or the decision may have reflected an economical choice on the part of the Philadelphia guardians to spare the expense of a constable's supervision over Armstrong the whole way to Massachusetts. Single, white, thirty-three-year-old Thomas Cochrane, on the other hand, had been transported in the reverse direction: born in Mifflin County, Pennsylvania, Cochrane spent his childhood in Pittsburgh before being "bound under indenture" and later relocating to "the State of Ohio and subsequently various other places" until "on the 29th of November he was sent by the Directors of the Poor of the City of New York to Philadelphia." It is not clear what motivated the directors to make this decision, as no settlement for Philadelphia is listed in Cochrane's records, unless it was perceived that better medical treatment would be available to Cochrane in Philadelphia, as he testified that "for the last two months . . . he has been in a bad state of health and is yet very feeble." Immediately upon arriving from New York, "the evening of the same day," Cochrane was "admitted to the Hospital of the Philadelphia Almshouse—Blockley."[45]

Similarly, Ann Sharp, a twenty-eight-year-old African American woman, had lived in New York with her husband, John Sharp, until "he was taken sick in October last," at which point "she supposes that he either went or was sent from New York home." She, meanwhile, "was sent from New York to Philadelphia Wednesday last by Mr. Hunter, Guardian of the Poor." Sharp had lived and worked in Pennsylvania for about six years as an adult, but she could also have had a claim to settlement in her birthplace, Wilmington, Delaware, or at her husband's legal residence in New York, which was apparently "about 150 miles from New York [City], up the East River." It does not appear that Sharp was removed an additional time after her examination in Philadelphia on 19 March 1827, as she remained there a few months later, in June, when she delivered a "legitimate child," a daughter she named Sarah.[46] Families were occasionally separated by orders of removal, as John and Ann Sharp discovered. Whether or not kin were removed together depended on a variety of factors: the legality of their marriage, dependent children, and the discretion of the city watchmen or overseers of the poor.

The laws of settlement and removal were gendered in their inclusion of coverture law in determining the legal residences of married women. As Linda Kerber notes, "a married woman could have no settlement separate from her husband." For the poor, then, "the law of vagrancy," and its attendant exclusions of nonresidents, "was shaped by the custom of coverture to the woman's disadvantage."[47] A married woman's settlement was determined not by residence factors of her own choosing but by her husband's; married women who were removed as nonresident paupers were taken to their husband's place of legal settlement.[48] Contemporary feminist and political commentator Clarina Howard Nichols argued against coverture in her home state of Vermont and was in favor of divesting married women's legal identities from their husbands' specifically to eliminate the "inhumanity of a system that could remove a native-born woman from her home."[49] And pauper removal was indeed a gendered issue, as Howard Nichols demonstrated: the removal of entire families "from among friends, to the care of strangers, at an expense which would have gone far to make them comfortable where they were, and at the risk of life too" might be avoided if, rather than legal settlements only being determinable by men, who might be intemperate or incapacitated, "the authorities who make laws had secured to [wives their] own earnings."[50]

Even a widow could be removed to the district where her late husband had established a legal residence, as was the case with Elizabeth Lee. She and her husband, James Lee, had been born and married in Ireland, migrating together to Quebec around 1820. They made their way to Pittsburgh and settled there when her husband found work at his trade as a glassblower. They rented a house from his employer and stayed there for over three years while he held that job until "two or three years after her husband left the employment of Mr. Bakewell, he died." In those intervening years, the couple had become destitute and, it appears, separated. James Lee "died beyond the Monongehela [sic] river . . . where he had resided . . . to the time of his death."[51] He had spent the same length of time he had held a job, paying rent and poor taxes, living hand to mouth outside Pittsburgh, and had left his wife. But when she, now a widow, found herself hundreds of miles away in the Philadelphia Almshouse in the dead of winter in 1830, the legal settlement recognized by the guardians of the poor was her husband's, "in consequence of the rent & taxes paid" by him in Pittsburgh. Rather than remove her in January's weather, Philadelphia's guardians elected to "charge her maintenance to" the directors of the poor in Pittsburgh. As she was "destitute of a home and not very well able to provide for herself," they saw fit to allow her to remain, at Pittsburgh's expense, until she might be able to manage on her own.[52]

What constituted "providing for oneself" was a discretionary determination made by justices of the peace and overseers of the poor. A young Irishman named Timothy Gribbins had been deemed capable of carrying out his own, seemingly informal, removal when he was sent from the New York City Almshouse to Philadelphia with enough cash for the trip. He testified that "in August last the Overseers of N York gave him 6/4 cents and sent him on to this city." It is not improbable that New York almshouse administrators may have seen greater potential for laborers finding work outside of New York City; Gribbins had worked "on the road" and at other odd jobs since coming to the United States prior to his admission to the almshouse in 1822.[53] The situation of thirty-nine-year-old James Ray was similar when he entered the Philadelphia Almshouse on Christmas Eve in 1827. He had been born a slave in York County, Pennsylvania, under the Gradual Abolition Act, and after his emancipation at age twenty-eight, he had worked there for some time and had also "been to sea." His work as a sailor was likely what landed him on Long Island prior to finding himself unemployed for the winter and sent by "the Overseers of the Poor of Brooklyn, Long Island" to Philadelphia, despite not having a legal settlement in the city.[54] Informal removals such as Gribbins and Ray experienced were not uncommon among individuals considered capable of providing for themselves, but with the very ill, pregnant women, and vagrants—all of whom posed a greater threat of expense or disorder—compliance with poor laws was of greater concern.

The nature of the jobs available for unskilled laborers often required an element of itineracy, which contributed to the instability many poor workers experienced. For this reason, John Steele, a house carpenter, was something of a familiar face in the Philadelphia Almshouse during the 1830s. He was first examined in 1829 at age fifty. Having been born in Ireland, he migrated with his family via Wilmington, Delaware, in 1803 and for a few years had been able to make a living, renting a house for his wife and children in Lancaster County. During the War of 1812, Steele enlisted in the army and, it seems, did not return to his family after that time. "He was discharged from the Army in 1817," he testified, but had since "wandered from New York to Ohio working at his trade." As it was late November with winter advancing, the Guardians of the Poor waited until February, when the weather broke, to issue an order of removal for himself and "three others . . . to the Almshouse of Lancaster County." Steele did not remain long but traveled to nearby Chester County for seasonal work, and when the following winter came, he was again admitted to the Lancaster Almshouse. "He remained all winter and left there last March," he testified, moving on to travel to "various places in pursuit of employment." This pursuit brought him back to Philadelphia yet again, and he spent the next several years moving between Philadelphia, Lancaster, Chester, and Lycoming Counties, working occasionally when weather permitted, and wintering in almshouses.[55] Henry McCluer, a fifty-nine-year-old Irish immigrant, followed a similar pattern. He resided for more than twenty years in Delaware, lived in Maryland, and traveled extensively with the army. Over the next seventeen years, he did not rent a house or establish a residence anywhere. After traveling to Philadelphia, McCluer, destitute, was removed to New Castle County, Delaware, on Christmas Day in 1822.[56]

Individuals' legal settlements were not always easily uncovered by city authorities. In 1829, Philadelphia received a request for financial support of a supposed city resident named James Caldwell who was under the care of the guardians of the poor in Pottsville, Pennsylvania. Further investigation was requested by the guardians, as according to almshouse officials in Philadelphia, "the order of removal proves nothing as to settlement" and almshouse steward Jeremiah Peirsol asserted that the guardians would consistently "abandon claims where there is not clear evidence of settlement in a place."[57] It is likely that many efforts to remove itinerant paupers like Caldwell remained incomplete if investigations were unsatisfactory.

Orders of removal, though legally binding, could be canceled, and often were in cases where a pauper's residence was in question. This was an especially common occurrence in cases concerning enslaved and manumitted blacks. As maintenance of paupers who had formerly been enslaved was debated in court, so, too, were removals of slaves who had become paupers. The Supreme Court of New Jersey heard a case between two towns' overseers of the poor, South Brunswick and East Windsor, in 1824, over the removal of "a negro man named Jack." Jack's identity before the courts was simultaneously that of pauper and of slave. His legal owner, John Mount, had moved out of the New Jersey to settle in New York in 1802 and left Jack in New Jersey, presumably to provide for himself. When Jack found himself destitute in South Brunswick, the justices of the peace of that township issued an order of removal to East Windsor, where Jack had resided with Mount some twenty years previous, as a slave. The court ruled that transferring an owner's place of legal settlement to a slave was only valid in cases of manumitted slaves. If South Brunswick did not wish to pay for Jack's maintenance, the law left them one option: "seek out the owner" to cover costs, as his legal responsibility required him to do for destitute slaves or manumitted former slaves unless he was insolvent. As for South Brunswick, the state supreme court reprimanded its overseers, reminding them that "the township must provide for a pauper needing assistance, though he may have no other claim than his poverty on their bounty. So in case of a slave." The order of removal "was quashed," and Jack was allowed to return to South Brunswick if he wished.[58] Slaves earned residency in the district in which they had been enslaved, which could, if one required poor relief, prove an asset after obtaining freedom. However, it also reinforced a lifelong association with one's enslavement.[59]

Settlement, Removal, and Vagrancy

An 1820 report issued by the Society for the Prevention of Pauperism (SPP) in New York outlined the difficulties of managing indigent transients within the pauper removal system, declaring it practically "inoperative." With an increasing number of immigrants arriving in New York City's port in the 1820s, as well as the seasonal system of rural labor (which favored the resident but not the itinerant worker, with no winter safety net but the almshouse in the city, or perhaps some outdoor relief), a marked "increase of paupers, by the ingress of such persons" was a grave concern for city officials and philanthropists at this time. Such laments were commonplace in the nineteenth-century United States, but the members of the SPP were especially concerned not only about the effects that "such persons" could have on residents, crime, and the economy but also that there might be no legal recourse available to them to fend off these paupers. Many indigent transients could not be removed because they had "no last place of residence" to be removed *to*. Or, the report went on, "if they have, their approaches to the city cannot be ascertained," which complicated efforts to follow the law's stipulation that a pauper be accompanied "constable by constable" back on the route that they had previously taken. New York's policies regarding pauper removal stipulated that constables escort "strangers" from their district to the next and pass their custody to the constable in the next district, until the pauper's legal settlement was reached. There was much debate among lawmakers and justices about exactly how this was to be carried out. As one lawyer argued, it was "repugnant to good order" for "constables... [to] be roaming over the state with paupers, seeking for some place of settlement."[60]

This SPP report advocated for a system similar to that of Massachusetts, which designated nonresident paupers in need of poor relief as being under the coverage of the state's budget rather than the responsibility of the pauper's place of legal settlement. But the SPP presciently described in 1820 what soon became even more apparent: that so many of the American poor could not be easily categorized within the system that was in place to assist them. With poor relief eligibility determined by residence, individuals without a legal settlement had no recourse to public aid. Itinerant paupers, the report argued, were "no more the poor of the city of New-York, than they are the poor of the city of Albany, or the county of Chetauque. They have no residence in the one place, more than in the other." New York's pauper removal system as it stood, the managers of the SPP argued, as a result of the incoming tide of poor migrants from England and Ireland, was "but little less objectionable, than that which Great Britain forced upon us by her transportation laws, while we were her colonies."[61] As is often the case when nations are resistant to immigration out of fear of economic degradation, incidents of what some historians refer to as "pauper dumping" were greatly exaggerated. Still, this exaggeration is instructive, as it was in part the perceived threat of being overrun by destitute migrants—in actions sanctioned by their home nations—that motivated American authorities to construct exclusive settlement systems.[62] Migration and movement, voluntary or involuntary, when involving the poor, often evinced a transformation of the status an individual held in the eye of much of the public. Whether conducted with charitable or punitive intentions, pauper removal was a method of carrying out legal proscription of transiency for the poor by linking class status with legality of presence.

The persistent definition of class status as defined by residency was reinforced in the laws governing individuals who might return to a location from which they had been removed as a pauper. In the State of New York's *New Conductor Generalis*, the manual for the justices of the peace, overseers of the poor, and other local officials, pauper removal was designed in such a way that it both diagnosed and sought to prevent vagrancy.[63] Paupers who returned to a location from which they had been removed were to be convicted as vagrants and punished accordingly as disorderly persons. In an explanation of what constituted such an illegal return, the manual clarified that "an order of removal only prevent[ed] a return in a state of vagrancy."[64] It may be assumed that the guidelines that removed paupers were expected to follow were made known to them by a justice or constable at the time of their removal. But the discretionary nature of vagrancy and disorderly charges would likely have not made it clear to a removed pauper what a return "in a state of vagrancy" may look like to any constable. Furthermore, justices required only the oath of one reliable witness to sentence a pauper to the punishment for recidivist vagrants in New York: sixty days in the local jail or workhouse at hard labor. New Jersey similarly took measures to prevent the return of vagrants and paupers into districts in which they had been arrested for vagrancy or from which they had been removed as paupers. In these states' official management of pauper removal, the often implicit connection between pauperism—especially mobile paupers—and vagrancy, is made explicit.[65]

For those who experienced the process of pauper transportation in this period, it may have been painfully clear that the same system that provided relief to the indigent, sick, and elderly also served as a penal institution for convicted criminals and paupers. The latter category were primarily vagrants, who, following conviction for vagrancy by a constable, were ordered by a justice of the peace to be transported to the county almshouse and held for a term at hard labor. The line between vagrant and pauper is especially blurred in these cases, as with forty-two-year-old Stephen Kelsey, who was described as a "pauper, under the Vagrant Act," when he was arrested and committed by a Kingston, New York, justice of the peace and transported eighteen miles to the almshouse for his term of incarceration.[66] Written into New York State's poor law was a provision wherein a justice was to determine whether a vagrant might be better suited to serving the punishment of thirty days of confinement in the poorhouse or in the jail.[67] Recidivist vagrant Cornelius Ylverston was variously incarcerated in the jail and the almshouse, well into old age.[68] In sentences where the former was chosen, such as in the case of Joseph Ruland, the conviction usually contained language that specified it "appear[ed] . . . that the said [vagrant] is an improper person to be sent to the poor-house," and thus should be committed to the common jail of said county" for a specified length of days. Severity of punishments varied, and some vagrancy sentences stipulated that the vagrant be put to hard labor, while others did not. Others, like Ruland, had bespoke sentences; in his case, he was to serve a total of twenty days in the common jail, ten of which he was "to be kept on bread and water only."[69]

The scale and cost of New York's pauper removal system was large enough to prompt a legislative investigation, led by Secretary of State

John Van Ness Yates, who found that New York spent upward of twenty-five thousand dollars in removing paupers in 1822 alone.[70] The Yates report, delivered to the legislature in 1824, emphasized the importance of reforming pauper settlement and relief provision procedures, painstakingly detailing "the expenses and operations of the laws for the relief and settlement of the poor," considering specifically the efficacy of pauper removal as opposed to almshouse aid. The report calculated that in New York State in 1822, 1,796 paupers considered as state residents "were removed . . . to different parts of the state." The researchers noted that 320 of these paupers were women, and 600 were children. It appeared that this figure included legal fees for 127 court cases in which orders of removal were appealed, dramatically increasing the total cost.[71] The authors of the report lamented the expense of litigating these removal appeals, which were paid out of already strained poor relief budgets, noting that the transportation of paupers "from constable to constable," until they arrive at their place of destination, gives rise to "great expense and trouble, to say nothing of its cruelty."[72]

"The removal of so many human beings," the report continued, "like felons, for no other fault than poverty, seems inconsistent with the spirit of a system professing to be founded on principles of pure benevolence and humanity."[73] This sympathy for the poor was not afforded to able-bodied vagrants, who could falsely appear to officials as "the poor and infirm," and thus, mischievously, be able to "partake of the same bounty" reserved for the truly needy. In proposing amendments to the poor law system then in effect, Yates advised the cessation of including "healthy vagrant[s]" in the removal process, opting instead to "command" vagrants "to return to the county where [they] belong."[74] If a vagrant did not comply, she or he would be punished by a term in the workhouse. This proposal would remove one route from the map of transiency that so many paupers and vagrants used. It is important to recall that distinctions between the "healthy vagrant" and the "poor and infirm" were not always readily discernible in practice. The names of convicted vagrants appear in the almshouse as indigents, not only incarcerated petty criminals. Justices of the peace and overseers of the poor frequently encountered individuals who could be perceived as "healthy vagrant[s]" in the summer, when work along the shore was available and provisions accessible, and "poor and infirm" come January, when temperatures dropped and the money had run out. The report's figures distinguish permanent paupers from occasional paupers, estimating that about a third were "the *permanent* poor," while two-thirds were only temporarily receiving relief "chiefly in the autumn or winter."[75] Ultimately, Yates's report swayed the legislature and led to New York's abolition of removal practices in favor of an expanded almshouse system that would provide care to indigent transients as well as residents. Some removal continued after the implementation of the 1824 law, as it allowed for the removal of paupers to their place of legal settlement if it was within the same county as the district from which they were being removed; an 1828 revision offered a status of "irremoveability" to all paupers within New York State.[76]

The states surrounding New York did not undertake the same reform process for their poor relief systems. Between one in four and one in six nonresident paupers were removed from the Philadelphia Almshouse during the 1820s and 1830s and sent across Pennsylvania and the Mid-Atlantic region.[77] By 1829, the influx of itinerant laborers working on canals and railroads had caused the already substantial population of seasonal farmhands and other workers to increase dramatically. Philadelphia was viewed by much of the rest of the state as capable of providing for these individuals, but the city's guardians of the poor were not pleased with the conduct of surrounding counties' overseers, who repeatedly sent "too many persons . . . from the country" to the city almshouse.[78] It was often difficult to locate the legal settlements of these persons, who were primarily itinerant laborers not maintaining employment in any one location long enough to gain official residence. The guardians' concerns were echoed by the city's mayor, John Swift, who advocated for strict enforcement of removal laws, commonly ordering the vagrants who were brought before him for sentencing to be sent "to the Guardians of the Poor" so that, as in the case of one man who had been in Philadelphia for only two days, they could "send him back to N. York where he belongs." Large cities like New York generated, received, and attracted so many thousands of indigent transients that they became targets of criticism. In 1837, Philadelphia's mayor stated publicly that "the paupers of that city" who were entering the city "in shoals" needed to be deterred. "A stop must be speedily put to these inroads," he wrote, "or we shall be overrun with the vermin."[79] Concerns were shared throughout the region, and in 1835 a bill was considered by New Jersey's Legislative Council that would "regulate the removal of paupers between the States of New-Jersey, Pennsylvania, and New-York," in recognition of the need for communication between the states that exchanged so many transients across their borders. The Council passed the bill, but the House voted it down, so it moved no further.[80]

Orders of removal could be issued without an individual's direct involvement with the poor relief system (for example, a stint in an almshouse or a vagrancy conviction), because any individual who appeared likely to become chargeable to the state could be apprehended by a justice of the peace and formally removed to their last legal settlement. In 1819, a case examining the legal grounds for and methods of execution of pauper removals came before the New York City Court of Sessions. The previous year, a pauper named Philip Thompson who possessed legal settlement in Quebec had, according to officials, "neglected to" return to Quebec, his "last legal settlement." Thus, the "commissioners therefore commanded . . . any constable of the city of New York to convey and transport the pauper from and out of the city . . . and so from constable to constable, by the nearest and most convenient route, to the said town of Quebec, in Lower Canada, and there deliver him to the overseers of the poor," with the understanding that the overseers in Quebec would be required by law to provide for Thompson.[81] The court declared this pauper-constable processional to be unlawful, as an act regulating pauper removal that was passed in 1813 did not allow for the burdening of each town through which a pauper may be removed with the expense of a constable's accompaniment and provision, when that pauper was not a legal resident of the state. "In the case of a foreign stranger," the court ruled, paupers that the city wished to remove were to be sent back on the path that brought them to their present location in New York.[82] Justices were instructed to "direct the pauper to be transported to the next city, or the first town in the adjoining county through which such stranger shall have been suffered to wander unapprehended." The court considered in detail the routes that were likely to have been taken by "every pauper who came here from Canada" and had been assumed to "wander through these towns." Constables should be required to describe the route to be taken in removals of paupers, as "Canadians may, and do often . . . approach the city through New-Jersey and Connecticut" as well as through towns in Westchester, Kings, and Richmond Counties.[83] The authorities were generally aware of the varying paths chosen by vagrants and paupers in their travels and argued against punishing, as it were, those towns through which indigent transients chose to travel, in favor of punishing those whose actions they deemed actually worthy of curbing: indigent transients themselves.

The law, then, seemed to recognize two varieties of pauper movement: illicit travel and supervised forced transportation. New York saw many poor migrants traveling south from Lower Canada, while Pennsylvania received Marylanders traveling north, both groups seeking work. With at least a dozen paupers transported each week in Ulster County from the 1820s to the 1840s and the consistent removal of paupers from the almshouse in Philadelphia, a common sight on Mid-Atlantic roads must have been bedraggled paupers, escorted under the watchful eye of a constable, on a path of forced migration, whether it was to the other side of the county or across an entire state and into another country. Indeed, New York's Court of Sessions discussed with familiarity processes of pauper migration and removal. The Thompson case was considered in 1819, at the start of the dramatic economic downturn that vastly increased the population of unemployed, homeless, and transient work-seekers in the United States, especially in the early industrial Northeast. These removal practices greatly affected the lives of the paupers they directly involved, and shaped populations and patterns of movement of thousands of paupers in the region. The location where the pauper Philip Thompson ended up is not made clear, though much of the case centers on his requiring medical care for a broken arm in the town of Kinderhook, which, when the next town north refused to convey him onward, provided for him until the issue could be resolved. Thompson was not convicted of a crime, as far as is discussed in this case, nor is he described as a vagrant or recipient of poor relief. He is said to have been removed from New York City for a combination of being likely to become chargeable and of lacking residence. And still, his transiency and poverty led to months of forced transportation by constables to a location that he had likely intentionally left to seek better economic prospects.[84]

The provision in poor laws for treating as vagrants removed paupers who returned to the location from which they had been forced out implies that compliance was not always easily won. In the first recorded examination of Jacob Merkel in the Philadelphia Almshouse, in January 1827, he admitted to having been there previously, in 1825, when he had "sworn . . . to his legal settlement being in Lancaster County" and had apparently been removed there. Since then, he had "been at different places but the longest time which he has lived in any one place was about 3 months."[85] Merkel returned again in January 1835 but still had not lived or worked anywhere long enough to gain a new settlement, and for whatever reason he remained unable or unwilling to remain and subsist in Lancaster County. Though Merkel had signed his own name to his previous testimony, he merely made his mark this time, perhaps indicating some loss of mental acuity or a physical injury in the intervening years.[86] It was less than a year until he again found himself in the Philadelphia

Almshouse, when he hinted that it had been the death of his wife that had brought on his transiency. After living in Lancaster for many years, it was after she died that he left, after which time he "sometimes followed boating" and "visited some of the counties of the state." He had lived in Philadelphia periodically but had not worked for anyone for one whole year since he left Lancaster over fourteen years earlier. The guardians of the poor were required to remove Merkel back to his legal settlement if he was well enough to travel, and though orders of removal for him do not seem to be extant, it is possible that it was returning to Philadelphia after his first removal that brought him to the almshouse under a watchman's sentence.[87]

Experiencing Pauper Removal

As David P. Delaney has summarized, "it is through mobility: as permitted, coerced or prohibited, that justice and injustice may be concretely realized—in the flesh."[88] The distances of travel that were involved in removing paupers to their places of legal settlement shaped the physical experiences of indigent transients, from illness to separation to corporal punishment for their mobility, as Sarah Turner experienced in Poughkeepsie. The majority of paupers who were removed from Philadelphia during the 1820s were forced to travel at least fifty miles, usually in the company of the enforcing constable or justice of the peace.[89] The data depicted here may suggest that transients who had traveled longer distances prior to their involvement with Philadelphia authorities were more likely to be subject to removal. Or it may point to a more common trend of longer-distance mobility as opposed to local movement among indigent transients who came through Philadelphia in this period. Regardless, the rigidly demarcated geographical boundaries that facilitated the systems of relief and punishment in the early republic could not account for the high level of movement undertaken by indigent transients.

Individuals who were contracted to convey paupers overland usually signed a binding agreement, such as the one David Taylor signed in the summer of 1828 to transport a man named Theodore McKenzie, by "order of removal . . . to Pittsburgh." The physical circumstances of removals were important to guardians of the poor and other law enforcement and almshouse officials involved in the process. This particular contract specified that McKenzie was to be well-cared for on the journey, and part of Taylor's twenty-five-dollar remission was to enable him to "furnish [McKenzie] . . . with sufficient food and lodging on the road." The removing institution was to cover costs for the full distance to their destination, or, in "the case of escape, or death . . . in proportion to the distance" traveled. He was received in Pittsburgh and remained at least a few days, despite lacking settlement.[90]

In a plethora of cases, the state of health of a pauper determined the course of action taken with regard to removal practices. This was manifest in a very material way in terms of available modes of transportation: Eleanor Dicky's place of legal settlement was Philadelphia, but she found herself under the charge of the Franklin County Directors of the Poor in 1826. Her removal was planned, but Philadelphia's guardians deferred to those with a view of her current state "to judge if her health should encourage the hope that she would be able to provide for herself." If this was the case, she was to be discharged at will; if not, Philadelphia would see to her care, provided that the Franklin directors would "send her down in a wagon at as little expense as possible."[91]

Destitute and ill, rather than disorderly, itinerant paupers were sometimes trusted with their own removals. In the same letter addressing Eleanor Dicky's removal, the journey of "Michael Reed and his daughter Ann Reed" from Philadelphia back to Franklin County was described. They were apparently "so far recovered . . . that they might make their way back to your county on foot. They were therefore discharged from this house with a good stock of provisions." Father and daughter had apparently been in the almshouse for two and a half weeks, as Franklin County was charged with their board for that length of time, totaling ten dollars in expenses. No written record of their settlement examinations remains extant, so little more is likely to be known about what brought them to the almshouse in Philadelphia, or what happened to them after their 150-mile journey on foot across Pennsylvania.[92]

Pauper removals to rural areas in the sparsely settled regions often proved challenging. The removal of Mary Craig from Philadelphia to Kiskiminitas in Westmoreland County required careful coordination. The guardians of the poor enlisted a physician to make a certified pronouncement as to the state of her health and its prevention of her removal: "to be removed two or three hundred miles," he wrote, would not be possible unless accommodation were made for her in a "vehicle, and short stages . . . of a kind" suited to her present condition, as she was "somewhat paralyzed."[93] In September 1831, she was to be sent "by a wagon owned by David Loye's, of Morrison's Cove, Bedford County" by a driver named Mr. Berry. Berry was to "take her to Greensburg," which was still nearly thirty miles from the township expected to take her in, but apparently transportation connections in that area were so weak that she could not be sent "in any other way, nor nearer to you." Craig was to be accompanied by an adult daughter who does not appear to have been in the almshouse with her mother, but who was also "a poor woman." The daughter may have been traveling with her mother as a means of transport as well as familial care, as she thought she might go, "perhaps, to Ohio, at her own expense."[94]

The materiality of indigent transients' experience can be examined by considering the significance of a single series of tangible objects: articles of clothing. Clothes not only played a prodigious role in determining the physical experience of transiency in terms of comfort and propriety but of course also held important signifiers of class and need to poor relief and criminal justice officials, social commentators, and the general public. Historians have described indigent transients as a floating proletariat, or mobile mass of wage laborers.[95] But as Michael B. Katz and Bryan Wagner have pointed out, the itinerant poor and vagrants of the first half of the nineteenth century were rather more of a "classic lumpenproletariat."[96] For Wagner, the term "lumpenproletariat" takes on greater importance than just social designation: it becomes a material embodiment of the physical features of a person, the very features that criminalize them and their actions. In the German from which the term is derived, "Lumpen" translates literally to "rags and tatters." Since "vagrancy has no empirical reference" per se, it is the "rags" that "stamp the vagrant as a vagrant by rendering all other properties irrelevant."[97] According to contemporaries, most vagrants were "covered only by a few rags" when they were jailed and were provided no additional clothing during their incarceration. In Philadelphia's carceral facility for vagrants, the Arch Street Jail, it was a "long-standing practice" to leave "vagrants and prisoners for trial nearly naked."[98]

The availability and appearance of clothing could determine eligibility for forced removal, as it did repeatedly in the Philadelphia Almshouse. John Kirby, in the winter of 1829, was set to be removed to Chester County on a given day, but the guardians postponed his removal, having "found when too late, that he had no clothing."[99] Henrietta Johnson, a young woman born in Pittsburgh, was only seventeen when she entered the almshouse. She was examined in the winter, having left Carlisle, where she lived with her grandfather, only a week previous, in late November 1826.[100] By mid-December, her removal back to Carlisle was imminent when the guardians realized that the woman with whom she had traveled to Philadelphia, "the first night after their arrival . . . took all her clothing and absconded from her."[101] Her removal was delayed, as she appeared to be completely "destitute of clothing." A week later, the guardians were eager to have Johnson out of the almshouse, and since "her situation [was] such as would render it inappropriate to discharge her," her removal was arranged. It is unclear whether she wished to remain in Philadelphia or return to Carlisle, but nevertheless "a passage in the stage" was "procured her" and she was "furnished . . . with such articles of clothing as were absolutely necessary." For this 125-mile trip in December weather, she was provided with one "lousy frock," one pair of shoes, one pair of stockings, a bonnet, and a shawl. While possession of clothing determined likelihood of forced removal for the transient poor, it was, of course, a matter of life and death for the persistent poor, too. When, for example, Peter Dougherty was unable to pay his house rent in late September 1835, he filed an insolvent debtor's petition, stating that the only real or personal property he possessed was his and his family's "wearing apparel," which, looking ahead to the winter to come, "he asks the court to allow him, as the inclemency of the weather at this season of the year especially requires that he should use it."[102]

Rosetta Hill was a nonresident pauper in the "coloured ward for sick women" of the Philadelphia Almshouse in 1834 when the steward of the institution declared her to be "incapable of earning a subsistence." She had spent the first twenty-eight years of her life enslaved in Lancaster County until, after a brief period of service following her emancipation under the provisions of Pennsylvania's 1780 Gradual Abolition Act, she traveled to Philadelphia to seek a new beginning. But before long, having fallen ill and received "injudicious treatment," she was unable to provide for herself, as overseers of the poor arranged her care and began the process of removing her as a nonresident pauper back to the county in which she had been enslaved.[103]

Former slaves like Rosetta Hill who were legally recognized as destitute were not exempt from the procedures of pauper removal. This process held greater implications for most African Americans, as law enforcement officials, legislators, and regional overseers of the poor sought to control their movements and labor, and for whom the concept of "legal settlement" was, as Joanne Pope Melish has argued, "either . . . empty" or "threatening."[104] As a result, many free blacks ensnared in the settlement and removal system shaped their testimonies to more effectively achieve their goals. For the sake of freedom, protection, or privacy, many people of color appropriated the examination process to assert their personal status.[105]

Conclusion

Residency restrictions for poor relief—and the preemptive policing of nonresidents that accompanied them—demonstrate how integral state conceptions of indigent transiency were to implementing poor laws and welfare policies. Pauper removal became less common later in the nineteenth century but continued to be practiced in some regions, including New York City, and remained on the books elsewhere, well into the twentieth century. Throughout the nineteenth century, pauper removals enforced a patriarchal mobility upon married and widowed women and subjugated the choices and movements of the poor to state control and state-approved transportation. In their efforts to limit the mobility of the lower classes through forced migration, the voluntary spatial transiency of the lower classes was criminalized and replaced with a state-sanctioned form of mobility.

Pauper removal was a method of carrying out legal proscription of transiency for the poor by linking class status with legality of presence, as an adjunct to the policing of vagrancy. Many paupers' relationships with the state were shaped by their experiences passing through the revolving doors of the almshouse and the prison, navigating a system that was both gendered and racialized. And in these practices, guardians of the poor were left to define community in the negative, by not only ejecting but also punishing unwanted individuals, and, in many cases, placing their own fiscal priorities above the needs of their charges.[106] As recent work by Hidetaka Hirota suggests, state-level pauper-removal practices "laid the foundations for state policies for the compulsory return, or deportation, of destitute foreigners already in America."[107] All the while, local government authorities exercised an inordinate amount of power over the lives of the poor and transient within their jurisdiction, governing where they had a right to move and to live.

Mobility and settlement status played a dominant role in determining how poor people interacted with the state. The 'wandering lives' that many paupers and vagrants led were viewed as threatening to the stability of community boundaries and marked their activities for punishment. Examining poverty and mobility in tandem reveals how central residential status was to the experiences and management of the poor, placing vagrancy at the center of debates surrounding welfare and subsistence migration in the early nineteenth century Mid-Atlantic. The decisions of workers to follow job opportunities, and thus, greater prospects of subsistence, across municipal boundaries reveals their understanding of the realities of the capitalist labor market that poor relief officials and city administrators seemed loath to recognize. Workers identified the challenges they faced in finding employment and carving out the means of subsistence for themselves, and responded accordingly, utilizing mobility, negotiations with employers, and the availability of poor relief and temporary shelter in order to make ends meet and in many cases, to survive. When possible, the poor utilized opportunities in growing urban and transportation infrastructure, especially the construction of canals and roadways, alongside agricultural and maritime labor, to provide for themselves. But in response to this necessary flexibility, authorities meted out punishment through the policing of the very mobility that had facilitated their survival. The stasis required by the existing poor relief system had not yet caught up to the demands of the early capitalist market system and its appetite for a mobile workforce, leaving poor relief administrators with a vastly growing population of targets and insufficient infrastructure to address their situations. The lives of the poor in the Mid-Atlantic during the early republic period were caught in between these two conflicting systems, of bare subsistence achieved via a peripatetic labor market and of punishment and aid stemming from highly fixed institutions. Ultimately, the market won: the reliance on mobile wage labor facilitated construction, expansion, harvesting, and the economic function of the region. Administrators continued to prop up an out of date system that was barely functioning, while the poor remained beholden to the moving target that was a subsistence wage, vulnerable to punishment for their poverty and their mobility.

4 /   "Since He Was Free": Vagabondage, Race, and Emancipation

In December 1826, an African American man named James Huston was admitted to the Philadelphia Almshouse. Huston had been born a slave in Delaware around 1786 and at some point "left his master," escaping across the border into Pennsylvania and using a pseudonym to avoid detection. Once there, he gained his freedom, sacrificing it only temporarily to work as an indentured servant for a few years at various places in Delaware County, Pennsylvania. With the "consent of his master," he then went "to Hayti as a sailor" for a year, earning enough money to pay off the remainder of his indenture. Since that time, he had "lived at various places, but not a year together with any one person." For Huston, freedom was costly, and it led him to the almshouse at age forty, homeless and sick. Huston's interest in traveling to Haiti as a sailor may have been a result of the ongoing discussion of the new republic and a Haitian emigration scheme for black Americans around the time he traveled there. It is possible that Huston heard some of these conversations, or participated in them, possibly bringing information on what Haiti was like upon his return to Philadelphia.[1]

The "vagabondage" of the emancipated—whether the movement of the illegally self-emancipated, like Huston, or that of one recently freed following legal manumission processes—was an active exertion that has been insufficiently explored in the context of regulated free and unfree labor in the antebellum era. But indigent transiency was a frequent byproduct of emancipation, and mobility was central to African American conceptions of freedom.[2] Mobility defined in large part how slaves and

African Americans interacted with the state.³ As Stephanie Camp has noted, at the heart of enslavement was a "geographical impulse" to control the spatial boundaries of the enslaved.⁴ For many people of color, especially the formerly enslaved in the nineteenth century, the right to be mobile both geographically as well as socially and culturally shaped their experience of emancipation and freedom.⁵ Enslaved people, in turn, developed ways to use their bodies, in part through physical mobility, as a "basic political resource."⁶ The right to move as well as to remain—when exile laws, labor laws, and black codes required or induced one not to—were two essential civil rights for people of color.⁷ Later in the nineteenth century, as Carter G. Woodson argued in *A Century of Negro Migration*, immediately following the Emancipation Proclamation freed slaves across the South "did wander about . . . believing that this was the most effective way to enjoy their freedom." This impulse shaped the next centuries of "African American life and cultural expression."⁸ According to Woodson, this choice was not unique to the United States, and "such vagrancy has always followed the immediate emancipation of a large number of slaves."⁹ Emancipation of enslaved persons and bonded laborers around the world has frequently involved legal efforts to retain labor control via vagrancy statutes that inhibit mobility. During abolition debates in England in 1792, one commentator claimed he foresaw a potential future in which emancipation would lead "the Negroes from all parts of the world" to "flock" to Britain, thus "increas[ing] the number of crimes and criminals, and mak[ing] Britain the sink of all the earth, for mongrels, vagrants, and vagabonds."¹⁰

In the antebellum United States, many communities attempted to curb the migration of newly freed slaves by restricting settlement to African Americans who could "register their certificates of freedom at a county clerk's office," and, in many cases, put up "bonds ranging from $500 to 1,000" to guarantee their ability to provide for themselves and abide by the law.¹¹ Massachusetts and New Jersey had legislated this process for their states since the late eighteenth century, and Massachusetts's law was especially concerned with preventing vagrancy by African Americans. Free blacks in Virginia after 1801 were effectively banned from leaving the county in which they resided without evidence of "honest employment" on pain of being "deemed and treated as a vagrant."¹² This association between free African Americans and dependence was widespread and ongoing.¹³

The long emancipation that began with late eighteenth-century gradual manumission laws in the United States reorganized labor systems and class structures on exponentially larger scales.[14] As Woodson reminds us, the dramatic reconstitution of labor in the South at the close of the Civil War prompted transiency among whites, too, who he notes "were also roaming and in some cases constituted marauding bands."[15] But this mobility had been ongoing for decades prior to the Emancipation Proclamation, as runaways, the unemployed, and indigent transients navigated the shifting landscape of the antebellum labor market. The coexistence of racial slavery, indentured servitude, and wage labor in time and place as well as within industries, as workers of varied races and ethnicities negotiated their voluntary and involuntary labor, effectively racialized lower-class status.[16] This process reacted with preexisting poor laws and laws regulating movement to create an environment where poverty and mobility were racialized. Poor white transients were often linked to people of color by authorities' perceptions of a shared class status that extended, often, to the means used to define contractual labor as well as freedom from bondage for blacks and whites with one profoundly important common tool: geographical mobility.[17]

There is a two-pronged juxtaposition of labor and mobility at work here: the frequency of transiency following release from bonded labor, on the one hand, and the common recourse by the poor to geographical movement as a means to achieve subsistence, on the other. Together, these connections led to the implementation of vagrancy and pauper removal laws to regulate labor, economic contributions, and public budgets.[18] This was done punitively via vagrancy law or under the guise of humanitarian aid via settlement-based poor relief. The figures of the fugitive slave and of the vagrant are at the nexus of this coercion and punishment, where both were subject to "locodescriptive policing."[19] Ira Berlin referred to these patterns as the "lessons of emancipation employed against the poor," but the antebellum origins of such efforts receive little attention. The origins of the postbellum black codes, particularly hallmark race-based vagrancy laws, are in the era of gradual emancipation, when similar tactics were used to curtail the movements of free people of color.[20]

This chapter will begin with the proposal that fugitive slaves should be counted among the populations of homeless and vagrant Americans in the antebellum era as a result of legal as well as experiential commonalities, to be detailed here.[21] Evidence supporting this argument is found in laws endorsing the recapture of fugitive slaves and the shared visual presentations of poverty and criminality inherent in vagrancy law, as demonstrated by *Prigg v. Pennsylvania* in 1842. It will then chart the transiency that former slaves as well as black and white former indentured servants often undertook after leaving bondage, going on to consider associations between race and transiency and subsequent criminalization of the freedom of movement for African Americans in varying stages of bondage. This casting of vagrancy as a racial characteristic is then seen in the enactment of manumissions processes that emancipated individuals via documents that disclaimed their likelihood to become vagrant. In addressing these topics, this chapter aims to highlight the relationship between personal status and vagrancy, and the ways in which individuals contested these designations and struggled to define their own statuses and identities.

Fugitive Slaves as Vagrants

Early American roads were a vital space for wanderers, runaways, and recent migrants crossing rivers and state lines in search of work and independence. Fugitive slaves were possibly the most vulnerable population on the road. In recent years, the historiography of the mobility of the emancipated has begun to address this. Roberta Ann Johnson has argued that runaway slaves have been left out of dominant narratives on the subject of homelessness to the detriment of the field and ought to be counted as part of the early American homeless population.[22] For enslaved people, Johnson explains, "although their living conditions were woefully deficient," residency and housing were not a concern, because they "were considered part of the 'community' (by the Whites), and, therefore, they were *not* considered homeless. On the other hand, Whites generally considered free Blacks to be homeless and suspect."[23] The transition to freedom, for many African Americans, introduced them to a new category of criminality under which they could be policed and punished. Free, and especially mobile free blacks, were assumed to be runaway slaves.[24] The African Americans who "organized to live in the forests, mountains, and swamps of the south" and in "freedom in the North" were often homeless or mobile for days, weeks, months, or even years, as they sought safe solutions in life outside of bondage. As a result, as Johnson notes, "runaway slaves represent an important chapter in America's homeless history."[25] This analysis affirms, in its historiographical perspective, that the act of running away was one of the most important means by which the illegally self-emancipated claimed freedom and independence.[26]

Considering runaway slaves as indigent transients and as a statistically significant portion of the nineteenth-century homeless population opens up new avenues of intellectual inquiry on fugitive slaves and the white and black mobile poor and suggests new ways of using records that document fugitive slaves. Both under the law as well as on the road, runaways, pauper migrants, and vagrants shared much by way of identity and occupation. These individuals used their bodies as means of resistance, sometimes by running away and sometimes by presenting their bodies to the law as evidence of their perceived identity. By seeing fugitive slaves as part of the larger homeless and poor migrant populations, we can learn more about the function of one's mobility in determining one's legal status, and about some experiences shared across racial lines as a result of one's class and labor status. One such example is in the examinations of paupers taken by guardians of the poor in Philadelphia. For the testimonies of African Americans in these examinations, it is admittedly difficult to identify who may have been a runaway among the population of self-identifying free blacks, as most were naturally keen to maintain their alibis as free persons, at least to officials. Admitting to having been a runaway slave, as James Huston did in his testimony above, could have led to harsh physical punishment and resale into slavery. But in using historians' estimates of the numbers of runaway slaves, somewhere around fifty thousand each year by the late 1850s, cross-referenced with sources such as these examinations of paupers, we can begin to see the cracks through which fugitives may have slipped.[27]

Such was the case of Samuel Burton. In 1829, Burton testified to the Philadelphia Board of Guardians that he had been born in Delaware County and worked there until he went traveling, ending up a year later in Philadelphia. When the guardians inquired with officials in Delaware County as to Burton's circumstances, the truth came out: his examination record was never signed, as his testimony was found to be "false," and his case closed with the statement "This man is a runaway."[28] The efforts of the guardians of the poor to secure legal and residentially appropriated poor relief for Burton thwarted his attempt at passing as a free laborer. Overseers of the poor often had little evidence to corroborate a pauper's claim other than their word, but that did not prohibit them from passing judgments of accuracy. Race complicated officials' assumptions of veracity in paupers' testimonies even further. A young woman named Mary Ann Smith was admitted to the Philadelphia Almshouse and believed that she may have a legal settlement in Lancaster County. She testified that "her father was black & her mother white," and at the time, in 1829, she was about nineteen years old. The guardians describe her as "a colored girl" with "an exceedingly impudent face." Most intriguing is the description offered of this young woman in the guardians' effort to "enable you to identify her." They went on to note that her origins were unconvincing because "she looks rather more like an Indian than a Mulatto. Her hair is longer than the Mulatto's, generally, & straighter."[29]

From the 1790s onward, free people of color utilized scant available opportunities to create subsistence for themselves, establish communities, and make important strides in northern race relations. Despite this social environment, during these years, "blacks represented no more than their share of the population" among those arrested for vagrancy in Philadelphia. Runaway slaves did raise the numbers of the illicitly mobile, but it is still noteworthy that it was not until the 1820s when blacks began to be targeted more effectively as vagrants.[30] In Philadelphia in the 1820s, 25 percent (166/668) of the institutionalized nonresident paupers in the almshouse were African Americans, double the population in the city at large. The disparity was even greater in the city's vagrant and debtor prison, Arch Street: during the same years, approximately 48 percent (2,325/4,848) of the convicted vagrants incarcerated there were African American.[31] Much of this disparity is likely due to the discretion of arresting justices, many of whom likely viewed African Americans as possessing criminal tendencies and may have, through the lax sentencing process for vagrancy, arrested a disproportionate number of African Americans for petty crimes that would lead to their incarceration in Arch Street.[32] Part of this difference could also be attributed to the fact that fugitive slaves were often incarcerated either as punishment or, along with some nonfugitive enslaved people, held there temporarily upon request of their masters, or while awaiting transportation back to their place of enslavement, though this practice seems to have diminished by 1820.[33]

Glimpses into the experiences of African American mobile paupers are found when one reads for gaps in the archive: in 1828, for example, one man named Samuel Reason testified that he had been born in Harford County, Maryland, and upon arriving in Pennsylvania, had no home and held no job to speak of for four years, before finding work with a rye manufacturer in the city.[34] Pennsylvania law targeted out-of-state migrants like Reason, in an effort to stem the tide of fugitive slaves and poor immigrants traveling onward from ports in Delaware or New York. In 1820, Pennsylvania passed a "law to prevent the increase in pauperism in the Commonwealth," which held individuals who brought African Americans into the state who could be considered likely to become destitute responsible for their care, thus freeing the overseers of the poor from providing for them. For African Americans who did not have such a sponsor, if a justice was not satisfied with their "account of themselves," they were to be prosecuted as vagrants.[35]

Fears of roving bands of vagrants and fugitive slaves motivated social commentary, preventative policing, and legislative action. Citizens and lawmakers in the antebellum Mid-Atlantic sought to curb the movements of what was seen largely as a homogeneous group of idle, unemployed people of color. This was especially pertinent in the southern border areas of the region. A grand jury convened at the Mayor's Court in Lancaster, near the Maryland-Pennsylvania border, just before the 1820 law went into effect, decried transient African Americans as a "source of well-founded apprehension of danger to the well-being of the city." The grand jury pinpointed what they saw as the source of this danger: "the numerous hordes of worthless Negroes congregated in huts about the suburbs of the city, who spend their time in idleness." The solution, they argued, was to "be vigilant in punishing such suspicious characters, black or white, who do not work and have no visible way of living, by committing them to prison as vagrants."[36] Similarly, in New Brunswick, New Jersey, in 1823, the city council, in an effort to impose limitations on the movements of the poor and of people of color in the city, deployed a committee to "ascertain the residence of Free Negros, Vagrants and paupers . . . with authority to take such steps for their removal."[37] This rhetorical movement from "worthless Negroes" to "vagrants" was not a leap in this period, as vagrants conjured up, in early nineteenth-century minds, images of shoeless travelers, black-faced Jim Crow on the stage, and roughly clad fugitive slaves on the roads.[38]

In nineteenth-century drama and verse, as in life, vagrants were common characters, often used to represent lifestyles that suggested that "itinerancy . . . threatened to inculcate popular disregard for legitimate public culture" in their association with idle low-lives. John Greenleaf Whittier used vagrants in his writings to depict the danger of the "other," while William Wordsworth's poetry often invoked vagrants as beggarly objects for sympathy.[39] Cultural representations of vagrants also antagonized perceptions of race, as in the blackface minstrel performance *Bone Squash Diavolo* by Thomas Rice of Jim Crow fame. Performed in New York, Philadelphia, and New Orleans in 1835 and 1836, the play displayed "the motley conventions of Atlantic urban street scenes," most notably through its protagonist, Bone Squash, a black "class-crossing vagrant" in a cast with all black characters except for one: a "white Yankee devil."[40] And many depictions of Jim Crow himself mirrored early nineteenth-century visuals of vagrants and showcased characteristics of transients.[41] Jim Crow became the stage voice of mobility, articulating the challenges of economic instability and social estrangement, the mobility that was associated with "the lumpenproletariat."[42] In was in this cultural climate that vagrancy became a central consideration in public discourse surrounding abolition and emancipation in the United States.[43]

The relationship between these two figures—that of the fugitive slave and of the vagrant—was not limited to proverbial association.[44] In the eighteenth and nineteenth centuries, poor laws often bolstered or replaced laws governing slaves, while vagrancy statutes similarly were used to control the movements of the poor and the enslaved.[45] In the landmark U.S. Supreme Court case *Prigg v. Pennsylvania*, which, in 1842, strengthened the federal laws allowing for the return of runaway slaves to their masters, the legal status of the vagrant was used to justify states' rendition efforts. The Court ruled that there could be "no doubt whatsoever that the States ... possess full jurisdiction to arrest and restrain ... runaway slaves, and to remove them from their borders ... as they *certainly* may do in cases of idlers, vagabonds, and paupers."[46] In other words, the increasingly empowered fugitive slave laws introduced in the United States during the antebellum years were predicated on the traditional function of vagrancy laws. The legal grounds that took the *Prigg* ruling from one that authorized slaveholders to capture their runaway slave property to one that authorized states to physically eject runaway slaves using public resources were settlement and removal laws. States were not only viewed by the Court as having the authority to "arrest and restrain runaway slaves" but also "to remove them from their borders and otherwise to secure themselves against their depredations" on the grounds of their legal capacity to pursue the same actions with paupers and vagrants. Peleg W. Chandler, a prominent Massachusetts attorney, spoke publicly about the connections between removals of paupers and of fugitive slaves, decrying both as abandonment of the government's duty to protect public welfare. The illogical conclusion of such laws, he wrote, would leave "every vagrant arrested in our streets ... transported to, and abandoned in, the streets of Savannah."[47] Fugitive slaves were vulnerable to far worse punishments for illicit mobility than were white vagrants, but the system that had circumscribed and punished the mobility of white vagrants for a century was modified and molded in order to facilitate the capture of runaway slaves and thus maintain slavery as an institution.

But the justifications of removal embedded in *Prigg*, built upon the protective basis of quarantine and police protection, were strong. The rights of a state to enact legislation governing the removal of the poor and criminal had been expressly stated in *New York v. Miln* of 1837, discussed in chapter 3. This extended to poor immigrants as well as native-born indigent transients, both of whom could be excluded if they lacked the legally recognized minimal means to prove they could provide for themselves. The legal language of maintenance and removal links the policing of vagrants, fugitive slaves, and paupers.[48] The policing of vagrancy and pauper mobility in the antebellum North set the legal stage for the Fugitive Slave Act of 1850, and as this evidence suggests, may have contributed to northerners' acceptance of fugitive slave capture and rendition as a function of government.[49]

Scholars who have studied the relationship between race and police power in the nineteenth century have noted the importance of this connection. In the words of Bryan Wagner, in the "antebellum courtroom," one "baseline that remains consistent . . . is the warrant that says statutes governing fugitives are legitimate whenever they can be analogized to vagrancy statutes. . . . Even before the fugitive slave, the vagrant was imagined in antebellum courtrooms as a self-sufficient cause for police action."[50] The line drawn connecting these two conditions effectively rendered the slave as an object of policing.[51] It is clear that in the courts as well as to legislators, racial distinctions that may have otherwise distinguished poor whites and runaway slaves were occasionally seen as separate from the defined vagrant identity that sent them on the road: as discussed in chapter 1, in 1837, at Pennsylvania's Constitutional Convention, one representative placed the two groups on equal footing, declaring both undeserving of suffrage, saying he "would never consent to bring down the standard of the laboring classes to the standard of the vagrant or of the black man."[52]

The legal language used to define vagrancy is found again and again, often verbatim, in regional petitions for the removal of runaway slaves and anti-abolitionist rhetoric. The actions described in vagrancy statutes highlight the experience of illicit mobility: visible destitution, the wearing of rags, traveling from place to place in pursuit of subsistence. Runaway slaves shared, largely, the same characteristics and goals, in addition to their pursuit of freedom.[53] Runaway slaves and, to a lesser extent, runaway indentured servants were among the most conspicuous travelers in antebellum public space, because their race, class, status, and social identity were readily visually readable. Both vagrant dockets and almshouse registers were populated by former and escaped bondspersons and white wanderers. One young black woman, Hannah Thompson, entered the

Philadelphia Almshouse with her daughter, Sarah Sammons, in January 1830. She testified that she had been "born, in Baltimore County, Maryland, a slave in the family of Samuel Noward." Thompson was sold to a Pennsylvania farmer as a teenager, where her servitude was then subject to gradual manumission law, and she was emancipated at age twenty-eight. "About a year" after her manumission, she "was delivered of a child in the Lancaster County poor house." For Thompson, mobility was not an immediate course of action upon gaining her freedom, but it did lead her east to Philadelphia not long after, where she encountered further destitution.[54]

In the interviews recorded with transient African Americans in the Philadelphia Almshouse, former slaves were often reluctant to admit to an earlier bonded status: out of 1,600 nonresident pauper examinations spanning 1822–44, only thirteen transients described themselves as formerly enslaved, totaling less than 1 percent.[55] Venus McClintock, a "Black married woman" in the Philadelphia Almshouse in 1828, "was born, in Strasburgh, Lancaster County . . . a slave in the family of John Freezer, who sold her when she was 14 years old, to George Withers of the City of Lancaster, to serve him till she was 28, which service she performed and was then free." Her first act of geographical freedom was travel to Philadelphia, where she was married. Her husband, Stephen McClintock, had also come to the city from farther west, having been born and raised in Harrisburg. Neither was able to find stable work in the two short years of their marriage, and Venus was alone when she was interviewed in October 1828.[56] Possessing knowledge of Pennsylvania's gradual manumission law gave some former slaves the legal grounds to assert their previous and present labor statuses. But some may have depended upon the level of awareness or compliance of their masters to share the parameters of their bondage with them.

While the narratives of some African Americans' transiency are localized and limited to the movements imposed by servitude or slavery, others chose or experienced more dramatic mobility. William Johnson was "born in Africa" and "sold" upon arrival in New Castle, Delaware, "to Welley Murry, and lived 9 months with him, then removed with his master to Harrisburg and lived 5 years there. Said master then went to McConnellsburgh three months after. His master died, then he was free." Johnson testified that he had "lived in Virginia, New Jersey, and everywhere hath not lived one year in any one place."[57] For Johnson, and many other freed blacks, the narrative of his transiency was the narrative of his bondage but also of his voluntary movement.

Samuel Scott was held as a slave by a lifelong legislator in both the Pennsylvania Senate and House of Representatives, Gabriel Hiester. Born in Delaware County, Scott "belonged to John Ferguson, who sold him to Edward Tilghman of Philadelphia, who gave him to William Graham, Esq. of Old Chester." Scott spent most of his childhood with Graham, but when he was nineteen, he was "sold to Doctr. Arthur May of Lancaster" and after eighteen months, sold again, this time to Gabriel Hiester, "with whom he served 7½ years when he became free by the laws of the State." Having been shuttled around southeastern Pennsylvania as a young enslaved man, Scott, now free and in search of work, amped up his transiency. He "lived at various places" after his manumission, "but not a year together with any one person," and, by 11 December 1826, held in the cells at the Philadelphia Almshouse, he had never "kept a house."[58]

Alfred Kennedy was described by the Philadelphia Guardians of the Poor in 1830 as a "yellow, single man" about "22 years old" who had been born a slave in Hunterdon County, New Jersey. He was sold "when he was a child to a man ... living in Princeton, N. Jersey." The final sale of his enslavement was to a man named John Chapman in Bucks County, Pennsylvania, from whom he was to be free at the age of twenty-one. During the year between his emancipation and his arrival in the Philadelphia Almshouse, Kennedy testified, he had "not worked a year for any one person ... since he was free."[59] As the examinations of Johnson, Scott, and Kennedy illustrate, slavery and emancipation both created different forms of mobility that shaped the lives and trajectories of slaves and free blacks.

The sight of runaway slaves on the road and in urban centers in the Mid-Atlantic was common and powerful enough to have become a trope, conjured in sarcastic police reports about the locales frequented by urban vagrants. An 1831 article in the *Philadelphia Inquirer* described a scene in which, late one night, "a colored man, barefoot, and very shabby dressed, applied to Mr. Jones, a respectable citizen, for some money or clothes." The man asserted that "he was a runaway slave, from the south." He told Jones that he "had thrown his shoes, which were worn out with walking so far, from the bridge into the Schuylkill" and hoped to acquire new clothes so that he could "disguise himself." Despite his "pitiful tale of his oppression, ... Mr. Jones conceiv[ed] it his duty to have him arrested." Between Jones and the city watchmen, the man was deemed "an impostor, known to use the same and other devices, to obtain charity," with a reputation among the city's "wharf-rats," and was convicted as a vagrant with the usual prison term.[60] Whether this unnamed vagrant's story was genuine or had been fabricated to elicit charity, it reveals the ubiquity of fugitive slaves identifying and being identified by others as indigent transients and describes the material circumstances perceived to be associated with the act of illicit mobility: barefoot, poorly clothed, and eager to go unnoticed. As the encounter with Mr. Jones demonstrates, indigent transients, including fugitive slaves, were not just victims of laws regulating their behavior and movement, but their identity narratives also played a role in how these laws were enforced.

Geographies of Servitude

Narratives of indigents' movements contribute to the historical construction of both noncitizen white and "Black geographies."[61] These spaces were not so clearly demarcated for the lowest classes of both races, as discussions in the historiography of race and bonded labor in recent years have demonstrated. Occupation and labor status were, of course, central determinants in the nature of poor individuals' mobility. And for free blacks in many northern states, indentured servitude often functioned as a replication of the circumstances of enslavement, albeit for limited terms. James Huston, after his self-emancipation into Pennsylvania, used his newfound right to enter into contracts to sell his labor under indenture as a strategic move toward a more complete freedom. But for many others, entering an indenture was not necessarily either voluntary or strategic.

Ebenezer Widdington, an African American man who was born in Philadelphia around 1817, was bound by his father "as an indented servt. to Samuel Brinkley, D.D. of Chester Co" when he was about twelve years old.[62] The circumstances of servitude precluded much liberty, but in Widdington's case, living at service with an established minister may have offered more physically sustaining surroundings than his previous circumstances. Records indicate that Widdington, along with his father and namesake, had been traveling, or attempting to establish themselves somewhere new, in Delaware, when the physical hardships of winter overcame them.[63] Both were admitted to the almshouse in New Castle County, Delaware, in 1826 as nonresidents, though they are not listed in the admissions register together. The father is described as age "39, African," admitted for having "frozen feet." His son's race was not noted by almshouse officials, only that he was just twelve years old and had "frosted feet."[64] The father remained in the almshouse for about a month, while the son stayed on for nearly two months; this is presumably when

Widdington Jr. was "bound by his father." But after serving "under indenture for 5 years" and securing release from his master, he again found himself as an indigent traveler, "living about—as he best could," until the winter of 1834, when he entered the Philadelphia Almshouse as a nonresident.[65]

The same year in New York State, a twenty-three-year-old white man named John Joseph was found unconscious on a public road. On 16 August 1834, he submitted to a "voluntary examination" by the overseers of the poor for Huntington, New York. Joseph testified that he "was born in Scotland, brought to America when an infant into New York." When he was nine years old, "the Almshouse Commissioners of New York bound him out" to a man in Delaware County, New York. He fulfilled his duties until, when he was about eighteen years old, "his master failed in business, and gave him his freedom." Joseph scraped by on what he could earn as he "worked about" in Delaware County for a couple of years until beginning to travel through southern New York State, starting with Ulster County, where he "worked . . . for about three months." From then on, his transiency was measured in months, then weeks, then days: he went on to Dutchess County "and there resided about four months and from thence he came to New York." While in the city, he became "unwell and was taken into the Alms House until he recovered." In late March 1834, "he was sent by the commissioners of the Alms House over to Long Island to work upon the farm belonging to them." He remained on the poor farm there for just shy of two months, when he "left and went to work in Springfield in Kings County a few days," to Buckram, Queens County, and "worked there about ten days" until he reached Huntington, New York. At some point on this trek, he must have again become ill: it was on 15 August 1834 that he had been "found lying in the road, sick" by Huntington resident Alexander Sammis and "brought to the Poor House."[66] The first five years of Joseph's life after indentured servitude had brought him at least three times to almshouses, across at least ten New York State counties, working dozens of daily, weekly, and monthly jobs as a wage laborer. He was far from unique in these experiences. Indeed, a man was apprehended for the same offense Joseph had committed, just a few counties farther north a few years later because "he did lie in the public street in a condition unable to help himself" and had apparently also been engaged in illegal begging. This man, Isaac Norman, was convicted as a vagrant and, deemed "an improper person to be sent to the poor house," was "confined in the common jail for thirty days."[67]

The stories of Ebenezer Widdington and John Joseph, whose transiency and poverty quite literally stopped them in their tracks, magnify the experiences of many former indentured servants. They participated in a process followed by thousands of fugitive and emancipated slaves, indentured servants, and former apprentices in this period, who comprised a significant subset of indigent transients in the first half of the nineteenth century in the United States.[68] The line between runaway slave and runaway servant was often blurred in carceral records, including vagrancy convictions.[69] Indentured servitude was on a legal decline in the post-Revolutionary period, with states gradually limiting its applicability to certain groups.[70] It was during this time that national opinion over the issue of consent in bound labor began to shift; under the eighteenth-century model, indentured servitude in the colonies and in the early republic was assumed to be voluntary. The post-Revolutionary economy was better suited to wage labor, and as the number of contracts for indenture waned, the use of indentures as labor security mechanisms began to shift. In 1788, New York limited legal contracts of indentured servitude to only foreign-born adults and children. The legislatures of Pennsylvania and Massachusetts echoed this in 1793 and 1795 respectively, though Pennsylvania's consideration of whether the indenturing of a child constituted involuntary servitude carried on for several years.[71]

Within indigent transients' narrative records, however, indentured servitude looms large as one of the most important driving forces in the lives of poor workers, especially in relation to their mobility. There is strong evidence to suggest that lifelong transiency and, for many, vagrant destitution were part of the legacy of release from slavery and indentured servitude. Former indentured servants were especially likely, from the late eighteenth century, to experience extreme poverty and transiency. Indeed, it has been estimated that approximately 80 percent of former servants in Pennsylvania during the last decades of the eighteenth century received poor relief at some time.[72] And this segment among the American homeless population did not disappear with the turn of the century. Among the nonresident paupers examined in the Philadelphia Almshouse between 1822 and 1844, over one-fifth (341/1,600) had served time as an indentured servant at some point in their lives.[73] Comparable sources from Huntington, New York, give figures that are much lower—about one-eighth (13/106) of the paupers examined there between 1811 and 1841.[74]

Native-born paupers were significantly more likely than recent immigrants to have served as indentured servants (about 90 percent of transient former indentured servants examined in the Philadelphia Almshouse during the 1820s were native-born), and many left immediately for the nearest urban area upon release from indenture.[75] Jonathan Smith was born in Huntington County, Pennsylvania, where he was bound to a shoemaker. As soon as he was "free," he traveled roughly two hundred miles "direct to Philad. for the purpose of procuring work." When he arrived, though, he had the misfortune to fall ill and was admitted to the almshouse for treatment as a nonresident under emergency circumstances.[76] Most indentured servants earned a legal settlement in the town or county where their indenture was served, as dictated by settlement law. But many former bondspersons chose instead to seek new opportunities in unfamiliar locations, possibly as a result of weak employment prospects in their place of settlement. This could have contributed to the larger numbers of the formerly indentured among the indigent transient population, as the residence system of poor relief would have decreased their chances at receiving aid outside of the location where they had served. It also highlights a major flaw in the residency-based poor relief system, because the places where the lower classes were more likely to find work so often differed from the places where the needy had earned the right to draw on relief.

While some indentured servants entered into bondage contracts of their own volition, others were involuntarily contracted as orphans or as part of a parent's punishment for vagrancy.[77] Reading backward into the lives of the individuals among these children can partially excavate some of the means of subsistence and types of experiences that the formerly indentured encountered. Irish-born Robert Caldwell came to the United States with his parents through Delaware. He was "bound by indenture to James Stephenson," a tailor in Norristown, Montgomery County, "at the age of eleven years" for a nine-year term. His indenture was transferred locally after a few years, and as soon as he was "free, he came to this city," Philadelphia, working as jobs were available, spending several years at sea. After his indenture, Caldwell did not live a single year in any one location until at least the age of forty-six.[78] Young James Nixon was described by the guardians of the poor in Philadelphia as a "yellow single man" who had been born in Bucks County and indentured at the age of eight to a farmer in Delaware County. He served there until the age of eighteen, when his indenture was sold to an attorney in Montgomery County. Reaching freedom around age twenty, he traveled to Philadelphia, but for the past three years had not "worked for any one person one year on wages, nor . . . rented a house."[79] This is a common description for life after bondage for young indentured servants, filled with temporary employment and travel. Compounding that transiency further, Caldwell's failure to gain a legal settlement in Philadelphia by the time he entered the almshouse there in 1827 led to his forced removal to Montgomery County, the last place of which he had been a legal resident. John Holson, a young African American man, had also been bound by indenture in Montgomery County before he entered the Philadelphia Almshouse in December 1827. He had been in the city for only four weeks before he and Caldwell were both sent back to Montgomery County, together. Holson had only been legally free for a few months before his mobility was again curtailed through this involuntary relocation.

It was routine for poor children to be bound out by overseers of the poor, family members, or other guardians, regardless of their possession of living parents, usually without their consent, as a means of survival.[80] The methods in which contracts for their service were drawn up demonstrate that in cases of the involuntary indenturing of paupers, vagrants, and their children, an individual's destitution stood in the way of their ability to consent to a particular labor placement. For many, the only means of withholding consent was through resistance. William Lynch was "about 9 years old" when he was "bound to Col. Jeremiah Moser" by indenture in Lancaster, Pennsylvania, for a twelve-year term. When he was fourteen years old, "he ran away from his master." For about the next seven years, he "followed the seas out of various ports," only once out of Philadelphia. It may have been on the return from that journey that he found himself destitute and was admitted to the Philadelphia Almshouse and examined in September 1828.[81] Mary Ann Jane McMahon was bound out of the Philadelphia Almshouse as a child to Charles Knox in Montgomery County. She lived with him for about a year and a half "when she ran away" and relocated herself to Philadelphia. Soon after absconding from her master, she served "twelve months in the penitentiary."[82] William Lytle was born in Franklin County, Pennsylvania, around 1802, where he was bound to a stonemason named Hoaks. Once he was "free," he traveled between Cincinnati, New Orleans, Baltimore, and Philadelphia, generally working a few months in each city before moving on.[83] Rebecca Benson was an eighteen-year-old "black, single woman" when she was admitted to the Philadelphia Almshouse in the winter of 1823. She was born in New Castle, Delaware, and "served her time there with Sarah Hayte" as an indentured servant. She "left" in 1821 (whether after completing her term of indenture or absconding is unclear), and she made her way to Philadelphia, where she did not work "one year in the employ of any one person since here." She was apparently pregnant, and either charged to the trustees of the poor of New Castle County or removed to their jurisdiction. She did end up back in New Castle, and apparently her circumstances had not improved. She died in the New Castle Almshouse on 9 March 1829.[84]

Phoebe Stull was born in Deerfield, New Jersey, around 1800 and bound as an indentured servant to a man in Salem County for eleven years. When she reached the age of majority, she left New Jersey for Philadelphia and remained there for about three years, until admitted to the almshouse there during the winter of 1822. She was determined by the guardians of the poor not to have obtained a legal residence in Philadelphia, indicating that she likely had not held steady work during her three years in the city. Stull's settlement was deemed to be Salem County, where she had served under indenture; it is unclear whether she was forcibly removed or requested to return to her legal settlement, but she was discharged from the almshouse following her examination.[85] Nearly eight years later, it appears that her poverty was again affirmed by Philadelphia authorities when she was convicted of "being a vagrant" on 21 June 1830. Her brief institutional footprint reveals a correlation between servitude and subsequent transiency, and the perennial connection between poverty and vagrancy.

As the cases of individuals like Phoebe Stull demonstrate, the poor were not necessarily spared the infelicities of indentured servitude merely by not entering into a contract for service, or even after completing one to full term. Between class-structured labor laws, vagrancy statutes, and a class- and race-based penal system even legally free individuals could be coerced into labor contracts or forced to work. In considering the trajectories of the formerly indentured described above, it is important to remember that indentured servitude was not an anomaly but rather, one of many common labor statuses among the poor.[86] And for African Americans, this was a particularly likely category into which they might fall in the first half of the nineteenth century.

The shared aspects of identity between vagrants, fugitive slaves, and runaway servants, both on the road and in the law books, were on the minds of contemporaries, who often conflated these identities. In 1817, the *Lancaster (PA) Journal* printed an advertisement for a runaway servant by the name of John Rubenthal, who was "supposed to have been enticed away" from his master, a printer named William Hamilton, by a journeyman "of a dark complexion" named Edward McKenzie. The advertisement offered a twenty-dollar reward for the apprehension of each man. In the repeated coverage of their flight, the headline "Fresh Intelligence!" was printed preceding a discussion of the tracking of the "westwardly course" that "the above vagrants" were said to have taken. The advertisement refers to the ease with which one could reinvent one's identity in this period; noting that "McKenzie passes for a shoemaker and Rubenthal as a taylor."[87] The notation of McKenzie's "dark complexion" may also suggest racial passing. By assuming a new name and a new set of clothes (whether owned, begged, borrowed, or stolen), runaway servants and fugitive slaves alike were able to reinvent their identities as soon as they had placed sufficient distance between themselves and their masters. But as soon as they embarked on the journey to carry them across that distance, in addition to whatever identity they assumed for themselves, they were also assigned another: that of the vagrant. In McKenzie and Rubenthal, the conflicted identity of the vagrant is clear. Presented to the public as simultaneously recognizable as vagrants and also "passing" under differing personas with the aid of visual changes—clothing, shoes, beards. This contradiction highlights the imposition of personal status that was created by the category of vagrancy, at the intersection of individuals defining their own identities and being defined by the laws they encountered.

Perceptions of Black Transiency

The categories which former slaves and servants populated as indigent transients were both a product of and an impetus for the law to codify racially charged discretionary policing. These efforts manifested as much in economic policing as in criminal, as vagrancy tied individuals, especially people of color, not just to a precarious economic standing but also to a social and criminal status tied to their race.[88] This policing was especially racialized in the southern and border states like Virginia, Maryland, and Delaware. From 1796, the Maryland legislature limited the legal rights and privileges of free blacks, tightening existing vagrancy laws to include provisions for resale into servitude.[89] The population of free blacks grew in the following decades as the economy weakened, providing fewer job opportunities. In response, the legislature expanded laws allowing blacks convicted on criminal charges, as well as insolvent debtors and underemployed vagrants, to be punished with a term of forced servitude. Maryland's legislative trajectory for curtailing the ingress and regress of free blacks echoed Virginia's 1801 law forbidding the presence of any free African American in a territory within the state where they were not registered with a legal residence, rendering the individual with "no honest employment . . . a vagrant."⁹⁰ The state also required free blacks to carry passes stating they were free, at all times when traveling outside of their place of legal settlement.⁹¹ Farther south, forced labor contracts for vagrants were possible methods for "reenslaving" free people of color, limiting the movements of poor whites and punishing both groups in the 1840s and 1850s.⁹² In 1826, the Delaware legislature implemented a nuisance law requiring all free blacks (who comprised 75 percent of the population of color in the state at that time) to carry passes.⁹³

Of course, with the conspicuous nature of racial identity, being required to carry a pass to state that one's visible race did not define one's freedom does not translate evenly to being required to carry a certificate stating one's labor and settlement status. For African American vagrants, the legal dangers of mobility were significantly greater than for white vagrants. Legislation was introduced in Maryland in 1839 that required constables "to take special oath to take up vagrant blacks and their neglected children." If any free black vagrant was found "to be without the necessary means of support and not of good and industrious habits he or she would be sold at auction as a slave for the current year."⁹⁴ The events that transpired as slave populations declined and free black populations rose in these two states during the antebellum era foreshadowed what was to come in the rest of the South following full emancipation at the close of the Civil War.⁹⁵ Between Delaware's racialized restrictive labor laws and Maryland's truculent punishments against poor African Americans, the centrality of vagrancy to white authorities' efforts at economic and spatial control is clear.

Especially in states where enslaved and free African Americans coexisted in substantial numbers, anti-abolitionist factions saw emancipation as a wellspring of vagrancy. Anti-abolitionists expressed in rhetoric and legislation a fear of roving, transient former slaves, free blacks, and others perceived as threats to safety or labor, including white vagrants and paupers. The result was that African Americans were viewed as especially deserving of coercion to labor, and especially vulnerable to vagrancy policing.⁹⁶ By the late 1830s, increasing abolitionist and anti-abolitionist pressures were coming to a head, and the results of the United States Census of 1840, which documented larger numbers of free blacks, sent some into a fury. An 1843 article in the *Southern Literary Messenger* described a feared potential future wherein the absence of the so-called benevolent force of slavery and resulting population of former slaves lacking the paternal care of a master would turn American roads into rivers filled with the destitute, diseased, and criminal. The author pointed to the effect that a large population of free blacks was having on Philadelphia, where residents were "perishing from want." Multiply these numbers, the article continued, and "where should we find penitentiaries for the thousands of felons? . . . The number of negroes would have a powerful effect in increasing their suffering. Pestilence and famine would rage among them with uncontrolled fury." If, as was assumed, African Americans grew "more vicious in a state of freedom . . . would it be possible to live in a country where maniacs and felons met the traveler at every crossroad?"[97] This racist anti-emancipation rhetoric showcased common perceptions that African Americans were less capable of earning a living than white people, and especially in free conditions. But it was not limited to people of color exclusively; abolitionists also featured in their vicious screeds.

Dozens of legislative petitions written by concerned citizens in this period articulated concerns over not just the presence of large groups of free blacks but also of vagrants and fugitive slaves. In some of these documents, concerns about slavery and abolition were linked with vagrancy. One petition to the Pennsylvania legislature suggested that the law should harshly punish and arrest as vagrants those who would go "prowling through the country calling themselves abolitionists, without any visible means of support, stirring up discord and dissension among the people."[98] Anti-abolitionists vilified abstention from labor as a racial characteristic that was believed to be allowed free reign among African Americans when not in bondage. By extension, they argued, abolitionists, in their support of vagrant free blacks, were participating in vagrant actions. In 1841, an identical petition was introduced ten times from different individuals across Delaware, from all counties, with a total of 386 signatories. This united effort has been credited to former Delaware governor Charles Polk Jr., who was then serving as a state senator.[99] The petition described a population of "lazy, irresponsible, lawless, and miserable free negroes and mulattoes" who were "by their indigence rendered irresponsible to the obligations of a contract" and posed a threat to the stability of the manual labor force.[100] The problem, as these citizens saw it, was that free blacks would not stay in one place and provide farmers with their labor consistently, as they had done under slavery.[101] The petitioners' complaints echoed phrases found in vagrancy statutes, describing African Americans as "a migratory tribe, without fixed abode, alternately roving from city to country, compelled to mete out a scanty subsistence." The petitioners requested that the legislature create laws that would "be more efficient in correcting and restraining the idle and roving habits of the negroes and mulattoes" through compulsory wage labor contracts.[102]

A few years later, twenty-four Delaware petitioners directly blamed this tendency toward movement on the influence of "the Abolitionists of the East ... making our State the Theatre of their action and abusive language, incendiary to the laws of our State." Legislative action, they insisted, was needed "to prevent our being overrun by vagrant negroes as well as slaves who are well known to be harbouring among us ... without any apparent business or means of support."[103] This relationship between race, vagrancy, and abolition continued into the Civil War itself, at which point, David Roediger notes, free blacks and abolitionists were both seen as synonymous with vagrants.[104] It is important to note that Maryland's and Delaware's statutes that inhibited the mobility and labor sovereignty of free blacks were not stopgap measures but, rather, permanent solutions reflecting actual legislative goals to induce people of color to move elsewhere.[105] This desire frequently manifested in the form of race riots, mob violence, and personal as well as community-wide attacks, in both North and South.[106]

Some contemporaries drew on the rhetoric of African Americans' "degraded state" and perceived incapability of providing for themselves to advocate for a more extreme form of mobility control: colonization and/or forced migration, either to Africa, the Caribbean, or the western territories.[107] In Great Britain as early as the eighteenth century, fears of mobile emancipated people of color led the government to propose colonization as a way to "limit the relief rolls by removing the poor and unwanted," especially black "vagrants and beggars." In the United States, too, support for colonization grew out of whites' beliefs about the behavior of people of color, especially the formerly enslaved.[108] In Virginia in the 1830s, a debate over abolition resulted in the state's serious consideration of the deportation of free African Americans, and Maryland considered similar policies.[109] Colonizationists won support for colonization by emphasizing what they saw as the "degraded" condition of free people of color, claiming that a disproportionate number were poor, relying on government aid, and participating in criminal activity. Even some abolitionists believed such claims because of the disproportionate representation of people of color in prisons and jails that resulted from discriminatory policing and carceral practices. In the first decades of the nineteenth century, some abolitionists, including members of the

Pennsylvania Abolition Society, even supported the targeted taxation of free people of color in order to create a fund to aid indigent people of color. Around the same time, calls for more restricted migration by people of color into Pennsylvania and for punishing "black criminals and vagrants" already within the state grew exponentially. Some Pennsylvania colonizationists claimed that people of color comprised "half the expenses of our criminal business and our paupers," while black abolitionists and advocates asserted the contrary, as the evidence bears out. Most of these schemes amounted to little more than inflated rhetoric, though some legislative appropriations for the removal of people of color were made in Pennsylvania by the 1850s.[110]

Regulating Indigent Transiency through Manumission

Beliefs that vagrancy, idleness, and mobility were racial characteristics, coupled with the very real necessity of many former slaves and free blacks to draw on public poor relief to meet basic needs, shaped discussions surrounding, as well as actual, processes of manumission. As a result, indigent transiency, especially in the form of vagrancy, was tied up with emancipation in several ways, both legally and experientially. New York and New Jersey addressed concerns about the poverty and transiency that were often results of emancipation by crafting laws that addressed those concerns within the manumission process. In these states, in the first decades of the nineteenth century, emancipation of slaves was carried out through the apparatus of the poor relief system. The process generally required that the enslaved person be subject to an examination and that the slaveholder file the paperwork of emancipation through the guardians of the poor or justices of the peace. These officials were obliged to determine whether she or he was likely to become chargeable to the town, county, or state, or if the individual had any latent vagrant tendencies that might be revealed upon manumission. Their goal was to ascertain whether or not the individual in question would be likely to be able to provide for themselves, in an effort to safeguard against a proliferation of formerly bound vagrants. New York introduced gradual emancipation in a 1799 law. Both New York and New Jersey required a manumitting slaveholder to consult the overseers of the poor for the town in which he or she resided prior to manumission. New York's "act concerning slaves and servants" containing this stipulation was passed in 1801, while New Jersey followed similar practices during this period, which were confirmed in a state supreme court case in 1824.[111]

The system was designed to protect public funds by mandating that the care of any former slave who may have become a pauper was to be paid for by the former owner or their heirs until the former slave's death. If a slaveholder wished to manumit a slave, New York State law would recognize this manumission if the slave were under the age of fifty, but the owner was required to "obtain a certificate signed by the overseers of the poor of the city or town where such owner shall reside ... certifying that such slave ... [was] of sufficient ability to provide for himself or herself."[112] As Sarah L. H. Gronningsater explains, "what lawmakers did," in an effort to diminish the hold that slavery had on New York State, "was replace slave law with poor law" via requirements for the demonstration of the personal ability and industry of those being manumitted that were meant to assuage fears of black dependency.[113]

The laws governing abolition and manumission echo the language of vagrancy laws in their utilization of personal industry as a prerequisite for freedom. Statutes throughout the North defined as vagrants all individuals who had "no visible means with which to maintain themselves and their families," who "live[d] idly and refuse[d] to work," or who went "from door to door, or frequent[ed] the streets and wander[ed] abroad begging; and ... those who [went] from one place to another ... following no trade, occupation, or business ... unable to give a reasonable account of themselves."[114] Furthermore, the manumission processes in these states render starkly literal the legal obligation to personal industry.[115] They effectively required that slaveholders, slaves, justices of the peace, and guardians of the poor all agree that the slave being manumitted was capable of self-maintenance and thus not likely to become a vagrant. These provisions can be seen as both protection against and facilitation of relief for indigent former slaves as well as a guarantee that the individual being manumitted would be capable of contributing their labor to the local economy. As Robert J. Steinfeld has explained, this is because workers' labor was viewed "as a common resource to which the community had rights." In exchange, workers, bound and free, "had legal obligations to make that resource available to community members on terms and conditions the community prescribed."[116] Nonworkers, then, were participants in idle vagrancy. For recently freed African Americans, this perceived obligation contributed to the climate of what famed abolitionist and former slave Frederick Douglass referred to as the transformation from individuals being held as personal slaves into "slaves of the community."[117]

Thousands of slaves were manumitted as part of this process, and the certificates of manumission created to document it contained variations on the theme of self-sufficiency to bolster descriptions of slaves' fitness for emancipation.[118] The language used by the overseers of the poor in these locations to justify the manumission of these slaves is consistent throughout and generally asserted the same baseline of independent subsistence, with some regional variations. A sense of the nature of these documents can be gotten from the 1824 case of Jim Hall and Beth Seigers, two slaves whose master, Richard Westcot, had written their manumission into his will. Hall and Seigers were examined in Gloucester County by two overseers of the poor and two justices of the peace and were declared "sound in mind and not under any bodily incapacity of obtaining a support."[119] This declaration may have been made at least in partial reference to the health of a slave, clearly an important consideration for legislators and overseers, who limited the window of years wherein a slave could be legally manumitted in New Jersey, between the ages twenty-one and forty (raised from thirty-five as stipulated in a 1786 law to forty in 1798).[120] When Phillis Wheeler was manumitted in Warwick, New York, in 1825, she was deemed by the overseers of the poor to be "capable of procuring her own maintenance."[121]

The function of manumitting through the overseers of the poor provided a legal record, maintained by the city or county, of all the manumissions which they facilitated. This enabled them to seek out the former owner of any indigent free black within that district in order to request payment for services rendered to their former slave. In New York and New Jersey, even slaveholders who manumitted slaves who had been declared capable of maintaining themselves through the appropriate channels could still be pressed to pay for the care of their former slaves who later became indigent, providing an extra layer of security for free blacks as well as the managers of poor relief funds.[122] It was in part through this combination of poor laws and manumission provisions that many free blacks were held in vulnerable legal positions.[123]

For free people of color and others with liminal residential statuses, these laws governing poverty and vagrancy were especially complex and disruptive. The case of one young African American woman named Jenny, who was convicted as a vagrant in New Jersey in 1833, reached the state supreme court that year. She had been arrested by a justice of the peace in Hillsborough for having "strolled from her place of legal settlement, and [gone] begging from house to house in the township." The arresting justice filed for the removal of Jenny as a vagrant to her last place of legal settlement, which was Upper Freehold, New Jersey. The overseers of the poor there were loath to provide for her maintenance in the poorhouse or jail, as Jenny's circumstances were familiar to them: she had been a slave for at least the last ten years "in the family of David Hay," a resident of Upper Freehold. Testimony was sought to corroborate this evidence, because as a slave, Jenny's right to maintenance by her master was protected by state poor laws. Indeed, according to a deposition by "Mrs. Cornell," it was likely that Jenny "owed service to him and was to have support from him," because "Hay was under contract to keep her till the age of twenty-one, for her services." Mrs. Cornell's testimony reached the heart of the incident that had brought about bureaucratic dispute when she accused Hay of having "carted [Jenny] from Upper Freehold into Somerset, and set her down there in the highway, and left her to beg for subsistence." Hay may have predicted that he could not have successfully manumitted Jenny because it would have been challenging to prove that she would be able to provide for herself independently. Or, if he had no knowledge of the law requiring him to do so, he may have been looking for a simple way to relinquish his responsibility to care for her. Either way, it was likely rare for a slaveholder to voluntarily transform his slave into a vagrant, as Hay evidently did, rather than to have one abscond from him into this status, but the confusion over Jenny's status was not unique. It illustrates the interconnectivity of slavery, vagrancy, and the systems of poor relief in this period.[124]

Jenny's case reveals the judges' willingness to view categories that readily appear to be mutually exclusive as coexisting: Justice Wall, in arguing that it was possible for a slave to gain a settlement in the district where they were enslaved, began one of his statements, "if the vagrant was the slave of Mrs. F. who resided in the township of Hillsborough," and went on to discuss the process of removing vagrants as criminal paupers as though the status of being enslaved was incidental to the court when the statuses of vagrant and legally settled were under consideration. In the view of the court, whether Jenny was enslaved or not, the overseers of the poor were authorized to remove her, "the vagrant," "to the place where she had commenced her wanderings."[125]

One of the few extant sources dealing with the removal of former slaves as paupers concerns the testimony of Thomas Tredwell, a "man of colour," before two justices of the peace in Huntington, New York, on 24 November 1820. Tredwell had been born a slave in the town of Flatlands in Kings County, New York. He had been sold several times throughout his life in nearby New Town before 1819, when, at around the age of thirty-five, Tredwell was "permitted by his master to go and work for himself." He then "worked at different places" during the "season past" before settling in Huntington with a wife and children. He had not yet earned a settlement there, however, and the justices ordered Tredwell and his family to be "remove[d] by Thursday next" but did not note his destination. Precedent suggests it may have been to his last owner, or at least to the town in which he had been held as a slave.[126]

The process of manumitting through the overseers of the poor could also produce situations where the ability of a slave to provide for themselves was defended by the slaveholder and upheld by the court. A 1790 law in New York made it possible for slaveholders to seek permission to manumit slaves from the Court of General Sessions if the overseers of the poor had declined to issue a certificate of manumission.[127] An 1809 case in Westchester County involved an enslaved woman named Nancy and a slaveholder named Benjamin Morgan who, as he testified in his petition to the court, was "averse to slavery and moved with compassion to liberate and manumit" Nancy. He had made several attempts to release Nancy through the overseers of the poor unsuccessfully because the overseers "did refuse to sign" the certificate of manumission. His assertions that Nancy did "appear to be under the age of fifty years and of sufficient ability to provide for herself" proved sufficient guarantee to the court, and Morgan's petition for Nancy's manumission was granted.[128]

The same records that were created to circumscribe manumission and limit the public's responsibility in providing for former slaves make it possible to chart their mobility as they came in contact with authorities outside of the districts in which they had been emancipated. There were marked regional differences in the movement of free blacks within northern states as a result of the landscape of abolition that had emerged at the end of the eighteenth century. Among the twelve formerly enslaved nonresident paupers who were examined for relief in Huntington, New York, in the 1820s, most had been born or bound in nearby towns on Long Island. Two had come from out of state, both from New Jersey, and four had come from farther distances in the large state of New York. The proximity of freed blacks' residences to the locations of their former bondage is not dramatically different from the persistence of whites who were examined for poor relief in Huntington during the same period, among whom only just over one-tenth were not local. Settlement laws, of course, could have served as incentive for these poor residents to remain near districts where they may have been entitled to relief.[129]

Conclusion

In the antebellum Mid-Atlantic, emancipation (both legal and illegal, of slaves and of servants), frequently prompted mobility. In turn, this mobility was racialized by law and colored by class, creating a legal and social environment in which the movements of fugitive slaves and servants were affected not only by their status as bonded laborers but also by the criminalization of poverty. The analogy employed by the U.S. Supreme Court in *Prigg v. Pennsylvania* that justified runaway slave capture and rendition on the grounds of states' abilities to "arrest and restrain, and to remove ... idlers, vagabonds, and paupers" demonstrates a perceived shared identity between paupers, vagrants, and slaves. It expands our understanding of fugitive slaves' and paupers' experiences in this period and raises new questions about the impacts of settlement and removal laws on indigent current and former slaves.

Authorities looked to poor laws and vagrancy statutes to manage the "massive dislocation experienced by former slaves" during the long emancipation process.[130] Did these punitive welfare laws inure northerners to the prospect of fugitive slave removal? What does it mean that the *Prigg* decision, by legally joining the categories of pauper, vagrant, and fugitive slave, casts slaves as members of the lumpenproletariat, categorized by and prosecuted on the prima facie evidence of poverty? The enumerated group concocted in law did, in fact, share many corporeal experiences. The seeds of the labor and settlement policies in the postbellum South can be seen in the laws and legislative petitions directed at free black workers and paupers described above.

Poor relief, vagrancy, pauper removal, fugitive rendition, and manumission were all linked by a context of the legal imposition of stasis on categories of persons deemed potentially harmful to communities, broadly defined. Vagrancy statutes, poor laws, and the regulation of manumission came together at an intersection where people both shaped their own identities and were shaped by the laws they encountered. And in the archives, the implicated individuals were rendered literally as strangers, blurring the lines between the homeless pauper, idle vagrant, and runaway slave.

While New York and New Jersey were the only states in the Mid-Atlantic to write protections against vagrancy directly into their manumission laws, the practice was not unheard of elsewhere.[131] In the petitions for legal residency made by African Americans in southern states that legislated the expulsion of manumitted slaves, similar language is found.

Petitioners, in their formal requests for residency, argued that the economic "industriousness" of "free blacks," "as well as their "respectability and "usefulness" ought to act as justification for their legal right to remain denizens of their state.[132] While states requiring these antivagrancy provisions in their manumission certificates sought to limit their liability in the event of the former slave becoming impoverished, poverty and dire material circumstances motivated many petitioners for residency to ameliorate their situations. Vagrancy was integral to the process of emancipation throughout the United States, even where legal provisions against slaves' likelihood to become vagrants were not written into manumission law. Although regional legal distinctions existed in the lived experience and treatment of race and labor status in the antebellum United States, race, class, and labor status were used throughout the nation to control and curb mobility.

5 / "Punishment for Their Misfortunes": Discretion, Incarceration, and Resistance

In August 1841 in Columbia, Pennsylvania, a woman named Cassey Newman was arrested for being an "idle" and "lazy" vagrant. She was convicted on the grounds that she "[would] not work for her living . . . [would] not work as other persons do and as she ought to." To commit the act of living without employment was an offense under Pennsylvania's vagrancy statute, which held that "all persons who . . . live . . . without employment, and refuse to work for the usual and common wages given to other laborers in the like work" were subject to thirty days of incarceration.[1] This language implied that any laborer who negotiated her terms of service may have been engaging in vagrant activity, a common feature of much vagrancy prosecution across the United States.[2] Vagrancy was a visual state; conviction rested upon another individual's recognition that one had no visible means of subsistence. This, of course, allowed for much leeway in constables' and justices' determinations of who should be identified as a vagrant, but average citizens, too, participated in the process. Commitments had to be made on the oath of an individual—the justice or a member of the public—making the process highly susceptible to inaccuracies and personal vendettas. In Cassey Newman's case, it was the latter; her conviction, as well as those of two other women, Sarah Thomas and Elizabeth Thomas, was thrown out. Elizabeth Thomas had been convicted for refusing to accept "work when work is offered to her," while Sarah, too, was imprisoned because she reputedly would "not work for her living as she ought to do," and further, did not have "visible means

"PUNISHMENT FOR THEIR MISFORTUNES" / 113

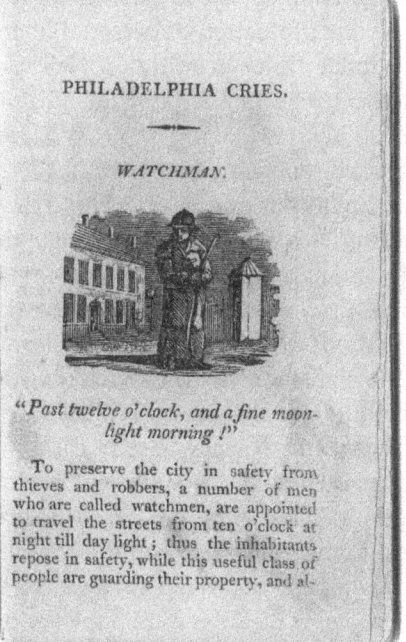

FIGURE 5.1. Watchman, in The Cries of Philadelphia (Philadelphia: John Bouvier, 1810). An illustration of a watchman, including a description of his duties, from an 1810 booklet documenting the sounds of Philadelphia's streets. Most apprehensions of vagrants in early nineteenth-century Philadelphia were carried out by the city's watchmen. (Historical Society of Pennsylvania in The Library Company of Philadelphia)

to support her[self]." The three women were each granted the writs of habeas corpus they had requested, and Judge Samuel Dale, upon review of their cases, ruled in their favor. "The complainant's wife," it appeared, had had a "quarrel" with the accused women, which led to the complainant's reporting of uncommitted crimes. "The prisoner has a fixed place of residence, and complainant has no knowledge but that she earns her living by labor," the judge wrote of the Thomases and Newman.[3] Furthermore, though the judge asserted that he was duty-bound to withhold from weighing in on the "merits of the proceedings of the justice," he could state, in indirect chastisement of the official, that "the summary proceedings against vagrants, under the provisions of the Acts of Assembly, should be conducted, strictly, according to the requisitions of those acts. An adherence to the principle is essential to the due protection of personal liberty."[4]

Judge Dale's acquittal of Newman and the Thomases acknowledged the purpose of the poor law in punishing vagrancy, while simultaneously acknowledging how easy it was for a law based on perception to be abused. Public involvement in the policing of disorderliness, vagrancy, and related crimes was a central facet of criminal justice for small communities, urban neighborhoods, and early police forces. This method for managing the actions of communities compounded already far-reaching, vague, and enumerative laws that criminalized the subsistence methods of the poor and migrant, leaving thousands vulnerable to criminal charges.[5] The free labor "duty to work" that arose as a distinct form of compulsion to replace forced labor was transplanted from the origins of vagrancy laws in early modern England, as Robert Steinfeld has noted, with labor viewed "as a common resource to which the community had rights." Because workers "had legal obligations to make that resource available to community members," those who disobeyed—that is, who did not provide their services to the public either at all or through acceptable means—were punished as vagrants.[6]

This chapter explores the function of the policing of vagrancy in the early nineteenth-century Mid-Atlantic by charting the experiences of convicted vagrants from arrest to incarceration to release. The breadth of actions and statuses that fell under vagrancy laws included not only indigent transiency but also other subsistence activities such as begging, scavenging, and petty theft. Constables, justices, and watchmen—to whom private citizens reported vagrants for conviction—were relied upon for their power of discretion in sentencing, with, in most cases, little to no further judicial process. This chapter argues that the nature of vagrancy as a crime chargeable on prima facie evidence increased the potential impact of the public's involvement in policing the poor. Not only could this lead to highly subjective sentencing for known individuals with unsavory reputations or in cases with personal vendettas at play, but it also placed transients, as strangers, at a further disadvantage. Because transients were less likely to be familiar to locals, they were vulnerable to having their strangerhood being interpreted by private citizens and constables as vagrancy.[7]

The reporting arrangements for vagrancy rested on individuals' abilities to define a vagrant's identity. This was complicated by indigent transients' frequent circulations between penal and aid-based institutions, as well as the quantitative and qualitative overlap between the groups that

FIGURE 5.2. David Kennedy, The Old Arch Street Prison Watercolor, ca. 1836/37. This watercolor depicts the Arch Street Jail around the time of its demolition. Inscriptions below the image read: "The Debtors' Prison," and "The Old Arch Street Prison, built in 1804. Demolished 1837. Occupied the south west corner of Broad and Arch street, the outside walls extended from Broad St on Arch to Schuylkill eigth [sic] now 15th street, 420 feet and from Arch to Cuthbert 150 feet, the building was the shape of a cross built of brick plastered and drawn in courses 4 stories high, the first was used for a kitchen dining and lodging rooms for the keepers families messers Reakert and Duff." (David J. Kennedy Watercolors Collection, The Historical Society of Pennsylvania, Philadelphia)

populated these institutions, in addition to the discretion afforded to justices and watchmen charged with apprehending indigent transients, who could sentence individuals to either the jail or the almshouse for the crime or expression of their poverty and mobility. Many individuals "moved between the almshouse and the prison, reflecting a cycle of poverty and imprisonment with no clear way out."[8] Apparent distinctions between vagrants and paupers are explored in this chapter by looking at the contrasting placements of indigent transients in almshouses and jails. Finally, the chapter will consider ten case studies focusing on writs of habeas corpus filed by convicted vagrants to assert their innocence and lobby for release from jail. Using the records from their cases, this chapter explores the arguments they used to proclaim their innocence and thus define what qualities could effectively prove that an individual was not a vagrant. When defending themselves against charges of vagrancy in court, the convicted drew on their own understandings of the law as well as, in some cases, the assistance of lawyers, to refute charges of idleness and immorality and to construct arguments that point to the social, cultural, and economic value of industriousness in antebellum communities.

Public Justice

Constables' authority rested in part upon the involvement of the public. While constables had an occupational and legal "especial duty" to preserve order, average residents, too, were enlisted. This duty resulted from the doctrine of "posse comitatus," which required "temporarily deputized citizens" to assist "law enforcement officers" in "keep[ing] the peace," a frequent occurrence "prior to the advent of centralized police forces," as Gautham Rao has documented.[9] In some cases in the early nineteenth century, the employment of posse comitatus was specifically tailored to the policing of vagrants. In Washington, DC, constables were charged to "endeavor to find out whether there be any such vagrants" within their jurisdiction, and to ensure their swift arrest.[10] Citizen vigilantes in Delaware were actually offered a cash reward of three dollars to report vagrants to authorities. There, in 1849, a racialized vagrancy law was implemented, whereby justices of the peace were tasked with apprehending any "free negro or mulatto, male or female . . . residing or staying . . . without visible means of support." The punishment involved a term as an indentured servant—leading some poor people of color back into a state of forced servitude as a result of their poverty and mobility.[11]

Because vagrancy statutes required only prima facie evidence to convict a person of vagrancy, any witnessing of the actions enumerated under a vagrancy statute whether on the word of a constable, magistrate, or passerby, could lead to prosecution. In Philadelphia, each time the conviction or commitment of a vagrant was recorded on the prison docket by a justice or magistrate, the grounds of the arrest were justified "on the oath of" either a reporting individual or informant, or the law enforcement official themselves. The extent of public or community policing is difficult to measure, but in the records of cities like Philadelphia, where the names of watchmen and magistrates are available (and most were thorough in their record keeping), it is possible to estimate how frequently passersby, neighbors, or victims reported vagrants to the authorities. There, spot checks of the prison's vagrancy commitment dockets from the 1820s and 1830s indicate that as many as one-third of such commitments may have been reported by citizens.[12]

Some cities authorized constables to search suspicious properties, including houses, for vagrants and other disorderly persons. This option likely afforded officials the ability to seek out squatters on private property and to remove drunks from disorderly houses. In practice, this gave justices and watchmen the option to search out, arrest, remove, and commit the indigent as vagrants on private property.[13] This practice was, as with most nineteenth-century policing, both gendered and racialized: women suspected of prostitution were often rounded up in this way.[14] Similarly, black women and men found in suspicious or illegal establishments such as dance halls or taverns were often extracted from the premises and convicted as vagrants.[15]

The legal privilege of law enforcement officers to remove suspected vagrants even from private property left many indigent transients in a vulnerable position. In the case of a vagrant by the name of Baldwin, the Philadelphia city watchmen brought him to the mayor to state his case after he had been "found by the watch after 10 o'clock . . . in some house towards the southern border of the city, where he was staying much against the will of the occupants." It does not appear that the occupants initiated his arrest, but he was discovered by a watchman. Thus apprehended, Baldwin "stated that he had no home—no residence in the city." When the mayor asked him where he lived, he responded "no where," having arrived in Philadelphia two days earlier from New York.[16] Squatting, or even indeed legally occupying a residence, in some cases, was insufficient protection against a vagrancy charge. Prison inspectors commonly found incarcerated persons "sentenced as vagrants, who, in legal contemplation, are not such." One report discussing the efficacy of prosecution asserted that while "a vagrant is a person without a home or visible means of subsistence . . . yet wives, husbands, children living with their parents, are sometimes sentenced as vagrants."[17] The visual and public nature of vagrancy, wherein a witness's word was enough to convict a vagrant, lent itself to easy convictions as well as mistaken prosecutions.[18]

Charitable goals also motivated the policing of vagrants by some citizens. The New York Association for Improving the Condition of the Poor (NYAICP), founded in response to the economic devastation that followed the Panic of 1837, aimed to "put an end to street begging and vagrancy" by discouraging philanthropic donations to the undeserving poor. Members investigated the would-be alms recipients and ranked their worthiness to receive aid against social and moral characteristics like industry and virtue. If an individual who did not possess the proper level of morality were to request alms from a member of the NYAICP, as one promotional letter for the organization asserted in 1847, the philanthropist would then find it her "duty to report [them] as a vagrant." The threat of this possibility, the letter argued, would be enough to cure those perceived as undeserving of their "begging and vagrant propensities."[19]

Public participation in the policing of an entire class of persons underscores the clarity with which vagrancy as a legal concept was entrenched in social perceptions in the early republic. Average citizens were seen as reliable sources for the accusation of vagrants and were regularly engaged in the process of prosecuting disorderly and vagrant persons. Of course, before the advent of ubiquitous professional police forces in the mid- to late nineteenth century, members of the public were commonly engaged in a culture of public reporting, and most crimes would have been witnessed by average citizens. But public involvement takes on different meaning in the context of the policing of vagrancy and the doctrine of posse comitatus, and may point to what Michael Meranze calls "mimetic corruption," a theory that was central to nineteenth-century theories on criminality. Many nineteenth-century Americans were wary of onlookers replicating witnessed criminality, and the prosecution of drunkenness, prostitution, profanity, and other disorderly behaviors can be seen as an effort to protect the morality of the public sphere.[20] Further, public participation in vagrancy policing solidified the visual signifiers of poverty, such as wearing ragged clothing or shoes or using unrefined language, emphasizing the distinction between the informer and the informant. This structure made it possible for the law itself to become a tool for the articulation and enforcement of class distinctions and power, allowing average citizens to shape and perpetuate class distinctions by identifying individuals as vagrants and reporting them to the authorities.[21] There were a few clear factors that increased an individuals' likelihood of facing arrest for vagrancy. These varied regionally and from person to person, but unfamiliarity, race, and destitute family groups were among the most common. The participation of onlookers in the policing of strangers and travelers further alienated the indigent and transient from civic life. Excluded from political life due to their rootlessness, transients—especially the poorer among them—were further excluded from communal life by policies that redefined passersby as impromptu justices.

As has been discussed in detail, vagrancy laws were notoriously susceptible to varying interpretations by those enforcing them—from justices to judges to jailers. In nineteenth-century Philadelphia's criminal justice system, discretion in policing was often inconsistently applied in the apprehension and sentencing of vagrants. Rather than arresting every individual who might have qualified as a vagrant, some arresting officials would effectively, if unofficially, induce indigent transients into leaving the city, in an impromptu form of pauper removal.[22] A cursory look at watchmen's returns in New York City's municipal records reveals a similar practice: individuals' arrests were recorded, but then, as in the case of John Green in 1825, the convicted vagrants were "discharged to leave the city." Similarly, that same year, Julia Freeman was arrested with the intention of sending her to "the commissioners of the almshouse" in New York, but she was instead "discharged to sail for Baltimore this day."[23] These informal warnings-out served to support not vagrancy laws but settlement laws, by policing denizenship through the removal of potential drains on poor relief or penal budgets. If such informal policing practices had been recorded more systematically, the actual population of vagrants in antebellum Philadelphia and New York City in particular might be much higher than written records now indicate.

The prevalence of discretionary arrests made under vagrancy laws left many poor families vulnerable to arrest. Across the antebellum United States, single and pregnant women, as well as children, were particularly targeted.[24] While public officials attempted to control women on the grounds of protecting public morality, indigent transient women were seen as especially problematic; vagrant women—especially pregnant women or women with children— were more vulnerable to warning and pauper removal practices throughout the entire antebellum period because they represented the potentiality of entire families of needy relief-seekers.[25]

Across state lines and through decades, married couples, parents and children, and siblings appear together on jail dockets. Groups of relatives did not comprise a large proportion among convicted vagrants, but their arrests were not exactly rare, either. Since the institution of early colonial vagrancy laws, the crime was not a single man's game (as it became at the end of the nineteenth century). Throughout the late colonial and early national periods, entire family units were convicted together: one early example from New Jersey in 1774 involved the arrest of "Catherine Land and her three children" on the same charge by a justice "as vagrants, strolling about, without any visible means of livelihood."[26] In some cases, the conviction of families resulted from a constable's view that each member had participated in the crime, or to avoid separating family members. In others, the law of coverture may have been interpreted to include a wife in her husband's punishment, or, for a husband to serve a punishment in lieu of his wife doing so.[27] Theoretically, under coverture law, wives could not be held responsible for illegal activities.[28] But in practice, married women were repeatedly convicted and punished in the early republic, especially for status and nonviolent crimes, including vagrancy.[29]

Vagrants in the Almshouse, Vagrants in the Prison

It was common for individuals to move between almshouses and jails, and officials were granted the opportunity to exercise tremendous discretion over how to punish indigent transients, as vagrants or as paupers, and in the almshouse or in the jail. But the internal processes at work during vagrants' imprisonment are something of a mystery, and few records give any idea of how they functioned on the inside.[30] Much of this story has remained unknown, as little documentation remains extant regarding Philadelphia's prison for vagrants, Arch Street Jail.[31] There were few distinctions between vagrants punitively confined or philanthropically detained, but the few extant sources documenting these processes provide insight into the carceral experiences of indigent transients. Examining what is available showcases the importance of classification and distinction in nineteenth-century penal reform, not only among the incarcerated but between different types of facilities. Jails and city and county prisons saw far less of the "age of the penitentiary" revolution than did state facilities in Pennsylvania, and the experiences of those detained within reveal the impact of that distinction.[32]

Following institutionalization, vagrants and other indigent transients were still singled out and rendered distinct from the general population of the propertyless and needy.[33] Female and male vagrants in the Philadelphia Almshouse were housed separately from the rest of the inmates, in separate rooms listed on the institution's weekly censuses as "vagrants cellars"; these cellars were further separated by sex, except in the case of children.[34] Vagrant children were held in the women's cellar. Highlighting this category of punishments for vagrancy illustrates pervasive early republic ideologies about labor obligations—and that they could extend to children expressly—as well as the deep-rooted nature of the legal class definitions that classified poor families as agents of social and economic unrest. This subjective incarceration was an extension of the subjective prosecution that generally preceded imprisonment for vagrancy.[35] This underscores the fact that the instability that defined the status of most indigent transients affected dependents not only through residency or income but also through criminal punishment and incarceration. And of course, many children were arrested and incarcerated on their own, as well: James McCoy, for example, who was described by a New York City watchman as "a small boy, no place to live at, found sleeping in a sandbox," was arrested for vagrancy in 1825. Adrian Allen, "a boy having no parents" who was "found sleeping under a workbench," was arrested as a vagrant that same summer, and both children served time in jail.[36]

Early republic Philadelphia seemed to be of many minds about where it was best to incarcerate vagrants arrested in the city. Between the 1790s and 1840s, the designated location changed at least four times. The longest-lasting of these, the Arch Street Jail, was a purpose-built building that, according to contemporaries, was "never considered sufficiently safe or well constructed to house prisoners."[37] This facility, which was in use for less than three decades, was designed to hold the overflow of the city's older Walnut Street Jail, which was by 1803 filled beyond capacity. Construction on the new prison began in 1804 and continued for several years while disputes over funding and allocations between the state, city, and prison inspectors in charge of overseeing penal facilities muddled the process. The county prison inspectors had made a case to the state legislature regarding the suitability of separating those incarcerated under their care according to the nature and severity of their crimes. "Because persons committed for various grades of crimes," they argued, including "fugitives [sic] from service, vagrants, servants, and apprentices" were "mingled together in a common crowd by which means the novice in view receives lessons from adepts in crime and comes out of prison prepared to follow the instructions and examples which have been given him," separation was essential.[38]

The solution determined by the inspectors and the state legislature was for criminal convicts to continue to be incarcerated at Walnut Street, while the "denomination of prisoners for trial, vagrants, runaway or disorderly servants and apprentices, and all other descriptions of persons (except convicts)" would be held instead at Arch Street.[39] Sometime around 1816, Arch Street began to receive the first arrivals of the debtors and witnesses, but, while construction and adjustments to the facility at Arch Street continued, the vagrants who had formerly been held at the Walnut Street Jail (which was adjacent to Sixth and Prune [now Locust] Streets) would be transferred to the debtor's prison, referred to as the "Prune Street Apartment." Around this time, a monthly average of 227 vagrants and untried prisoners were sentenced to be incarcerated there.[40]

In 1816, the county prison inspectors also opened a discussion with the managers of the Philadelphia Almshouse about the guardians of the poor sending disorderly and vagrant persons to the almshouse instead of the prison, perhaps in an effort to relieve the crowded and unsanitary conditions in the prison facilities. This discussion may represent the beginning of the practice of allowing the use of discretion by guardians and city watchmen sending vagrants and other homeless or disorderly individuals to either the jail or the almshouse for incarceration.[41]

After April 1823, vagrants and prisoners awaiting trial were sent to the Arch Street Jail. The first census of inmates following their transfer listed 103 vagrant and untried men and 73 vagrant and untried women in the facility; these numbers rose steadily throughout that summer. By July, there were 270 vagrant and untried prisoners incarcerated at Arch Street.[42] By the following year, more than eight thousand vagrants and untried prisoners were recorded on the inspectors' lists of the incarcerated. While this number is certainly lower after recidivists are removed, there were still thousands of individuals plucked off of Philadelphia's streets as vagrants in these years. For Arch Street's vagrant inmates, the punishment of incarceration in this institution usually followed some form of movement or mobility: most were detained for the crimes of "strolling" and "wandering," being persons "having no residence," and "being destitute of a home."[43]

Members of the internationally renowned Prison Discipline Society observed in 1830, that the "Prison on Arch Street [was] another New York Bridewell," an assessment that would have been cause for alarm, as New York City's carceral facility where vagrants were held had a reputation for filth, destitution, and desolation.[44] The most significant difference was that hundreds of debtors were also incarcerated at Arch Street: 817, according to the Society, were held there during an eight-month period spanning 1829–30. Beyond that, the prison's defining characteristic was that it held "vagrants and untried prisoners, of all colors and degrees of crime . . . assembled in one common room," where prisoners were kept "with privations so great as to form a severe punishment for their misfortunes and poverty."[45] According to the inspectors, throughout 1823, the first year of Arch Street's full operation, "two thirds" of the inmates "were vagrants, disorderly persons, and disturbers of the peace."[46] These individuals were receiving punishments "dealt out," as one observer noted, "not to convicts, but to men whom the law holds as innocent, they not having received a trial by a jury of their peers" and to vagrants, men and women alike.[47] An annual average of two thousand vagrants, debtors, and untried prisoners were held at Arch Street. While the prison contained a separate apartment to confine debtors, the rest of the prisoners mingled, with the result that "the reputed pirate and murderer" might be found "seated beside a youth confined for a drunken brawl."[48] Legislators and reformers had condemned intermingling of prisoners at Arch Street's predecessor facilities, and the prisoners' shared confinement contributed to calls for a separate system that might not breed, as it was feared, further crime.

Strong distinctions were drawn by prison inspectors between criminal convicts and Arch Street's noncriminal prisoners. In 1824, a Philadelphia grand jury found that "the arrangements made for the safety and health of the convicts [at Walnut Street Jail] are as well calculated for those objects as the extreme scarcity of room in the . . . apartments of the vagrants and untried prisoners." Discomfort was a design feature for the punishment and housing of vagrants and debtors as a deterrent against recidivism.[49] Authorities claimed that convicts held in Philadelphia's high-profile Eastern State Penitentiary by the late 1820s and 1830s were "of a different class," possessing "higher intelligence," better social habits, and better hygiene than the average "miserable vagrant" confined in the Arch Street Jail.[50] The conditions in the two institutions reflected this perception. A legislative committee investigating the issue in 1833 questioned whether offering greater "provisions and comforts" to incarcerated vagrants would encourage "idleness and profligacy" yet asserted that they were entitled to be treated at "least upon an equal position with the convicts."[51] Arch Street Jail was designed to house vagrants with adequate space and provisions. But in practice, vagrants were left "nearly naked," with scant material comforts.[52] As the purpose-built vagrants' prison, the facility's condition and features can be read as a contemporary comment on the punishment vagrants were thought to deserve.

According to some calculations, during the 1820s, as much as three-eighths of the population of Philadelphia had been jailed for debts owed. With such a high proportion of the population subject to debt imprisonment, the institution's visibility, and thus, social distaste for it as an outmoded and cruel imposition, grew in the 1820s and 1830s. As public opinion began to turn in the late 1820s, the number of releases from petty debts owed increased. Records indicate that as many as three thousand debtors had their obligations discharged by courts in Philadelphia over just a four-year period between 1827 and 1830.[53] If this is the case, then three thousand more insolvent and indigent persons were at liberty in the city in those years than previously, possibly contributing to the increase in the number of vagrants incarcerated in the almshouse in that period. Most states were slow to adopt any dramatic limitations on imprisonment for debts, and this affected the labor market in myriad ways. Not only was the ability of the incarcerated individual to contribute his or her labor circumscribed, but parents—especially free men of color—often resorted to offering their children as indentured servants to work off their debts.[54]

Because justices and city watchmen in New York and Pennsylvania were both commonly left to decide where to incarcerate vagrants, in almshouses or jails, vagrants were a ubiquitous group within not only the Arch Street Prison but also the Philadelphia Almshouse in the 1820s and 1830s. One indigent transient, a woman named Catharine Morrison, entered the Philadelphia Almshouse in the winter of 1822 as a homeless widow. Now twenty-eight years old, she had been born in New Jersey and traveled to Philadelphia around the age of twenty. There, she had married a local man named William Morrison and lived in the city with him before moving to New York City. There, her life took a turn. She testified to almshouse officials that it was there, "in the summer of 1820," that her husband died "of the Yellow Fever," and their "house was consumed by fire." Morrison returned to Philadelphia after her husband's death, and after about a year in the city, she entered the almshouse, apparently in need of medical care, where she was examined in the surgical ward. Shortly after her arrival, in February 1822, she was forcibly removed from Philadelphia by a city official—either a justice of the peace or an almshouse agent—and escorted to her place of legal settlement. The removal was not lasting: a year later, Morrison was back in Philadelphia, arrested for being a "strolling vagrant." She was sentenced to serve "one month" in the county jail "or GP," under the guardians of the poor, in the almshouse.[55]

Some vagrants arrived in the almshouse upon sentencing, while others were released from jail to the almshouse during or after serving their term at Arch Street. In regular monthly censuses taken in the Philadelphia Almshouse between 1827 and 1833, vagrants comprised around one-tenth of the total population.[56] They were held in two separate areas of the facility, in cellars segregated by sex, and young children regardless of sex were placed in the female vagrants' cellar. Out of twenty-nine censuses, the number of female vagrants surpassed the number of male vagrants in all but one. No more than three children are listed as part of the almshouse's vagrant population at any given time, and this small number was housed with the women. This low number may be a result of the frequency with which the children of vagrants and paupers were forcibly apprenticed or bound out under indenture rather than held in the almshouse for an extended period.[57] The highest figures are found over the winter of 1829, when as many as 125 vagrants were confined together in the two cellars. During these years, the vagrant population differed significantly from the general population of almshouse inmates: the proportion of men in the latter was higher than that of the women for the whole period between 1800 and 1850, and while the number of women remained largely stagnant, there was greater fluctuation among the proportion of men, converse to that of the vagrant population of the almshouse. One explanation for the large proportion of men may be due to the greater likelihood that welfare officials would deny outdoor relief to men, leaving institutionalization the only remaining option for men in need of poor relief.[58]

Since these vagrants could have found themselves in the almshouse cellars in a number of ways and sparse record keeping obscured their identities, little more than inferences can be made about the individuals who were counted in this census, except in a few cases. The stories of Isaiah White and Alexander Bishop illustrate that the result of discretionary policing was discretionary incarceration: White was a transient, veteran, vagrant, and pauper. He was first arrested with three other men for "being idle vagrants" on 1 December 1827.[59] Of this group, one man was released on bail or indenture after only two weeks, while one other served his full sentence and was discharged after thirty days. On 28 December, during a visit by "the visiting inspectors," White and the other remaining man, Alexander Bishop, were "sent to [the] almshouse" on the inspectors' order.[60] Arriving there as vagrants, White and Bishop would have been counted among the thirty-three men listed in the census on 29 December 1827. To the inspectors, they must have appeared more like paupers than like vagrants. But neither Bishop nor White were examined for settlement once they arrived in the almshouse—at least until White found himself there again, possibly as a result of a further vagrancy conviction in 1837. He testified that he had been a bound apprentice until the age of twenty-one, around 1785, when he went to work for his father, a store owner, in Chester County, on wages. He later lived for a time in Harrisburg and identified as a "weaver and gardener." He "enlisted in the army" in 1811 and "remained in it . . . stationed the whole of the time in the state of Louisiana." After he was discharged, he "continued laboring about in Louisiana" wherever he could find work, until he returned to Pennsylvania in 1827. It is plausible that it was upon his return to the

North, likely through Philadelphia, that he was arrested as a vagrant. His transiency continued when he "went to the state of Ohio," then back to Chester County, where he was apparently employed on wages at the Chester County Poorhouse as a gardener. Employment in an almshouse apparently did not pay enough to keep one out of the almshouse as a resident, however. White left there and made his way to Philadelphia, where he "worked about until harvest time" before applying and obtaining admission to the "Hospital of the Philadelphia Almshouse."[61]

The ease with which White and Bishop were externally defined and redefined as vagrants and as migrant paupers is a testament to the interrelation and flexibility of the two categories. Many indigent transients spent time in Philadelphia's almshouse and jail before continuing to move. Others were more locally transient—still lacking in the stability of home and permanent residence but drawn or kept to one location by other factors. Such was the case with Mary Porter, who was repeatedly arrested as a vagrant in Philadelphia throughout the 1820s and was well-known in the almshouse. Born in Ireland, she had migrated to Delaware as a child with her family, but they had remained in New Castle only a few days. The family spent six years in rural Lancaster County before moving to the city, where they remained for about seven years. Around the age of twenty, she relocated to Southwark, where she met and married Irish-born John Porter. The couple lived "for a few weeks" in Southwark, and then for "7 or 8 months" in Moyamensing, before settling in Lancaster for five years. When her husband died sometime around 1822, she left Lancaster with their two children and went to Philadelphia, likely in search of work or a former contact.[62] It was after this time that she was found on the street "having no residence" on 25 February 1823. She was admitted to the almshouse as a nonresident and examined on 13 March 1824, when her legal residence was determined as Lancaster. If this information, and the likelihood of her removal, was made known to her, it could explain why she "eloped" that same day. Two weeks later, she was again arrested as a vagrant.

Porter reentered the almshouse in the winter of 1825 but "was removed from the Philadelphia to the Lancaster Almshouse on the 22nd of February." By this time, she was no longer described by officials as a "widow with two children," and it is possible that her children were bound out during her first stay in the Philadelphia Almshouse. In 1826, she was again admitted there, and an order of removal was issued to send her back to Lancaster, "but she eloped." She did not return until the following autumn, when another removal attempt was made. Porter managed to return to Philadelphia yet again, and in January 1827 was the subject of correspondence between the steward of the Philadelphia Almshouse and Lancaster's overseers, who noted that "Mary Porter is again returned to this house and is now able to be removed. She will be a constant source of expense to you while suffered to remain in this city." She was arrested as a vagrant on 23 October 1827.[63] Porter's activities cease to be recorded in the vagrant docket and examination books after this, so her fate is unclear, but as a previously removed pauper, she would have been vulnerable to harsher sentencing for frequently returning to a city "in a state of vagrancy" from which she had been formally removed, as the law stipulated.[64]

Legal Resistance

Mary Porter's choice to elope repeatedly, absconding from the custody of justices and guardians, can be read as resistance to the policing of her movements. Resistance was a common feature of vagrancy prosecution. During a vagrancy sweep by New York City magistrates in 1825, a man named John Johnson, apprehended alongside six others for "living idle without employment and having no visible means of supporting themselves," resisted arrest to the point of "a fall" which "injured his knee." One repeat offender from Philadelphia must have refused to reveal her identity strongly enough for the constables to record her identity on the vagrant docket as "I got no name" twice in one week, with the comment "alias Henrietta Blake" inserted later after further questioning.[65]

Prosecution and incarceration for indigent transiency was a means by which many of the poorest members of antebellum society came in direct contact with institutional processes, as their own identities, described in the terms of the law, became institutionalized. In a legal system where indigent transients were regularly convicted and incarcerated on prima facie evidence, with no witnesses, with few other actions resembling due process involved, and with short prison terms, it is somewhat remarkable that any number of vagrants were able to use the law to appeal their charges. But some did manage to defend themselves in the courts. In fact, it could be argued that it was the discretionary nature of vagrancy policing that aided their defense, as will be explored in this section, by highlighting the subjectivity of their sentencing.

The dominant means of release available to incarcerated vagrants who believed themselves to be wrongfully convicted was petitioning for writs of habeas corpus. When individuals appealed their charges, they were able to articulate, through the language of the law as well as their own expression, the criminalization of poverty. The defenses offered up by convicted vagrants on their own character emphasize that they perceived that personal industry was what distinguished their own actions from a vagrant's actions. In order to refute a vagrancy conviction, they struck at one of the key features of the crime: idleness. This process documents the nineteenth-century link between morality and market participation through the dichotomy between idleness and industriousness. The following case study explores the definitions and redefinitions of identity that emerge in the habeas corpus petitions of vagrants.

Between 1836 and 1841, at least ten convicted vagrants in Lancaster, Pennsylvania, pursued writs of habeas corpus in hopes of ending their incarceration.[66] In the case of vagrancy, especially, with its myriad definitions, clauses, and applications, habeas corpus petitions serve as an articulation of why their actions did not amount to vagrancy, or why their identities belied a conviction as a vagrant. Unfortunately, because these convictions occurred outside of the courts, detailed records are rare for this period. Watchmen, constables, and justices of the peace were largely independent actors in the carrying out of their duties, and justices in particular generally worked out of their homes. As such, dockets or arrest records were not often maintained in a central location. The few that are extant afford a closer look at the proceedings of vagrancy convictions and absolutions of convictions. At least nine of the ten petitions were successful; in the other case, the record of the petition's outcome has not survived.

John Harkins was arrested for vagrancy on 11 June 1836, and he remained in jail for three days before his release was secured.[67] Harkins was convicted by Justice of the Peace Thomas Lloyd, who asserted, upon delivering him to the constable for removal to the common jail, that he was "an idle and disorderly person and a common vagrant" and should be sentenced to hard labor for one month. As was the case for formally charged vagrants at the time, he "had no opportunity of defense." Harkins may have requested an audience with a lawyer or made some written pleas while incarcerated in order to orchestrate his request for a writ of habeas corpus. In the next two days, he managed to secure the writ on the grounds that he had been unjustly "restrained of his liberty," and his case was brought before an alderman for the City of Lancaster. Harkins, the alderman recorded, believed his incarceration "to be ... altogether unjust, illegal, and suppressive." His case was heard by two judges from the Court of Common Pleas on 14 June, where he testified that the justice had proffered the charge of vagrancy against him, though "he had been taken upon an execution . . . for debt." Before the court, three "respectable witnesses" testified in favor of Harkins's character and against the claim that he was a "common vagrant," on the grounds that he was known "to be an industrious man, and possessed of a trade and means of sustenance." He was discharged that day.[68]

John Harkins did not make a lasting impact on the historical record, but the nature of his defense says much about laws pertaining to vagrants in this period, as well as to the lives of vagrants who may have met the standards of the law more than he himself did. To assert that he was "industrious" was to refute the statute's accusation of idleness; the same was true of possessing means of subsistence and knowledge of a trade. The latter, of course, did not guarantee employment or income. Since the exact circumstances of Harkins's arrest are unknown, we can only speculate as to what led to his arrest as a vagrant. It could be that he was having difficulty getting sufficient work at his trade and had neglected to pay a creditor, or, perhaps, he merely looked to the justice like a debtor or "idle" man.[69]

On 28 October 1837, Martha Ann Ramsey was convicted with the same language of the vagrancy statute as John Harkins had been: for "being an idle and disorderly person and a common vagrant." She, too, was sentenced to thirty days imprisonment in the Common Jail, at hard labor. She spent about a week in jail before her case was heard before the county Court of Common Pleas. Deliberations were minimal; Ramsey was presented before the court as a household laborer, and the judge found that there was sufficient "proof that the defendant is industrious and not a vagrant" and discharged her.[70] The crime of which Ramsey and Harkins were convicted was, in effect, unemployment, or the withholding of labor from the marketplace, construed, in the context of this burgeoning capitalist society, as idleness. Testimony to the contrary was enough to contravene this claim against their character, but only after the assertion that industriousness and labor contribution pointed to moral behavior and thus could not qualify as participation in vagrancy.

Many indigent transients like convicted vagrant Martha Ann Ramsey were defined first as idle vagrants and then redefined as industrious defendants. Others, like Ramsey, were externally assigned the role of disorderly vagrant, a role that was summarily contradicted once they had managed to prove that they possessed a "dwelling" to call home, which they managed as "industrious housekeeper[s]."[71] This conflict of identity is important on a cultural level, in recognizing that antebellum authorities exercised control over the lives of the lower classes, by compelling individuals to provide evidence that they were not impoverished to the point of homelessness or begging. This compulsion to prove an individual's innocence as opposed to guilt is indicative of the tone of early nineteenth-century policing and is far from a revelation. But in the steps that followed the initial interaction with authority described here, that is, arrest and the assignment of carceral punishment, the distinction between the criminal vagrant and the pauper vagrant is highlighted.

Most convictions for vagrancy in this period, as in Ramsey's case, were for idleness and disorderliness, and most of the actions listed under the list of arrestable offenses as vagrant actions in the 1836 Pennsylvania Poor Law could be grouped together as "idleness." Beyond that, however, part of the law's revision that year involved the formal designation of beggars as vagrants; and of course, as has been discussed, any individual who did not possess "visible means" of subsistence was liable for arrest as a vagrant. So, too, were loiterers and the unemployed. The broad definitions of disorderly conduct employed in this period covered activity far beyond modern understandings of the term and were used to describe appearing drunk in public, the wearing of expensive-looking clothes by black men, or women walking down the street without chaperones.[72]

Whatever the specific offense, occasionally constables sentenced vagrants to lesser terms. On 11 September 1837, three women were arrested together and sentenced to ten days of incarceration each, at hard labor, in the county jail. The convictions of Eliza Henry, Martha Loney, and Mary Brown, were identical. While Harkins and Ramsey had been convicted on the oath of the justice of the peace himself, Henry, Loney, and Brown were convicted before the justice on the oaths of three men, James Shantridge, Robert Chalfant, and Jonathan Figelo, "with being disorderly vagrant[s]." The women spent the night in jail but filed a petition for a writ of habeas corpus the very next day, stating "that they have each been committed to the jail ... and sentenced as disorderly vagrants" unjustly, "request[ing] and pray[ing]" that a writ of habeas corpus be granted to enable the petitioners to present their cases to the court, "that they may be dealt with as to right and justice belong." The writ was granted them, and the judge, "on hearing proof that all had dwellings and families and were industrious housekeepers and not vagrants," released them on the same day.[73] The actions that led to the arrest of these women are unclear, but the offenses for which women faced vagrancy convictions often involved activities akin, at least in the public eye, to prostitution.

Assumptions of such activity, however, were sometimes deemed unfounded even by contemporary courts. When Elizabeth Fasnacht, a woman arrested as a vagrant in the winter of 1837, requested a writ of habeas corpus, a prominent local attorney got involved in her defense. But the justice of the peace who had sentenced her was so adamant that she deserved to be jailed for her behavior that he wrote to the attorney requesting that her case be reconsidered. "There has been complaints at different times respecting this woman keeping a tippling house, and a house of the most infamous character," he wrote. There had been previous offenses that he had allowed to "rest" because of "Elizabeth having an infant. . . . but since that, [her] conduct was so intolerable that the people in their neighborhood would bear with it no longer." He accused Fasnacht of selling liquor, bawdy activity, fighting, and having "almost every night . . . men and women, white and black, of the most abandoned characters" in her home. These activities were offenses in their own right, but the justice of the peace had chosen to arrest Fasnacht for being an "idle, disorderly vagrant." It may be this inaccuracy that afforded the courts the grounds for releasing her. In Fasnacht's explanation of her wrongful incarceration, she objected explicitly to the fact that the charges she was brought up on were criminal in nature, asserting that she was "unjustly confined . . . for some . . . supposed criminal matter" with which she had not been involved. The judges of the Common Pleas Court may have agreed, as they chose to discharge Fasnacht on 14 February because "from other testimony produced it appears that the said Elizabeth has a home and is a regular working woman and does not come under the meaning of the vagrant act."[74]

Similar pleas were made by others wrongfully incarcerated for vagrancy. One such case, a habeas corpus petition filed in New York in 1838 led to a state supreme court case, *Emma Sands vs. The People*.[75] Emma Sands was arrested for prostitution but was committed for vagrancy. While incarcerated, she filed for and was granted a writ of habeas corpus, and her conviction was overturned. The presiding judge declared that the vagrancy law that had allowed her incarceration, which had been passed by the New York State legislature in 1833, was unconstitutional. But even without New York's legal conflation of vagrancy and prostitution, the behavior of women, sexual and otherwise, was closely monitored by male citizens and regulated by law enforcement. The moral proscriptions of the law linked poverty with immorality, rendering homelessness and prostitution equally valid activities to prosecute under the umbrella of vagrancy laws. For women, the sorts of immoral actions most commonly punished under vagrancy law included sexual activities but also appearing in public, in the presence of men, wearing clothing deemed inappropriate, neglecting to don a hat, but most commonly, walking alone in public, especially at night.[76] Under the function of vagrancy laws in New York City, poor women's regular activities were classified as prostitution.[77]

Convicted vagrant Sarah Cooper was categorized as a vagrant because, like Cassey Newman, and Sarah and Elizabeth Thomas, her control over her own labor was not manifest in a way that was read by law enforcement as compliance. Cooper claimed that her conviction "as a common vagrant" had occurred not by being "apprehended on the streets as an idle person" but, rather, by being "induced under the hope of procuring employment to go to the house of one of the constables of the City of Lancaster by whom she was immediately arrested and carried to gaol."[78] The result of Cooper's petition is unknown, but her statements may corroborate scholars' claims of constables' manipulation of sentencing, release, and resentencing to add to their own fees, which would increase their incomes with each commitment.[79] Samuel Waits, the constable who convicted Cassey Newman, charged thirty-seven cents for "bringing prisoner before justice," another thirty-seven cents for her commitment, and seventy-two cents for mileage, totaling $1.47.[80] If Cooper's claims were valid, they could be evidence of authorities' utilization of their knowledge of the desperation of the poor to pad their wages.[81]

The defenses put forward by these accused vagrants in Lancaster appear to be representative, as similar cases are found elsewhere in the region. When John Kennedy was allegedly wrongfully convicted of vagrancy in Philadelphia in 1819, after several days in jail, a man named John Holliday came forward to testify on oath that Kennedy was "in general a sober industrious man, maintaining himself by his own industry." This testimony convinced the mayor, Robert Wharton, and Kennedy was released.[82] Within the space of one conversation with a stranger on the street, or a city constable, the poor, isolated as a separate class of "persons ... liable to ... penalties," could be redefined as criminals.[83] In vagrants' habeas corpus petitions, definitions of personal identity are articulated by individuals who have been rendered vulnerable by the state. In the testimonies presented before the courts in these cases, the singular fact of not being homeless served as sufficient evidence to warrant release from jail. These cases, then, allow the circumstances of arrests that would otherwise be recorded as little more than two lines on a jail docket to illustrate individuals' interactions with the social manifestation of vagrancy law. Their cases indicate both the sorts of actions that early police viewed as vagrant as well as the means of tactical resistance used by the convicted.

Conclusion

The habeas corpus cases discussed in this chapter show vagrants resisting the definitions assigned to them by both police and the penal system, tactically maneuvering within the context of state control over their physical movements and actions in order to assert their own, self-defined identity. That surviving records of instances where accused vagrants refuted their assignations in courts of law in the antebellum period show such efforts to have been fairly successful demonstrates that there was a limit to the power of discretionary policing that rested with the judiciary. But because most vagrancy cases did not include direct judicial involvement, the characteristics and actions that led to the arrest of indigent transients continued to circumscribe their freedom. This underscores that for many Americans in the early nineteenth century, poverty was a "constraint . . . as effective as legal slavery."[84] The most effective means of combating these constraints, as this chapter has shown, was the designation of oneself as industrious, as a full participant in the labor force.

The stories presented here—from street-level arrests to incarceration in almshouses to imprisonment in jails to the resistance of vagrants through the legal system—should complicate how we understand the management and punishment of the nineteenth-century poor.[85] They demonstrate how the early republic state writ large conceived of its power over the poor, and the foregoing discussions illustrate the ways in which state apparatuses were used to control the labor and movement of the poor and transient. Furthermore, a look inside of small city and county penal facilities like the Arch Street Jail and consideration of their purposes, management, and inmates, demonstrates that the history of carceral practice in the nineteenth century remains incomplete if we do not look at the administration of poor relief as part of the story. The overlap in the function of, and inmates held within, Arch Street Jail and the Philadelphia Almshouse in particular demonstrates substantial proximity of purpose in each facility.

6 / "It Was amongst the Vagrant Class... That Cholera Was Most Fatal": Mobility, Poverty, and Disease

John and Jane Welsh were arrested together as vagrants on 5 August 1832, in the midst of a bacterial and social maelstrom. Committed to the Arch Street Jail on "the fatal Sunday," as it was soon described, they became characters in "a tale of horror."[1] Newspapers were describing piles of bodies lining the streets, with gravediggers unable to keep up with the demand for their services. The infamous cholera epidemic of that year had reached the United States in early summer and had been raging in Philadelphia for nearly three weeks at the time of their arrest. A month earlier, New York City's Court of Sessions had released all misdemeanants who were incarcerated in the city's almshouse, but cities farther south had not yet reached the point of crisis to prompt them to do the same.[2] Hundreds in Philadelphia had succumbed to the disease by the time the epidemic waned in late August, but not before Jane Welsh died alone in prison, on the same day she had been committed. John Welsh, meanwhile, was sent to the hospital, possibly to meet the same fate.[3]

As indigent transients, John and Jane Welsh were members of a social group described as a "class of people who have no provision for cleanliness whatever—namely, 'vagrants,'" according to John Snow, the English physician often referred to as the "father of modern epidemiology." Snow made this claim in a discussion of the cholera epidemic of 1832, when he wrote that "vagrants are notorious for contracting fevers, and carrying them about from place to place," because "nothing assists the communication of disease more than the want of personal cleanliness."[4]

To Snow, vagrants were both the greatest victims and the greatest perpetrators in the spread of disease. Snow's knowledge and experience as a pioneer anesthetist and epidemiologist, who had developed the first theory to pinpoint an organic source to explain the contagious nature of cholera, were sought around the world, including in the United States, throughout the nineteenth century. In his treatise on the disease, *On the Mode and Communication of Cholera,* he asserted that vagrants were so susceptible to cholera because of the "crowded state" in which they were generally held in almshouses and prisons. Studying the communicability of the disease years later, Snow noted that, during the 1831–32 epidemic in England, cholera had made its first appearances in "the courts and alleys to which vagrants resort for a night's lodging."[5] By the time the epidemic had waned that year, Snow wrote, it had been "amongst the vagrant class ... that cholera was most fatal."[6]

Snow's statements were not merely hyperbolic descriptions of the havoc wreaked by disease among the poorest communities with the least sanitary conditions. Nor were they limited to England's experience of the epidemic. In the 1830s, germ theory was all but meaningless, contagion was far from understood, and an individual's health was viewed by the general public as a by-product of their social class and socioeconomic stability. Within this climate, vagrants had a complicated relationship with disease and health in general, the interrogation of which can provide valuable insight into the corporeality of poverty and mobility. Indigent transients comprised an especial public health concern, as a population suffering from exposure, hunger, and a profound lack of the most basic human necessities, as a direct result of not just their poverty but also their transience. In the nineteenth-century Atlantic world, they were also central to societal and medical understandings of the dissemination of disease and the relationship between poverty, criminality, and health in the period when epidemiologists began to make their most profound discoveries. Like the disease itself, ideas about cholera traveled from continental Europe, to England, and then to North America. On both sides of the Atlantic during and following the 1832 cholera epidemic, researchers, physicians, writers, and the general public covered reams of paper and spent hours debating the origin, movement, and devastation of cholera. This process resulted in increased governmental regulation of health, enhanced urban planning and efforts at community sanitation that continue into the twenty-first century. Explanations for the epidemic's targeting of specific demographics—vagrants, the poor, nonwhites, recent immigrants—revealed competing modes of scientific

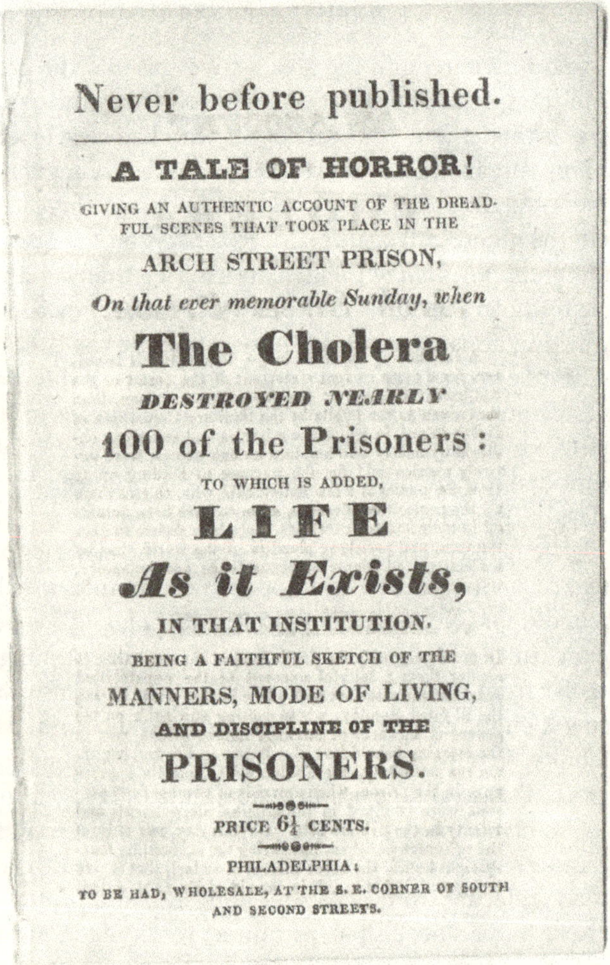

> Never before published.
>
> ## A TALE OF HORROR!
>
> GIVING AN AUTHENTIC ACCOUNT OF THE DREADFUL SCENES THAT TOOK PLACE IN THE
>
> ### ARCH STREET PRISON,
>
> *On that ever memorable Sunday, when*
>
> # The Cholera
>
> *DESTROYED NEARLY*
>
> ### 100 of the Prisoners:
>
> TO WHICH IS ADDED,
>
> # LIFE
> # *As it Exists,*
>
> IN THAT INSTITUTION.
>
> BEING A FAITHFUL SKETCH OF THE
>
> ### MANNERS, MODE OF LIVING,
>
> AND DISCIPLINE OF THE
>
> ## PRISONERS.
>
> PRICE 6¼ CENTS.
>
> PHILADELPHIA:
> TO BE HAD, WHOLESALE, AT THE S. E. CORNER OF SOUTH AND SECOND STREETS.

FIGURE 6.1. Tale of Horror! Giving an Authentic Account of the Dreadful Scenes that took place in the Arch Street Prison, a sensational pamphlet printed in Philadelphia in 1832, not long after the city had begun to recover from the epidemic, documenting the events at Arch Street Jail. The distinctive experience of Arch Street during the epidemic—and the vagrants within it—was central to the way nineteenth-century Philadelphians narrated and remembered the epidemic. The authors detailed the conditions of the prison and the experiences of its inmates. It offered laments for lives lost, praises for heroic physicians, and recommendations for prison management. (The Library Company of Philadelphia)

and moralistic thinking that narrate the changing social climate of the nineteenth century.[7]

Scholars such as Charles Rosenberg have documented the attention paid by contemporaries to the trajectory of nineteenth-century cholera epidemics across Europe to England and onward to North America.[8] With the knowledge of the spread of the disease came understandings of contagion, of course, but also identification and prevention techniques that affirmed preexisting perceptions of connections between morality, class, and physical well-being.[9] This chapter explores those connections throughout the Mid-Atlantic, charting the ways in which, as Snow discussed, vagrants were pinpointed as carriers of disease, and particularly associated with the spread of cholera, as evidence of a shared transatlantic culture surrounding indigent transiency. The continuity of definition and response contributes to the potent colonial and cultural legacy of British influence on American vagrancy law, poor relief, and epidemiology.

This chapter begins by examining indigent transients' medical case files, almshouse records, and newspaper coverage in order to investigate the corporeal experiences they faced while homeless, mobile, confined in almshouses, and incarcerated in prisons. It also utilizes the records of prisons and almshouses where vagrants were incarcerated during the 1832 cholera epidemic and reports generated by inspectors and other officials during this period to argue that the punishment and incarceration of vagrants was illustrative of the pathologization of poverty at work in early nineteenth-century social management.[10] With high recurrence of epidemics of cholera and other similarly viewed diseases in later decades, social and cultural understandings of disease transmission became less tenable, just as scientific explanations began to gain more ground. At the center of this discussion lies the Arch Street Jail, Philadelphia's carceral facility for vagrants, and the site of the highest mortality during the 1832 epidemic.

Corporeality of Indigent Transiency

John Snow's explanations of vagrants' living conditions contributing to their vulnerability to disease addressed only the tip of the iceberg. Daily and little-considered material struggles defined vagrants' lives, most of which were worsened by transiency. Among the most significant of these was the most basic: environmental exposure. Scholars have often had to rely on the crudest of data when considering the impact of environments on populations in the absence of firsthand accounts, especially when studying the lowest classes.[11] Accurate statistics that reveal how many suffered or died from exposure in this period are difficult to ascertain, especially because coroners investigating causes of death often attributed deaths resulting from environmental exposure to supernatural or inevitable causes, possibly in order to preserve their or their city's reputations.[12]

Hundreds of transients were admitted to almshouses and public hospitals in the United States each winter suffering from exposure throughout the first decades of the nineteenth century. Their names appear on admissions registers next to the notation of their "disease," often recorded as poor or destitute, signifying some pathologization of poverty.[13] Many, like the Delaware father and son wanderers Ebenezer Widdington and Ebenezer Widdington Jr., were admitted with "frozen" or "frosted" feet.[14] In some cases, such causes for admissions to the almshouse are broken down along the division between residents and nonresidents. Race and ethnicity, in turn, while still noted in the record, faded next to the category of residence that had a more tangible impact on their admission and treatment. The black and white itinerant poor experienced a shared "vulnerability" to exposure and "disease . . . as a consequence of spotty nutrition, exposure, and the vagaries of itinerant living."[15]

In the New Castle County, Delaware, almshouse from the 1820s to the 1840s, the distinction is clear: residents were most frequently admitted for illness, destitution, pregnancy, and injury. Nonresidents, meanwhile, were more likely to be admitted with the description of "indigent travelers," many of them with frostbite. Nonresidents tended to spend less time in the almshouse, whether voluntarily or through coercion or death.[16] One of these nonresidents, Harmon Lively, was admitted on 5 February 1826, described as "African," aged twenty-nine, with "frozen feet," and died two days later. James Fitzgerald and James Criser were admitted together in December 1835, both with "frosted feet"; Fitzgerald died after eleven days in the almshouse.[17] Similar policies of designating residents and nonresidents in almshouse records were followed throughout the Mid-Atlantic.[18]

Some examination records reveal glimpses of the material wealth of the indigent transients who were admitted to or incarcerated in antebellum almshouses. One woman, a presumed former slave listed as "Virgin Mary, black," possessed at her death one coat and one single shoe stocking. A man named John Williams, who died shortly after arriving at the almshouse, owned little more: one pair of shoes, a vest, two handkerchiefs, a coat, and a hat—which were noted as "all very much worn and ragged."[19] The illicitly mobile in the early nineteenth century traveled on foot year-round, leading many to almshouse hospitals for treatment of frostbitten extremities. One group, reportedly wandering through the Codorus Hills in Pennsylvania, was described by the *York Gazette* as a dangerous "corps of vagrants ... said to consist of four or five persons, one or two of whom are coloured people," who despite their supposed threat of "depradation [*sic*]," were apparently destitute, "badly clothed ... scarcely covered with any thing but nakedness."[20]

Incarceration of the poor often, of necessity, involved the provision of health care. Some records note this occasionally reluctant offering. In the prison records for a man named James Coarsey, it is clear that the Philadelphia watchmen who committed him viewed him with contempt. Born in New York, by age fifty-six he was hunched over from years of labor as a shoemaker and, more recently, from a winter spent sleeping out of doors, exposed to the elements.[21] On 24 January 1823, he was arrested on the oaths of two men for being not only an "idle, disorderly vagrant" but "an old convict having no home or visible means to make an honest living." He was sentenced to the vagrant's usual month's incarceration but actually remained in the Arch Street Jail for several days after his time was up, "he having been sick," and was released on 28 February.[22] The medical care available in prison was limited, so the detainment of Coarsey beyond his original sentence because he was unwell may suggest an awareness that even less comfort or care would be available to Coarsey on the other side of the prison's walls.

Prison inspectors in Philadelphia reported that "many persons" in Coarsey's position, incarcerated and ill, "gain admission into the Alms House, soon after their discharge from the Arch Street Prison," in addition to those "sent directly from the Arch Street jail to the Alms House," who, jail officials claimed, numbered "perhaps not more than 20 in a year."[23] The inspectors were concerned that the conditions in the jail were actually degrading the health of the vagrants and untried prisoners incarcerated there, with the result of them being discharged in worse health than when they had been committed. This was not a condition unique to Arch Street, of course; city and county jails, by and large, were not healthful places, as a vagrant known as Homan discovered in 1824 in Kingston, New York. That year, Joseph Deyo, the city's jailer, wrote to the overseers of the poor of Shawanagunk, New York, the legal residence of one of the jail's inmates, to advise them that: "Homan the pauper from your town who is confined in jail here does not appear to be as well as he was." He had evidently "refused to eat anything," and Deyo "did not think" the treatment of a visiting physician had been effective. Deyo suggested that the overseers "send him to the asylum in New York" because, as he saw it, Homan "never will get better in this prison." But Homan was destitute, and "his clothes [were] all worn out." Deyo asked that the overseers assist him in his efforts to have Homan properly outfitted with more adequate clothing so that he could be transferred to a more appropriate facility. The prison, seen as an effective means of influencing the intellectual correction of the disorderly and criminal, was far from ideal for the care of the mentally and physically ill.[24]

The sick poor often received medical care in almshouse hospitals. A sample of case studies from the clinical ward of the Philadelphia Almshouse reveals that some of the most challenging physical experiences of indigent transients were often the result of basic efforts at survival. One single volume of case records, charting the medical histories of almshouse residents treated from 1824 to 1825, acts as a window into those episodes. The volume was compiled by the resident physician and attending student physicians, narrating the illnesses and treatments of thirty-three patients. Of those thirty-three, eleven patients—one-third of the cases—were admitted for environmental exposure, usually to cold. In many cases, it was a lack of shelter that led to their infirmity.[25]

One of the eleven patients treated for exposure, Patrick O'Flaherty, was born in Ireland around 1791 and migrated to North America in 1807. He landed in Quebec and settled briefly there, joining the British army sometime between 1807 and 1811, when he deserted service in favor of joining the army of the United States. He was discharged from American military service in 1814 at Sackets Harbor in New York. He traveled onward to Washington briefly, before settling in New York State for "about 8 or 9 years." He "left there in August" of 1822, and by 25 February 1823, he had been admitted as a nonresident pauper in the Philadelphia Almshouse. His legal settlement was somewhere in New York, but almshouse records do not indicate whether an order of removal was issued to return him there.[26] In any case, he left not long after but was back in Philadelphia and back in the almshouse, this time in the clinical ward, by the end of 1824. The physicians' notes describe him as "Aged 35 years—A Laborer." The previous month, he "took cold from night exposure" and "was treated . . . before entering this institution," but his condition did not improve. He "entered the House" on 13 December 1824 "with a cough, pain in breast, expectorations sparing & difficult & breathing extremely laborious." Within a week, he had begun to improve, and was continuously treated with mercurial cathartics and opium. O'Flaherty convalesced in the clinical ward of the almshouse hospital until 18 January 1825, when his case record closes with the physicians' remark "this patient is well."[27] O'Flaherty's case notes specify that it was exposure to the cold overnight—sleeping out of doors—that led to O'Flaherty's hospitalization. After receiving treatment and being released, he would likely have faced yet again the same conditions that had brought him there in the first place.

That same winter, Catharine Shearer fell victim to the elements. She was twenty-four years old when she was admitted as a nonresident to the clinical ward of the Philadelphia Almshouse on 10 November 1826. According to the physicians' notes, she was a "native of Pennsylvania" who was "brought up to housewifery and has generally enjoyed good health." At the end of October, however, "after exposure to wet and cold," she was "attacked with rigors, followed by pain in the head, back, and stomach, and a well defined paroxysm of fever." The fever and other symptoms continued for several weeks until she was admitted to the almshouse. Hugh Thompson, a forty-year-old shoemaker "was taken with fever from exposure to cold, accompanied by pain in breast and a cough."[28] Another shoemaker, twenty-five-year-old William Kane, "was for a considerable time exposed to the cold & damp weather" on an immigrant ship sailing to the United States.[29] Twenty-five-year-old laborer Robert Martin and forty-three-year-old John McGuire were both admitted experiencing "severe pain in different parts of [the] body" following excessive "exposure to cold." Catherine Riggins had "been sick upwards of 3 weeks," her "indisposition" attributed to "exposure to wet and cold" before she was taken with the same painful symptoms.[30]

The individuals whose treatment was recorded in these case histories were both resident and nonresident, persistent and transient; exposure was a danger faced not only by the mobile or unemployed but by the local and employed as well. In urban America in the early republic, poverty often translated into walking the city searching for day work, taking health-absorbing employment as a washerwoman despite the conditions, or following canal construction to bring in daily wages, and many experienced poor working conditions that endangered their health.[31] Free and poor African Americans were disproportionately affected by such maladies as a result of the subsistence activities, such as collecting bones and picking cloth, to which they were usually limited. Twenty-five-year-old black woman Susan French, for example, "had been collecting bones and rags in the street" when she became ill with the symptoms of extended environmental exposure.[32]

This single volume of case histories offers a glimpse of the challenges and consequences of transiency and poverty in the early American republic, with such a high proportion of the poor lacking the basic ability to ward off the cold. The current historiography of poverty and welfare does little to help us understand Patrick O'Flaherty's, or Catherine Shearer's, or Susan French's, stories, and less still that of a man identified by the arresting official only as "Wilcox," who was "found" by police in January 1837 "sleeping upon a snow bank." According to the watchman, Wilcox was "nearly frozen" when he was found. The event that followed is even less explicable: the watchman woke him up, arrested him as a vagrant, and escorted him to the prison, where he would serve a thirty-day sentence. The watchman possessed the right of discretion in committing Wilcox to the almshouse or the prison and elected punitive incarceration. Whether or not indoor imprisonment of either variety may have been somewhat welcome to Wilcox at that stage, with precedent to sentence the man to serve his commitment in the almshouse, his arrest suggests a punitive interpretation of Wilcox's poverty on the part of the watchmen, possibly as a result of an interpretation of Wilcox's morality or sobriety resulting from his circumstances.[33] These Philadelphia case histories highlight the deprivation that informed societal perceptions of the poor and demonstrate that, for those struggling to acquire the "means of subsistence," the effects of indigent transiency often manifested physically.

Vectors of Disease

Common wisdom in the nineteenth century held that the poor were "inherently dirty," a conception that, as Kathleen M. Brown has explained, "coalesced around reports following epidemics of high death rates and squalor in poor urban neighborhoods."[34] Vagrants were viewed as vectors of disease, as the vehicles that threatened to bring the filth of the slums to the thoroughfares.[35] In times of public health crisis, as Joanne Pope Melish notes in relation to a yellow fever epidemic in Providence, Rhode Island, "the 'laboring poor' themselves were considered a kind of secondary infection."[36] Attributions of the spread of cholera to poor migrants confirmed upper-class suspicions of the lower sorts that dominated social theory in the early republic.[37] Just as vagrancy laws and the impetus and methods for policing vagrants had been imported to

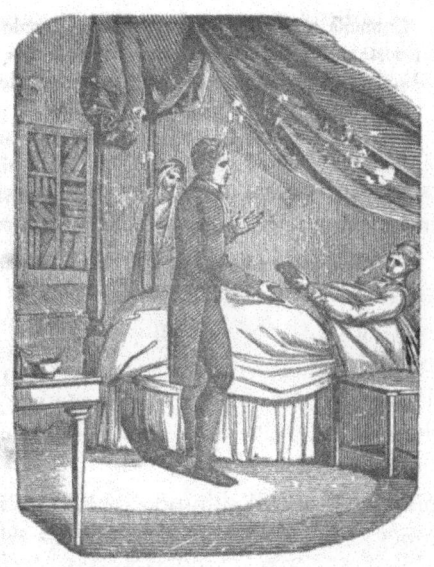

EPIDEMIC CHOLERA.

This frightful form of Cholera Morbus, which made its appearance on the Banks of the Ganges, in 1817, and successively through various countries and islands of the East, after having crossed to the Western shores of Europe, made its first appearance on our continent, on the Banks of the St. Lawrence, in 1832;— soon afterwards appearing at New York, and speedily extending its ravages to our City. About the middle of July, the vagrants and prisoners in the Arch Street prison (at that time,) located at the corner of Arch and Broad Streets, became suddenly affected with Spasmodic Cholera, and a large number died, within a few hours of the attack. The humanity of many of our citizens, was distinguisingly displayed on that occasion, and JOHN SWIFT, Esq. the late Mayor, deserves to be mentioned, for his courage and fortitude, at that time.

FIGURE 6.2. An entry for "Epidemic Cholera" in Daniel Bowen's illustrated History of Philadelphia (1839), published less than a decade after the 1832 epidemic. Bowen placed vagrants' experience with the epidemic at the center of his entry on the disease, emphasizing the significance of the crisis at Arch Street Jail in the city's memory.

the United States from Britain, so too had associations between poverty, filth, and disease. The consequence of this was a transatlantic trend of using "metaphors of disease and reproduction" to encourage the arrest of vagrants as "a form of crime prevention."[38]

Across the Atlantic world, vagrants were viewed as naturally likely to spread disease, especially cholera, and many early public health agencies established limitations on their movement in order to prevent the spread of disease.[39] The associations between poverty, dirt, and ill health were condensed in the image of the vagrant, and Britain set the precedent for associating vagrants with the dissemination of cholera.[40] This association was potent enough to comprise the subject matter of Romantic poet Samuel Coleridge's poem about the 1832 epidemic "Cholera cured before-hand," wherein Coleridge addresses cholera as the personification of an "offal-fed Vagrant."[41]

The deadly epidemic that killed hundreds of thousands by 1832 was believed to have begun in India the previous year and progressed to Europe through Russia and Poland.[42] When the disease appeared in Edinburgh, Scotland, the first official response by the city was to designate vagrants as enemies of health and order all magistrates to walk the length and breadth of the city in an effort to "arrest . . . all beggars and vagrants" in order to keep them, and the disease they were believed to carry, confined. The English public tracked the movements of vagrants, too, and newspapers carried reports like the following from the Manchester *Guardian*, which claimed that it was "by means of Irish vagrants from Sunderland" that "the cholera has been twice brought amongst us." According to this paper, the fault lay with an "Irish vagrant" who apparently had gone "to Sunderland to collect rags and beg."[43] It was with the start of the 1832 epidemic in Great Britain that public health administrators and—down the line, law enforcement and the general public—began to claim and act upon the idea that vagrants were responsible for cholera's movement across Britain and eventually, across the United States.[44]

The news of the spread of disease in Europe, and through maritime networks, on to the British colonies of Lower and Upper Canada, was followed closely with almost daily reports printed in American newspapers.[45] Presses printed editorials bemoaning the lack of preparedness for curtailing the movements of "persons, who are supposed to contribute greatly to the spread of the disease, beggars and vagrants," recommending that cities take pains to manage the threat posed by "hosts of beggars and vagrants."[46] When cholera finally did reach the United States after months of predictions and fear, American officials reacted similarly to those in the Canadian Provinces and Great Britain. After a single case of cholera on Lake Erie, the first course of action taken by the city officials was to increase the number of members of the "police committee," who were immediately engaged in "ferreting out every thing in the shape of nuisance, or anything calculated to increase the danger of the borough, especially vagrant and intemperate persons." Five vagrants were arrested on the first day, a product of this "vigilance and liberality" and "general purification."[47]

One observer in Montreal summarized the prevailing view, describing "the wandering companies of needy vagrants whose very garments looked as though they might carry infection and death about with them."[48] In Quebec City, it was anticipated that the presence of "wandering companies of . . . vagrants" and "scores of half clad and worse fed families" might "originate" cholera in the city, or at least "operate as quick conductors of it."[49] Many ports and river towns enacted quarantines for incoming goods and ships in the lead-up to the disease's arrival.[50] But the primary concern during the 1832 and 1849 epidemics, as William Baly later argued, was that the early nineteenth century's growing international commerce made standard quarantine procedures ineffective against the spread of disease, due to the extent of interchange at all levels, from humans to goods. "The march of the epidemic is dependent mainly on human intercourse," he argued, and cholera was likely to be spread via the "bodies of troops, dirty vagrants, and foul clothes."[51] Information received about the direction in which the disease was moving mingled with perception and fears of outsiders: in Baltimore, it was generally perceived that disease would arrive from "the Washington and Philadelphia roads."[52]

The poorest—whether "wandering companies of needy vagrants," "half clad . . . families," or "dirty vagrants"—wherever cholera appeared, suffered the greatest losses and highest mortality. Cramped conditions, poor sanitation, and poor nutrition were all accurate explanations for the disproportionate impact of the epidemic on this class. But cramped quarters could only explain so much: communicability of the disease relied upon movement, and few groups were more mobile than vagrants. These conditions are especially important in considering how the susceptibility of vagrants to cholera shaped contemporary views of the vagrants' prison in Philadelphia, the Arch Street Jail, where the 1832 cholera epidemic was the defining event in that institution's history.

Perpetrators and Victims

By late spring of 1832, American presses had been printing news of the spread of the disease for months, and fears were abundant. Montreal and New York City had some of the highest mortality rates in North America. Montreal lost around four thousand residents, while New York City lost 2,782. Baltimore was reported to have lost 853, many of whom were residing in the city's almshouse, where the mortality rate was disproportionately high. Philadelphia had one of the lowest mortality rates of the stricken cities that year—only one in 173 persons—but the mortality at one particular location, the vagrant prison at Arch Street, raises many questions.[53] At Arch Street, the prison where Jane Welsh died in August 1832, it is estimated that as many as one in three persons died of cholera in the few short weeks it took up residence there.[54] The narrative constructed around poverty and the cholera epidemic of 1832 has been discussed by historians and scholars of epidemiology in detail, and much of this analysis can be extended to carceral institutions.[55] Compared to the almost completely spared Walnut Street Jail and Eastern State Penitentiary, the significantly higher mortality rates at the Arch Street Jail served as confirmation of contemporary views about the epidemiological ramifications of destitution.[56]

Incarcerated vagrants were viewed as sources of disease, distinct from other prisoners sharing crowded and unsanitary conditions. During a 1798 epidemic of yellow fever, the Philadelphia Prisons Board of Inspectors feared that vagrants incarcerated in the Walnut Street Jail would "endanger the health of the Prisoners," and vagrants were isolated to prevent the spread of disease.[57] In 1823, a cholera epidemic brought an excessive death toll to Philadelphia, with 265 lives lost, many of them at Arch Street.[58] An 1824 report by the Inspectors of the Prison of the City and County of Philadelphia foreshadowed the disaster that repeated itself with intensity less than a decade later. According to the inspectors of the prisoners at Arch Street, "two thirds... were vagrants, disorderly persons, and disturbers of the peace." It was "to this cause"—the presence of so many vagrants in one institution, as opposed to other varieties of criminals, they argued—that the high "quantum of disease" in that institution was to be attributed.[59] This assessment seems to have been delivered as a foregone conclusion without remedy. The fact that similar evaluations were made after the 1832 epidemic suggests a deeply rooted association between the bodies of vagrants and disease. Interrogating these associations further suggests that assumptions about vagrants and other petty criminals played an integral role in how contemporaries constructed their own narratives about cholera, as well as the ways in which vagrants and other indigent transients experienced the physical toll of their poverty and mobility.[60]

According to physicians' and prison inspectors' reports, cholera reached Philadelphia in 1832 in the body of a female vagrant. She, who remains unnamed, had "only been a day or two in the house" when she fell ill on 13 July. She was believed to have been among the group "who had recently entered the jail" and were the ones who apparently "suffered the most." They were "principally old vagrants, who were constantly in and out of the jail."[61] As of a mid-July report, as many as 298 people were incarcerated in the prison at the time, 127 of them women.[62] The prison's vagrancy docket lists seven women committed for vagrancy between 10 July and 12 July who may have been the woman in question. Of these seven women, only one of them was listed as a fatality: Eliza Gray was arrested on 12 July, and by 4 August, at the height of the disease's presence at Arch Street, she had died. But epidemic cholera was known for its unexpected and incredibly swift progression. Death often occurred within hours of a victim showing symptoms, so it may be unlikely that the report pinpointing a female vagrant who had only been in jail a day or two is correct, unless of course she was treated and recovered.[63]

Within two weeks of the first case, it was reported that "the epidemic cholera broke out decidedly in the Arch street jail." Around that point, on 30 July, the inspectors recommended "that one or more resident physicians be appointed for Arch Street Prison during the existence of the cholera," to provide care for victims in the prison. They also aimed to decrease physical contact between prisoners by making "such alterations in the workshops of the Arch Street Prison, or other rooms as may be necessary" to ensure that "as few prisoners as possible may sleep together during the ... prevailing sickness in Philad."[64] As the death toll rose, the inspectors aimed to prevent more prisoners from entering Arch Street in the first place, requesting "police officers" to "use the necessary means to keep the prisoners in confinement in the City Watch house until further orders" were issued by Arch Street officials. They were concerned with finding "a suitable place for the reception of vagrants committed by the legal authorities," in the present state of affairs.[65]

On 5 August, the grisly situation in the prison led to the authorization of the warden to release the nonviolent prisoners, as had been done in New York City. The prison inspectors were called in and determined that "the urgency of the case" warranted this action. Some vagrants and other petty criminals were released upon their word, while the city's recorder of deeds and an attorney for the Court of Quarter Sessions, Joel Barlow Sutherland, "released as many from the criminal side, as their powers would admit of."[66] Formal processes were also followed for the release of the debtors who were held in the prison, for whom "some medical gentlemen and others, private citizens, as well as the county commissioners, advanced sums of money to release the debtors."[67] As a result, it was understood that no deaths occurred "in the debtor's appartment [sic], owing to the humane conduct of several individuals, who by discharging, or becoming responsible for the debts, released the greater part of the inmates on that side of the prison."[68]

One Philadelphia physician, Dr. Richard Harlan, described what it was like to work with the sick in the Arch Street Jail on one of the highest death-toll days, writing that at least "60 were sick at one time, the suffering and agony of the dying wretches was an awful sight." According to his count, "26 died there that day," 6 August, and so far, on the day he was writing, another twenty-six had succumbed, but he knew there would "probably be more tomorrow." His time, he lamented, was "usefully, at least, if not profitably employed, night and day," because of "cholera, cholera, cholera!!!!"[69] At this time, the almshouse increased its humanitarian efforts, offering admission regardless of residence in acknowledgment of the damage caused by the epidemic. Following its abatement, one representative from the Philadelphia Almshouse began to work through the backlog of correspondence that had accrued during the crisis, writing that one letter "would have been given immediate attention were it not for the great press of business at that particular period of time, attributable in a great measure to the prevalence of the epidemic which mired itself over our city."[70]

At the time the first female vagrant in Arch Street became a cholera victim in mid-July, there were 310 prisoners incarcerated at Arch Street. The inmates were divided by sex, with 110 women in the female apartment and 170 men in the male apartment. Since the Arch Street Jail still served as the facility for the incarceration of debtors, an additional 30 prisoners were held in the designated debtors' apartment.[71] Among those imprisoned at Arch Street during the epidemic, the names of some of the most frequent recidivist vagrants appear on the docket. As has been demonstrated, the line between poverty and vagrancy in this period was especially thin, and many of these individuals left a paper trail not just in prison records but also in almshouse and settlement examinations, making it possible to reconstruct brief biographies for several persons among Arch Street's cholera victims.

Patrick Cane was an Irish immigrant who arrived in New York in 1817. He stayed there for about two months, but finding insufficient prospects for work, left there, spending two months in Trenton, New Jersey, before continuing on to Philadelphia. There he remained, working "for different persons for a few months" at a time. Cane spent some time in the Philadelphia Almshouse in the winter of 1823.[72] He continued this lifestyle over the next several years until, on 10 July 1832, Cane was arrested for "being [an] idle vagrant." He was sentenced to one month's imprisonment, but cholera intervened, and Cane became one of the Arch Street Jail's numerous fatalities that summer.[73]

Another one of these victims, a woman named Susan Hunter, had served prison time for vagrancy convictions repeatedly. In 1830, she spent the month of February timing out her sentence as an "idle vagrant," and she later spent the month of March 1832 also jailed for vagrancy.[74] Her last conviction amounted to a death sentence: when she was arrested on 3 August, prisoners at Arch Street had been dying of cholera for three weeks. Two days after her conviction, Hunter became one of the many victims of what was apparently referred to in the prison as "that ever memorable Sunday" mere hours before prison inspectors began to release some prisoners in an attempt to spare their lives.[75]

Some fears of transients as vectors of disease were well-founded: when prisoners were discharged from Arch Street Jail during the epidemic, many "went into the neighborhood of the city, fell sick, and died... on the road," some "on the Lancaster turnpike not far from the town," others in abandoned lots in the city and "on the commons."[76] An editorial printed in the midst of the crisis decried any efforts to relocate sick transients to the almshouse or elsewhere in order to receive care for fear of "spreading the contagion." To the authors, it was clear that the disease would have ripped through the almshouse if cholera-infected patients were brought there. But concern lay also outside of the buildings: there was fear that the residents might return to the vagrant lifestyle that had led them there in the first place and that they may "burst away, and spread around the country, going into the farm houses."[77] This concern was real: one man who had come in contact with cholera patients while in the Arch Street Jail, and was released by the inspectors as part of their humanitarian efforts, did just that. He apparently began walking in search of work immediately, following the Schuylkill River into Montgomery County, where he joined a crew at the Plymouth Locks. He became ill shortly after his arrival and was dead by nightfall. In the process, fifteen other people became sick, nine of whom died.[78]

The canals were an especially dangerous place to be laboring, as poor hygiene in close working quarters sickened many. Residents of New Jersey blamed canal workers in particular for spreading cholera after the epidemic reached the state via the Delaware and Raritan Canal near New Brunswick. "Irish laborers" and the "shantees" in which they lived in close quarters, with "their filthy habits and great numbers," were also held to blame in Somerset County and Trenton.[79] The Irish were consistently associated with dirt, disease, disorder, and transience throughout the nineteenth and into the twentieth century in the United States.[80] *Niles' Weekly Register* of Baltimore reported with interest in the epidemic's impact at Arch Street, but with little attention to the class or criminal status of those incarcerated there. Instead, writers from Baltimore focused their narratives of the spread and decimation by the disease on racial distinctions: "In all places where persons of color abound, the disease has affected them most severely," the *Register* reported, "because of their own imprudence, as the want of attention and necessaries when sick." In general, nonwhite and non-native-born Americans were viewed as more likely to succumb to diseases like cholera and were thus feared as infectious.[81]

Panic about the spread of cholera was underscored by knowledge of stories like the above and that the lower, mobile classes were simultaneously the most vulnerable and the most likely to spread the disease. One single disease carrier in the vicinity was enough to stoke the fires of fear up and down the East Coast. One could infect hundreds. Regional newspapers pinpointed individuals as well as groups, citing migrants and "sick transient persons" as the most likely culprits.[82] Recent immigrants and other noncitizens were viewed as especially threatening, in part due to their unknown origins and in part due to the fact that cholera indeed had been spread by human movement. With strangers and noncitizens being categorized as impure, citizenship came to signify purification.[83]

There were figurative and literal implementations of this purification process. One observer argued, in the years following the epidemic, that if arrangements had been made for each vagrant entering Arch Street to "take a bath" as was "the first act imposed upon a convict as obligatory" at Eastern State, the extent of disease and death at the prison might have been prevented. The dangers of uncleanliness were within and without: the author declared that many vagrants were "sometimes ejected from the prison in a state of more abject filth and destitution" after serving their sentence than they had been upon commitment.[84] If this was the case, it was likely the result of a failure on the part of the prisoners' custodians, who under a 1790 law were required to ensure that "every person who shall be ordered to hard labor shall be separately lodged, washed and cleansed . . . if such person be a convict, the clothes in which he or she shall then be clothed, shall either be burnt, or at the discretion of two of the inspectors be baked, fumigated, and carefully laid by, until the expiration of the term for which such offender shall be sentenced to hard labor, to be then returned to him or her."[85] These prisoners, among the rapidly growing "population of the city and its suburbs" being confined "as vagrant and untried prisoners, at the Bridewell," experienced distinct suffering, according to the Philadelphia Society for Alleviating the Miseries of Public Prisons, from those held in the penitentiary.[86] Part of the reason for their miseries was the lack of space and proper facilities "where the vagrants might be suitably classed" before being "compelled to hard labor."[87]

The attentiveness devoted to each prisoner under the separate system, in addition to the actual physical separation in confinement, gave some the impression that the convicts held at the Eastern State Penitentiary were "of a different class."[88] Some outsiders viewed these inmates, with their supposed "higher intelligence," better social habits, and better hygiene, with more respect than the average "miserable vagrant" confined in the Arch Street Jail. One editorial, printed in the *Philadelphia Inquirer* months after the cholera epidemic had ended in the region, argued that some deaths may have been prevented if some of the practices followed at Eastern State had been implemented at Arch Street. But the visiting inspector of Arch Street Jail, Dr. J. R. Burden, claimed that leading up to the epidemic, "the whole building was in fine order, few private dwellings equalled, none exceeded it in cleanliness." Rather, the events that proceeded were the result of the physical status of the inmates themselves, according to Burden: "The character of the inmates, most of whom are vagrants of dissolute habits and of broken down constitutions, victims of unwholesome and scanty diet, and destitute of proper clothing."[89]

Following the epidemic, the state legislature formed a special committee to "investigate the local causes of cholera in the Arch Street Prison." During their investigation, "none of the committee, or . . . other members of the legislature who accompanied them to the Arch Street Jail, entered the apartment in which the untried prisoners and vagrants were confined during the day, without the most marked disgust at the filth, destitution, and personal misery in which the majority of the prisoners were found." They smoked cigars to disguise the smell of the poor, unwashed prisoners held within.[90] Shortly thereafter, the committee issued a report that was read before the Pennsylvania House of Representatives on 21 February 1833. The legislature was concerned primarily with the excessive mortality rates at the Arch Street Jail and how these losses may have been linked to the "sufficiency of the legal provisions for the maintenance of untried prisoners and debtors." The committee, chaired by a physician and legislator named Dr. J. H. Gibbon, recommended significant changes in the state's treatment of the vagrants, petty criminals, and sundry untried prisoners who found themselves in Arch Street and other penal facilities in the state. So long as providing greater "provisions and comforts" would not encourage "idleness and profligacy," and provided ample employment on the inside, such individuals were to be placed "as least upon an equal position with the convicts," specifically those held at the Eastern State Penitentiary, who seemed to experience less physical hardship in the course of their incarceration than did the petty criminals and untried prisoners housed at Arch Street. Of course, poverty could not be eradicated by a single act of legislation, the committee recognized. But it was also noted that "the character of some of our laws, as well as in their mode of administration" affected "disadvantageously, the poorer portions of the community," which was within their power to change.[91]

The committee's acknowledgment was tied directly to both the high concentration of contagious disease within the population of vagrants and untried prisoners, as well as the dissemination of disease by them. The committee implied that lawmakers were partially responsible, as regulations and administration "peculiarly expose[d] them at all times to the influences of epidemic disease, and unduly increase the number who tenant the jails." The state recognized its at least partial role in creating the population of the incarcerated destitute and debtors. But rather than adjusting vagrancy laws or placing tight restrictions on debt imprisonment (as most other nearby states had done by 1833), the recommendation offered by the committee was not to decriminalize poverty but rather to provision the poor, when in state custody, as sufficiently as the criminal.[92]

The legislature's report summarized many of the interpretations about vagrants' lives, status, and health that comprised contemporaries' received wisdom on the subjects. Many of their assessments were echoed by the visiting inspectors of the Philadelphia County prisons, both following the 1832 epidemic as well as the next time cholera struck the city in 1849. Then, the inspectors wrote that "the experience gained in 1832 was of some avail."[93] The primary recommendation to the legislature to improve responses in future epidemics was to suggest a more attentive means of managing the vagrant population. "The want of a house of industry," instead of only an almshouse and jail, "was very apparent during the prevalence of the epidemic," they wrote, and could have prevented the disease from spreading within the population most likely to succumb to it. An institution "where the houseless vagrant might be fed, clothed, worked, and kept the proper length of time" would have, according to the inspectors, been tremendously beneficial to those providing treatment and indeed, to the population of "victims of unwholesome diet, and destitute of proper clothing."[94]

The inspectors echoed early republic reformers who believed in the benefits of hard labor and penitence for the criminally inclined. While vagrants were not generally considered part of the convict population, they argued that length of sentences ought to be one area where they could be treated on par, in order to enable vagrants to more fully imbibe the ameliorative qualities that incarceration had to offer. "The vagrant is not imprisoned long enough to make that change in his physical constitution by diet, comfort, and work, as will enable him to resist disease," they wrote.[95] For the inspectors, longer sentences in a purpose-built institution might remedy that. They described vagrants as significantly more likely than convicts to become victims of cholera, writing that it would be "fair to presume that" even the few convicted criminals at Arch Street who did contract the disease could have been spared if they had "been beyond the atmosphere of a vagrant prison."[96] This sort of institution, according to the inspectors, was unique because the bodies of vagrants were unique: "At the approach of an epidemic," they wrote, "the vagrant prison is always the cause of deep anxiety; it is the nucleus of diseases. In the time of the cholera in 1832, the mortality was dreadful; whilst at the convict prison, situated at a distance, there was but a solitary case."[97]

Conclusion

The identities of convicts and vagrants were so distinctive for the Board of Inspectors as to warrant incarceration in separate institutions from each other, because of the different ways in which they experienced disease. Their poverty and criminality, then, were defined, on both sides of the Atlantic, as extensions of their bodily dispositions. On this basis, criminals were understood to have greater agency over their actions— illegal or not—and, seemingly, over their susceptibility to disease. Vagrants, meanwhile, were clearly the victims of the side effects of poverty and class and, as a result, lacked the agency to resist contamination.

The consequences of the physical conditions of vagrancy and incarceration were starkly visible in the Arch Street Jail in 1832. Commentators placed the onus for the high death toll at Arch Street on those in charge of treatment in the latter institution, who afforded their charges fewer physical comforts, but also on the social class of the inmates themselves. This disparity could also be seen as a marked distinction between the old and new systems of punishment that emerged in the early American republic. The moniker of the early nineteenth-century penal revolution appears markedly incomplete when considering vagrancy, not only in policing but in incarceration as well.[98]

The legislative committee that inspected the Arch Street Jail following the cholera epidemic mused in their report to the state that the need to punish vagrancy might perhaps be prevented if the poor received more assistance. They argued that "certain physical comforts are essential to morality" and that contrary to popular opinion, "crimes *do* originate from the misery, the distresses . . . of the poor." Thus, "to be prevented there must be an improvement in their condition and information," they asserted: "The very sight of the prisoners in the Arch Street Jail, gives an opinion of the operation of such causes. We fear that too frequently the combined influences of ignorance and of want have more effect in causing their offences, than the voluntary desire to outrage the regulations of society."[99] After seeing the devastation wrought by the 1832 epidemic, the inspectors asserted that "there can now be no doubt" that "the physical condition affects the moral character . . . as well as of the reverse reaction."[100]

The discussion surrounding—and punishment of—vagrancy provides a clear illustration of how early Americans were developing their understanding of what policing could and should, and could not and should not, do. Much of this played out in the debate over imprisonment for debt. In Philadelphia, the presence of debtors in Arch Street during the epidemic heightened concerns over the dangers—as well as futility—of incarcerating debtors.[101] Even in a city known worldwide for its scientific reputation and its inventive methods of penal incarceration, Arch Street stood apart, seemingly untouched by the movement toward separation and reform as the methods and goals of imprisonment that was the order of the day. It continues to provide a valuable lens through which to look at the role of vagrancy and, more broadly, class in the narratives constructed about the 1832 epidemic, as well as the ways in which vagrants and other indigent transients experienced the physical toll of their poverty and mobility.

Conclusion

In 1851, the Board of Inspectors of the Philadelphia County Prison, in their annual report to the Pennsylvania legislature, posed a question central to the policing of vagrancy: "Why put a man in a cell because he has no home?" The inspectors made a case for policy change, arguing that the current laws governing vagrancy neither deterred crime nor aided the indigent transients incarcerated for vagrancy, who, they asserted, "deserve the designation of unfortunate rather than of criminal."[1] In the Mid-Atlantic during the early republic, the answer to this question had been that punitive incarceration for vagrancy should act as a deterrent to others among the poor, idle, and criminal classes. Punishing vagrants was meant to deter the poor from excessive mobility and idleness, for these practices challenged authorities' perceptions of how the poor should behave, as well as how sources of labor should be allocated, and common economic resources managed.[2]

Mobility was crucial in the lives of the poor because it opened up employment opportunities and allowed them to establish their own social and economic networks. But it was also central to the laws that governed the relief available to them, and their vulnerability to criminal punishment, as has been documented here.[3] For transients, incarceration held an additional layer of punishment aside from being jailed, as a very literal means by which their movement was inhibited. This, in turn, reinforced the ideas put forward in settlement laws, state constitutions, and welfare policies that excessive mobility was an illicit activity.

Incarceration, even when as short-lived as the sentences resulting from most vagrancy convictions, functioned as an impediment to geographical movement that sent the message that the homeless, transient, and unstable had violated the social contract.

By exploring the relationship between welfare, mobility, crime, and punishment in the Mid-Atlantic during the early nineteenth century, this book has argued that the concept of indigent transiency played a dominant role in shaping poor relief laws and practices, the evolution of policing, and penal policies in the early American republic. Vagrants and pauper migrants engaged in geographical movements that violated the intentions for interstate ingress and regress first laid out in the Articles of Confederation. Fugitive slaves and runaway servants used their bodies to participate in illicit forms of mobility that often involved a transition from the oppression of an unfree labor status to the oppression of poverty. Many of these individuals were subject to forced movement sanctioned by the state that superseded the choices they had made about their own movement and stasis.

Indigent transiency was linked, in the first decades of the nineteenth century, with definitions of citizenship, social epidemiology, and the provision of relief to the needy. This study has attempted to represent transients' stories, acknowledging that many of these stories were originally recorded by authority figures and mediated through several layers of power dynamics. Many of the questions addressed here have great potential to be explored on a much larger scale. For example, how does the United States' management of indigent transiency compare with other nations that lack strong roots in British jurisprudence? What is the extent to which regional differences between North and South, and the eastern and western territories, might point to uniquely American interpretations of vagrancy?

By recognizing the critical role of mobility in the experience and regulation of the poor, this study has begun to place vagrants and other indigent transients at the center of inquiries about the provision of welfare, the emancipation of slaves, and the evolution of policing in the nineteenth century. Citizenship, in this period, was construed as a function of residency, leading to the exclusion of transients and other nonresidents from community and civic life, and, in turn, from welfare provisions integral to their livelihood. Indigent transients, through pauper removal and forced transportation, were simultaneously punished for their geographical mobility and forced to participate in a state-sanctioned form of mobility. Because of this construction of community, transients—with

CONCLUSION / 159

their movement and instability—as well as others who occupied the interstices of early nineteenth-century society posed a serious challenge to the state. This transiency was guarded against in myriad ways, from requiring the ejection of nonresident paupers from towns where they might deplete poor relief funds in New York, New Jersey, and Pennsylvania, to the inclusion of disclaimers against vagrancy in the certificates of manumission of slaves in New York and New Jersey. This simultaneous construction of criminality and strangerhood for indigent transients was particularly profound in the context of the spread of cholera, a significant fear in the nineteenth century, as many in the Atlantic world linked the mobility of disease with the mobility of the lower classes.

In these ways, state and local legal systems policed the lives of the poor by limiting the movement of their bodies, especially for African Americans. This reflected the logic of the marketplace, voiced as concerns about vagrancy, dependency, and labor. Under this framework, abstention from labor, either voluntarily or involuntarily, translated into the definition of one's actual freedom by the metric of one's labor status.[4] Poverty was linked with vagrancy, race was linked with poverty, and vagrancy was linked with criminality. Through these connections, the state determined how, for whom, for how long, and for how much pay individuals labored, and punished those who did not labor. In the early American republic, personal industry, achieved through an acceptable form of labor or employment, was one of the few characteristics that could protect an individual from a vagrancy conviction.

The findings laid out here uphold one central claim: that indigent transiency, in its many forms and through the varied forms of its management, contributed significantly to understandings of citizenship, labor status, freedom of movement, the spread of disease, and the transformation of punishment in the early American republic. These conclusions suggest that historians could do more to find the antebellum precedents of the late nineteenth-century phenomena of the "tramp" and the criminalization of poverty and blackness. The historiography on these subjects should reach back further chronologically, with deeper analytical intentions, than it has previously done. This makes it possible for historians to chart a course from Elizabethan poor laws to American colonial settlement policies and early national vagrancy laws, the postbellum black codes, the "tramp scare" of the 1890s, hobohemia of the 1930s, loitering statutes, and late twentieth-century urban stop-and-frisk policies.[5]

Indigent transiency is an important concept for American historians because investigating it reveals how the choices and movements of the poor shaped laws and the responses of authorities, driving welfare reform and influencing carceral practice. Looking at indigent transients as a group allows us to see legal and lived connections between poor white people, free people of color, slaves, and servants that offer unique revelations about the early American republic. Namely, it becomes clear that mobility and, conversely, the privileges gained by stasis, mattered—significantly—to nineteenth-century Americans. This knowledge should influence how we read laws governing the poor, consider the black codes, and think about the penitentiary revolution. And it should remind us of the importance of local government officials in this period, who played a very large role in shaping how towns and counties functioned, and how people within their borders lived.

Twenty-first-century debates over migration contain many of the same features as those from the nineteenth century, harnessing fears of indigent transients and targeting international immigrants. In early 2017, a federal proposal to deport any recent migrants who received a certain amount of public aid was announced. The proposal assesses these individuals in the language of the discretionary laws employed in the eighteenth and nineteenth centuries that aimed to remove previous migrants and prevent migration by individuals deemed "likely to become a public charge." Such considerations emphasize the ongoing relevance of the legal and historical origins of welfare laws as well as those governing migration.[6] The historical roots that prompted indigent transiency and the ways in which it has been treated under the law remain profoundly relevant in the twenty-first century. As Americans continue a national conversation about the policing of behaviors and of individuals, there is little doubt that it will continue to remain so.

Acknowledgments

My sincere thanks go to the scholars who guided this project in its earliest stages, James Campbell and Elizabeth Clapp, who offered astute observations, editing suggestions, and all-around good cheer. The project was continuously improved by their feedback, as well as that of Clare Anderson and George Lewis. I'm grateful to Clara Platter and Amy Klopfenstein at New York University Press for their editorial and practical prowess, and to the anonymous readers whose suggestions improved the final product immeasurably. While completing the research and writing for this project, I was fortunate enough to receive essential financial support from the following organizations and institutions, through grants, fellowships, and employment: the Library Company of Philadelphia and Historical Society of Pennsylvania, the Prindle Institute for Ethics at DePauw University, the Peter Parish Memorial Fund awarded by the Association of British American Nineteenth Century Historians, the College of Arts, Humanities, and Law at the University of Leicester, the Society of Historians of the Early American Republic, the Maryland Historical Society, Drexel University, and the Archives of the Pennsylvania House of Representatives. Thanks also to Pennsylvania State University Press for allowing portions of my article "Vagabonds and Paupers: Race and Illicit Mobility in the Early Republic," originally published in their journal *Pennsylvania History: A Journal of Mid-Atlantic Studies*, to be reprinted here.

I am grateful for the assistance of archivists across New York, New Jersey, Pennsylvania, Maryland, and Delaware, who aided a fellow archivist and researcher in locating documents that others considered impossible to locate or, indeed, nonexistent. Profound thanks also to all of the scholars who kindly shared their time, interest, and enthusiasm at conferences and other events over the last few years, especially at SHEAR and BrANCH. The conversations I was fortunate enough to have with Seth Rockman, Tim Lockley, Ruth Wallis Herndon, Lisa Wilson, Mike Wise, Jasper Maasen, Christian DeVito, Paul Gilje, Alec Dun, Katy Roscoe, Keri Leigh Merritt, Chris Florio, Samantha Seeley, Brian Luskey, Beverly Tomek, Jonathan Wells, Kirsten Wood, Annie Anderson, Rob Gamble, Wendy Wilson Fall, Katy Lasdow, Charlene Boyer-Lewis, Kunal Parker, and many others over the past few years have been challenging, helpful, and have improved my work immeasurably. Thanks especially to Sarah L. H. Gronningsater, who has been a font of poor law knowledge, a sounding board, and a cheerleader at crucial moments. She also deserves the credit for finding the invaluable Sarah Turner whipping case in Poughkeepsie – thanks, Sarah! A special thank you to the 2016 Prindle Institute for Ethics summer fellows, who talked with me in great detail about how best to excavate usually unheard voices from the archives in the Indiana summer heat: Rabia Belt, Anne Balay, Julia Miele Rodas, Christopher Hager, Heidi Morse, Jeff Mullins, Rhondda Robinson Thomas, and Ashley Kerr. I'm also grateful to mentors and colleagues at Rutgers University who have welcomed me with open arms and had wide-ranging conversations on this project and many others, including: Johanna Schoen, Jennifer Jones, Barbara Cooper, Paul Clemens, Andy Urban, Trinidad Rico, Francesca Giannetti, Jamie Pietruska, Mia Bay, Ann Gordon, Jennifer Mittelstadt, Marisa Fuentes, Deborah Gray White, and others.

My sincere thanks go to friends and colleagues from Queen's University Belfast, who in many ways shaped my thinking about the topics discussed in this book, and about American history more broadly: Catherine Clinton, Anthony Stanonis, Louise Canavan, Jonathan Lande, and Olwen Purdue. Catherine has offered far more intellectual, academic, and career-related support, not to mention cups of tea and positive chutzpah, than anyone could be expected to, and I remain in her debt.

Abigail Raymond and Christopher Schaeffer, beloved friends conveniently located near the archives in Philadelphia, provided me with countless opportunities to sleep on their Ikea couch and listened to tales of archival woe. Lynne Calamia, Quaker historian and Philadelphia transplant, provided invaluable conversation, emotional support, and vegan cookies from Wholefoods. Molly Sheffer offered advice, humor, encouragement, and invaluable cat-sitting services. Sincere thanks to the Jordies, who provided essential distractions and frequent chances to hug their Boston terriers, and to the O'Brassills and Kulfans, who offered unflagging confidence. During the preparation of this manuscript, I spent countless hours listening to Pablo Casals's Bach cello suites, followed by the entire discography of Fugazi, on repeat, with my cats perched on my desk. I am grateful for these essential components of the writing process.

Most of all, I am grateful to my husband and comrade, Christopher Kulfan, for providing life-sustaining cooking, good humor, support, and sanity while I worked on this project. He accompanied me on numerous jaunts to archives and conferences, tolerated my frequent absences, and both enthusiastically and carefully read the full manuscript. All he asked for in exchange was homemade pizza and lifelong partnership. I intend to continue to provide both.

Abbreviations

DPA	Delaware Public Archives
EXPA	Examinations of Paupers, Guardians of the Poor, PCA
GPP	Records of the Guardians of the Poor, PCA
HSP	Historical Society of Pennsylvania
HTCA	Huntington Town Clerk's Archives
LCHS	Lancaster County Historical Society
LCP	Library Company of Philadelphia
MCR	Medical Case Records, GPP, PCA
MDHS	Maryland Historical Society
MSA	Maryland State Archives
NYCM	New York City Municipal Archives
PCA	Philadelphia City Archives
PI	*Philadelphia Inquirer*
PPL	*Philadelphia Public Ledger*
UCCA	Ulster County Clerk's Archives
VAG	Vagrancy Dockets, Philadelphia Prisons System, PCA
WCA	Westchester County Archives

Appendix

Table A.1. Population demographics for the 1,600 nonresident paupers examined in the Philadelphia Almshouse between 1822 and 1844

Women	636
Men	964
People of color	395
Former indentured servants	341
Born in the United States	386
Out-of-state residence or extended travel	581

Source: EXPA, 1822–1844, PCA.

Table A.2. Convictions recorded by justices of the peace in Kingston, New York, 1839–1844

Larceny	
of nonsubsistence items	13
of food	12
of clothing or firewood	7
Vagrancy	69
Other Crimes	13

Source: Convictions, UCCA.

Table A.3. Vagrants incarcerated in Arch Street Jail after its opening in April 1823

Date	Men	Women	Total
May 5, 1823	103	73	176
May 19, 1823	108	96	204
June 2, 1823	120	106	226
June 16, 1823	136	101	237
June 30, 1823	119	127	246
July 14, 1823	140	130	270
July 28, 1823	131	122	253
August 25, 1823	143	121	264
September 22, 1823	133	112	245
October 6, 1823	122	29	151
October 20, 1823	122	74	196
November 3, 1823	122	76	198
November 17, 1823	119	78	197
December 1, 1823	125	74	199
December 29, 1823	94	51	145
Total	1,837	1,370	3,207

Source: Inspectors of County Prison, Minutes 1821–1827, Philadelphia Prisons System, PCA. These figures do not consistently correspond to the commitment docket for vagrants in the county prison records at the Philadelphia City Archives and do not account for recidivism rates.

APPENDIX / 169

Table A.4. Vagrants incarcerated in Arch Street Jail, 1824

Date	Men	Women	Total
January 12, 1824	98	53	151
January 26, 1824	89	65	154
February 16, 1824	97	68	165
February 22, 1824	92	54	146
March 8, 1824	87	51	138
April 5, 1824	100	44	144
April 19, 1824	111	60	171
May 5, 1824	111	78	189
May 20, 1824	131	91	222
May 31, 1824	152	105	257
June 14, 1824	149	129	278
June 28, 1824	119	88	207
July 12, 1824	114	88	202
July 26, 1824	126	115	241
August 9, 1824	128	108	236
August 22, 1824	158	125	283
September 6, 1824	168	129	297
September 20, 1824	147	122	269
October 7, 1824	148	116	264
October 18, 1824	117	90	207
November 1?, 1824	98	62	160
November 14, 1824	98	48	146
November 20, 1824	94	56	150
December 13, 1824	109	67	176
December 27, 1824	93	64	157
Total	2,934	2,076	5,010

Source: Inspectors of County Prison, Minutes 1821–1827, Philadelphia Prisons System, PCA. These figures do not consistently correspond to the commitment docket for vagrants in the county prison records at the Philadelphia City Archives and do not account for recidivism rates.

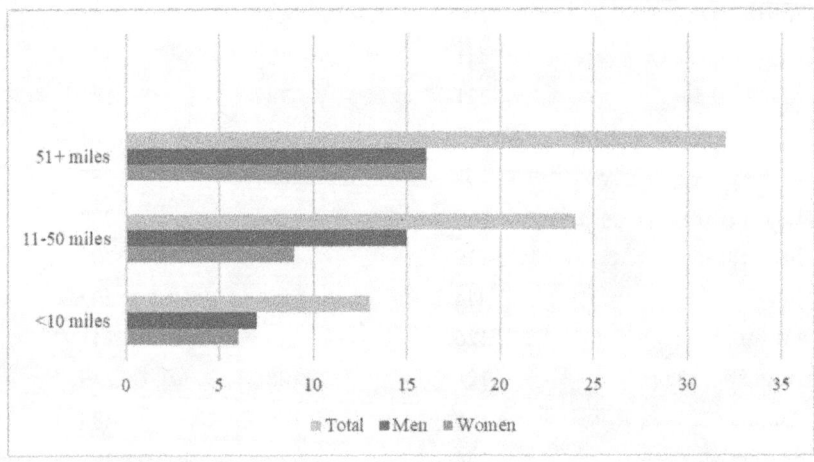

FIGURE A.1. Distances Paupers Removed from Philadelphia, 1822–1825. (EXPA, 1822–1825 and Letter Book, 1824–1829, GPP)

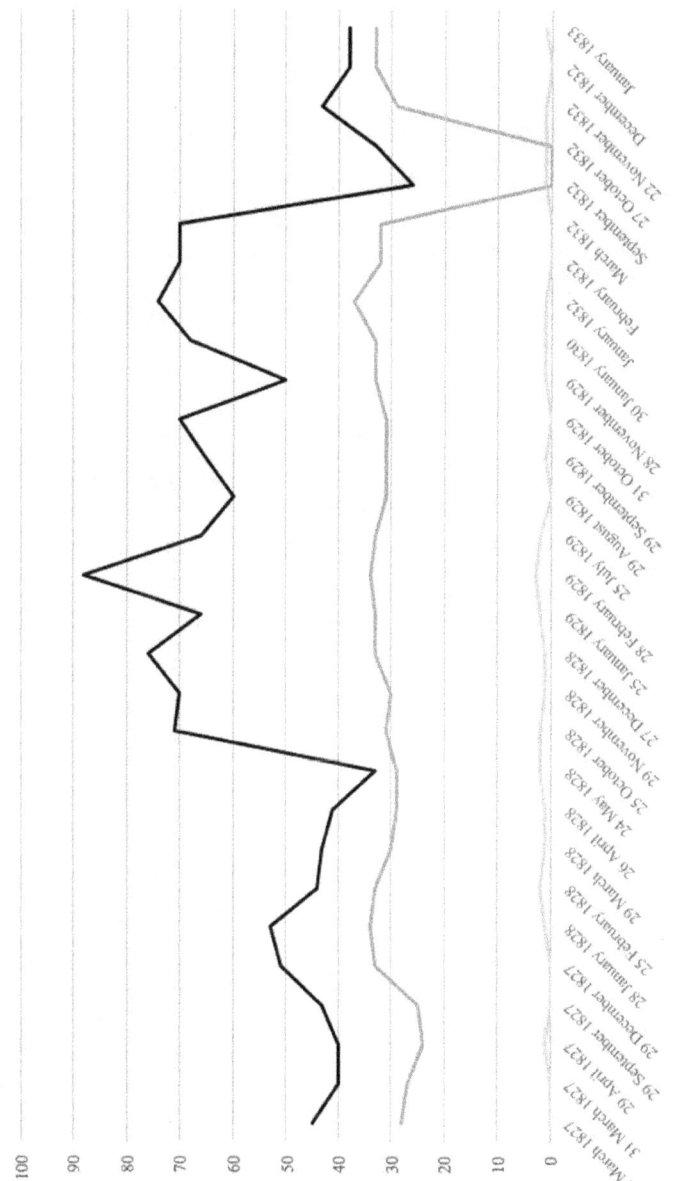

FIGURE A.2. Monthly Census of Vagrants Incarcerated in the Philadelphia Almshouse Cellars, 1827–1833 (Almshouse Weekly Admissions and Census, 1827–1833, GPP)

Notes

Notes to Introduction

1. "A Would Be Sailor," *Niles' Weekly Register* (Baltimore, 1841), vols. 59–60, 1841, 368.

2. This term is used to describe the varying means employed by the poor to make ends meet, notably in S. King and A. Tomkins, eds., *The Poor in England, 1700–1850: An Economy of Makeshifts* (Manchester: Manchester University Press, 2003).

3. "City Police," *PPL*, 6 June 1843.

4. Actual and fictional accounts of cross-dressing and female sailors were fairly common in the early nineteenth century (see Birgit Spengler, *Literary Spinoffs: Rewriting the Classics—Re-Imagining the Community* [Frankfurt: Campus Verlag, 2015], 182–83; and Sandra Frink, "'Strangers Are Flocking Here': Identity and Anonymity in New Orleans, 1810–1860," *American Nineteenth Century History* 11, no. 2 [2010]: 163).

5. Markus D. Dubber, *The Police Power: Patriarchy and the Foundations of American Government* (New York: Columbia University Press, 2005), 51–59; David Montgomery, *Citizen Worker: The Experience of Workers in the United States with Democracy and the Free Market during the Nineteenth Century* (Cambridge: Cambridge University Press, 1995), 29, 61; Gunja SenGupta, *From Slavery to Poverty: The Racial Origins of Welfare in New York, 1840–1918* (New York: New York University Press, 2010), 97.

6. On the lives and experiences of vagrants and other indigent transients in American history, see Kenneth Kusmer, *Down and Out, on the Road: The Homeless in American History* (New York: Oxford University Press, 2002); Tim Cresswell, *The Tramp in America* (London: Reaktion, 2001); Todd DePastino, *Citizen Hobo: How a Century of Homelessness Shaped America* (Chicago: University of Chicago Press, 2003); Mark Wyman, *Hoboes: Bindlestiffs, Fruit Tramps, and the Harvesting of the West* (New York: Hill and Wang, 2010); Frank Tobias Higbie, *Indispensable Outcasts: Hobo Workers and Community in the American Midwest, 1880–1930* (Champaign: University of Illinois Press, 2003); Seth Rockman, *Scraping By: Wage Labor, Slavery, and Survival in Early Baltimore* (Baltimore: Johns Hopkins University Press, 2009),

Billy G. Smith, *The "Lower Sort": Philadelphia's Laboring People, 1750–1800* (Ithaca, NY: Cornell University Press, 1990); Billy G. Smith, ed., *Down and Out in Early America* (University Park: Pennsylvania State University Press, 2010); Billy G. Smith and Simon Middleton, *Class Matters: Early North America and the Atlantic World* (Philadelphia: University of Pennsylvania Press, 2008); Jen Manion, *Liberty's Prisoners: Carceral Culture in Early America* (Philadelphia: University of Pennsylvania Press, 2015); Simon Newman, *Embodied History: The Lives of the Poor in Early Philadelphia* (Philadelphia: University of Pennsylvania Press, 2003); Simon Newman and Billy G. Smith, "Incarcerated Innocents," in *Buried Lives: Incarcerated in Early America*, ed. Michelle Lise Tarter and Richard Bell (Athens: University of Georgia Press, 2012), 60–84; Ruth Wallis Herndon, *Unwelcome Americans: Living on the Margin in Early New England* (Philadelphia: University of Pennsylvania Press, 2001); Cornelia H. Dayton and Sharon V. Salinger, *Robert Love's Warnings: Searching for Strangers in Colonial Boston* (Philadelphia: University of Pennsylvania, 2014); Eric Monkkonen, *Walking to Work: Tramps in America, 1790–1935* (Lincoln: University of Nebraska Press, 1984); and Priscilla Ferguson Clement, *Welfare and the Poor in the Nineteenth-Century City* (Cranbury, NJ: Fairleigh Dickinson University Press, 1985).

7. Paul R. Ocobock, "Vagrancy and Homelessness in Global and Historical Perspective," in *Cast Out: Vagrancy and Homelessness in Global and Historical Perspective*, ed. A. L. Beier and Ocobock (Athens: Ohio University Press, 2008), 22; Margo De Koster and Herbert Reinke, "Controlling Migrants and the Rise of Modern Policing," in *The Oxford Handbook of the History of Crime and Criminal Justice*, ed. Paul Knepper and Anja Johansen (Oxford: Oxford University Press, 2016).

8. On Anglo-American poor laws, see Christopher Tomlins, *Freedom Bound: Law, Labor, and Civic Identity in Colonizing English America, 1580–1865* (New York: Cambridge University Press, 2010); Priscilla Ferguson Clement, "The Transformation of the Wandering Poor in Nineteenth-Century Philadelphia," in *Walking to Work: Tramps in America, 1790–1935*, ed. Eric H. Monkkonen (Lincoln: University of Nebraska, 1984), 59; Raymond A. Mohl, ed., *The Making of Urban America* (Lanham, MD: Rowman and Littlefield, 2006), 8; Michael B. Katz, *Poverty and Policy in American History* (New York: Academic Press, 1983), 157–58, Benjamin Klebaner, *Public Poor Relief in America, 1790–1860* (New York: Arno, 1952); Clement, *Welfare and the Poor*; Robert E. Cray, *Paupers and Poor Relief in New York City and Its Rural Environs, 1700–1830* (Philadelphia: Temple University Press, 1988); Mohl, *Poverty in New York;* William I. Trattner, *From Poor Law to Welfare State, 6th Edition: A History of Social Welfare in America* (New York: Simon and Schuster, 2007); James D. Schmidt, *Free to Work: Labor Law, Emancipation, and Reconstruction, 1815–1880* (Athens: University of Georgia Press, 1998); Mimi Abramovitz, *Regulating the Lives of Women: Social Welfare Policy from Colonial Times to the Present* (Boston: South End, 1988), 137; Joan Underhill Hannon, "Poverty in the Antebellum Northeast: The View from New York State's Poor Relief Rolls," *Journal of Economic History* 44, no. 4 (1984): 1007–16; and Kenneth J. Winkle, *The Politics of Community: Migration and Politics in Antebellum Ohio* (Cambridge: Cambridge University Press, 2002), 2, 60–61, 175. On nineteenth-century associations between poverty and health, see Erin O'Connor, *Raw Material: Producing Pathology in Victorian Culture* (Durham, NC: Duke University Press, 2000); Charles Rosenberg, *The Cholera Years: The United States in 1832, 1849, and 1866* (Chicago: University of Chicago Press, 1962); Kathleen M. Brown, *Foul Bodies: Cleanliness in Early America*

(New Haven: Yale University Press, 2009); and Alan Kraut, *Silent Travelers: Germs, Genes, and the Immigrant Menace* (Baltimore: Johns Hopkins University Press, 1995).

9. Seth Rockman, ed., *Welfare Reform in the Early Republic: A Brief Documentary History* (Long Grove, IL: Waveland, 2014).

10. Gary B. Nash, "Poverty and Politics in Early American History," in *Down and Out in Early America*, ed. B. G. Smith (University Park: Pennsylvania State University Press, 2010), 14; Susan Klepp, "Seasoning and Society: Racial Differences in Mortality in Eighteenth-Century Philadelphia," *William and Mary Quarterly* 51 (1994): 473–506.

11. *The second annual report of the managers of the Society for the Prevention of Pauperism, in the City of New-York* (New York, 1820), 65.

12. EXPA, 1822–1844.

13. Beverly C. Tomek, *Colonization and Its Discontents: Emancipation, Emigration, and Antislavery in Antebellum Pennsylvania* (New York: New York University Press, 2011), 176–77.

14. According to Michael Katz, pauperism originated as an administrative category. And in the words of Priscilla Ferguson Clement, "to nineteenth-century Americans, paupers were the unworthy poor, those who preferred to rely on public and private relief rather than work . . . such paupers were quite distinct from the worthy poor, who drank sparingly and labored willingly, but who, through no fault of their own, became impoverished due to illness or unemployment" (Katz, *The Undeserving Poor: America's Enduring Confrontation with Poverty*, 2nd ed. [New York: Oxford University Press, 2013]; Clement, *Welfare and the Poor*, 51). On increased mobility in this period, see Clement, "Transformation"; and Bourque, "Poor Relief," 195.

15. On the relationship between burgeoning capitalism and poverty in early America, see Rockman, *Scraping By*; Katz, *Undeserving Poor*; *The Economy of Early America: Historical Perspectives and New Directions*, ed. Cathy D. Matson (University Park: Pennsylvania State University Press, 2006); Seth Rockman, "What Makes the History of Capitalism Newsworthy?" *Journal of the Early Republic* 34, no. 3 (2014): 439–66; Sven Beckert, "History of American Capitalism," in *American History Now*, ed. Eric Foner and Lisa McGirr (Philadelphia: Temple University Press, 2011), 314–35; and *Capitalism Takes Command: The Social Transformation of Nineteenth-Century America*, ed. M. Zakim and G. Kornblith (Chicago: University of Chicago Press, 2011).

16. As Seth Rockman explains, for the early American poor and working class, "class experience was waiting every February for the harbor to thaw so that low-end jobs might resume. Class consciousness was knowing the proper pose of deference to get hired. Class struggle was trying to meet the rent and scavenging for firewood to stay warm during winter" (Rockman, *Scraping By*, 11). Indigent transients were, as Jeffrey Adler notes, a contemporary challenge to "the delicate web of mutual obligation that provided relief for the poor," because they moved too frequently to meet tax requirements or to gain legal settlements that would entitle them to aid. Stephan Thernstrom and Peter R. Knights's landmark 1970 study of nineteenth-century Americans' mobility was arguably the first concerted effort to determine why geographical movement was such a defining feature of life for the lower and middling classes. They asserted that, for the laboring classes and indigent transients, spatial mobility was not a one-way move but, rather, was a continual feature of their lives, part of an ongoing search for employment, safety, and community. Indeed, the study to follow here confirms Thernstrom and Knights's assertion that "long

distance or leapfrogging mobility seems to have been more common than short-distance movement in the antebellum period." Their findings challenged the idea of the ghettoization of the poor in slum neighborhoods, allowing further work to point out that the poorest were often the most mobile. This discovery has received little historiographical follow-up, and indeed, scholarly perceptions of poverty are still skewed by community-based studies, where the privilege of stasis and residency are not often accounted for. In 1979, Charles Stephenson made this very assertion in asking the question, "Who ruled?" in the nineteenth-century polity. His answer: "those who stayed in the town." This statement is profoundly true, as the challenges faced by transients in the nineteenth century, especially indigent transients, clearly show. This underscores the importance of considering those who populated the in-between spaces—those who traveled between towns—when questioning the operation of the antebellum polity and distribution of power. These transients, as Marcus Rediker and Christopher Hill remind us, were "carrier[s] of information and ideas between different groups of laboring people" and other members of the lower classes. On this subject, the research presented here is in conversation with recent work published by Ruth Wallis Herndon and Amilcar E. Challú, which suggests that, though "scholars have long recognized that poor people were attracted by the early American city," it has not been acknowledged that "they continued to be mobile after they arrived," which classifies continued transiency and exchange, not just one-way migration, as a key fixture in the lives of the poor (Rockman, "What Makes the History of Capitalism Newsworthy?"; Adler, "Analysis of the Law," 214; Stephen Thernstrom and Peter R. Knights, "Men in Motion: Some Data and Speculations about Urban Population Mobility in Nineteenth-Century America," *Journal of Interdisciplinary History* 1, no. 1 [1970]: 32; Charles Stephenson, "A Gathering of Strangers?': Mobility, Social Structure, and Political Participation in the Formation of Nineteenth-Century American Workingclass Culture," in *American Workingclass Culture: Explorations in American Labor and Social History*, ed. M. Cantor [London: Greenwood, 1979], 41; Marcus Rediker, "'Good Hands, Stout Heart, and Fast Feet': The History and Culture of Working People in Early America," *Labor/Le Travail* 10 (1982): 141–42; Christopher Hill, *The World Turned Upside Down: Radical Ideas during the English Revolution* [New York: Penguin, 1972], 48–51; Ruth Wallis Herndon and Amilcar E. Challú, "Mapping the Boston Poor: Inmates of the Boston Almshouse, 1795–1801," *Journal of Interdisciplinary History* 44, no. 1 [2013]: 62–63).

17. Seth Rockman, "The Unfree Origins of American Capitalism," in *The Economy of Early America: Historical Perspectives and New Directions* (University Park: Pennsylvania State University Press, 2006), 352; Seth Rockman, "Work, Wages, and Welfare at Baltimore's School of Industry," *Maryland Historical Magazine*, 102 (2007): 572–607.

18. Lars Maischak, *German Merchants in the Nineteenth-Century Atlantic* (New York: Cambridge University Press, 2013), 123; Max Grivno, *Gleanings of Freedom: Free and Slave Labor along the Mason-Dixon Line, 1790–1860* (Chicago: University of Illinois Press, 2011), 51–52.

19. For a discussion of economically driven definitions of community and the moral definitions of poverty and industriousness, see Katz, *Undeserving Poor*, 5–6; Schmidt, *Free to Work*, 53; Steinfeld, *Invention of Free Labor*, 60; William J. Chambliss, "A Sociological Analysis of the Law of Vagrancy," *Social Problems* 12, no. 1 (1964):

67–77; and Seth Rockman, "Class and the History of Working People," *Journal of the Early Republic* 25, no. 4 (2005): 528.

20. Jen Manion's work has demonstrated for historians of the early republic "how incomplete our understanding of state authority has been without attention to the actions, thoughts, and experiences of those subjected to its reach" in a "triangulation of authority, resistance, and imprisonment." Vagrants were viewed "as a threat to democracy," and the "expansive application of vagrancy laws . . . solidif[ied] the criminalization of poverty" (Manion, *Liberty's Prisoners*, 6, 86–93).

21. On the legal history of vagrancy law, see Caleb Foote, "Vagrancy-Type Law and Its Administration," *University of Pennsylvania Law Review* 104, no. 5 (1956); William J. Chambliss, "A Sociological Analysis of the Law of Vagrancy," *Social Problems* 12, no. 1 (1964); Jeffrey S. Adler, "An Historical Analysis of the Law of Vagrancy," *Criminology* 27, no. 209 (1989): 209–29; Schmidt, *Free to Work*; A. L. Beier, *Masterless Men: The Vagrancy Problem in England 1560–1640* (London: Methuen, 1985); Kunal M. Parker, *Making Foreigners: Immigration and Citizenship Law in America* (Cambridge: Cambridge University Press, 2015); Amy Dru Stanley, *From Bondage to Contract: Wage Labor, Marriage, and the Market in the Age of Slave Emancipation* (Cambridge: Cambridge University Press, 1998); Mary Farmer-Kaiser, "'Are They Not in Some Sorts Vagrants?': Gender and the Efforts of the Freedmen's Bureau to Combat Vagrancy in the Reconstruction South," *Georgia Historical Quarterly* 88, no. 1 (2004): 25–49; Michael Cohen, *At Freedom's Edge: Black Mobility and the Southern White Quest for Racial Control, 1861–1915* (Baton Rouge: Louisiana State University Press, 1991); Keri Leigh Merritt, *Masterless Men: Poor Whites and Slavery in the Antebellum South* (New York: Cambridge University Press, 2017); and Clement, *Welfare and the Poor*, 46, 98.

22. As Tim Cresswell has argued, mobility in the United States was viewed "as a right—as a geographical indicator of freedom . . . intertwined with the very notion of what it is to be a national citizen—to be American," because the "ideology of America as uniquely mobile is a very powerful one" (Cresswell, *On the Move: Mobility in the Modern Western World* [New York: Taylor and Francis, 2006], 51).

23. Jen Manion argues that "the excessive enforcement of vagrancy laws reflected local rather than state or national values of punishment. Constables and watchmen filled the prison with people to get them off the streets" (Manion, *Liberty's Prisoners*, 118). For a discussion of the tenuousness of federal power, see Gautham Rao, "The Federal "Posse Comitatus" Doctrine: Slavery, Compulsion, and Statecraft in Mid-Nineteenth-Century America," *Law and History Review* 26, no. 1 [Spring 2008]: 4).

24. Allen Steinberg, *The Transformation of Criminal Justice, Philadelphia, 1800–1880* (Chapel Hill: University of North Carolina Press, 1989), 276.

25. In a study of a form of geographical movement, a regional scope is most useful to effectively reflect the extent and diversity of mobility that was occurring. This study does not aim to provide a comprehensive overview of poor laws or vagrancy statutes across this region, nor is it a comparative study between the states it discusses in greatest detail, particularly Pennsylvania and New York. Rather, it uses the available sources across this region to investigate indigent transiency, those who experienced it, and efforts at managing it. The states that comprise the Mid-Atlantic region (New York, New Jersey, Pennsylvania, Delaware, and Maryland) included the most bustling ports, greatest population diversity, and evolving systems of poor relief and criminal punishment in the early nineteenth-century United States. The term "Mid-Atlantic"

is frequently used by scholars to denote the states that lie between New England and the Upper South. It is a generally descriptive term for the region that has tended to carry less meaning than others do, as Randall Miller and Beverly Tomek have argued. Scholars, they note, "agree that the Mid-Atlantic lacks the social and cultural cement of a self-conscious regionalism that holds people to place and each other as it does elsewhere." Still, when the journal *Pennsylvania History: A Journal of Mid-Atlantic Studies* published a special issue of the journal devoted to defining the term in 2015, it featured a description of the function of the Mid-Atlantic as an analytical category based on the following characteristics: within the region, cities were the "central agents for . . . development . . . much more so than either New England or the South, both of which lacked the ports that facilitated trade and thus dictated settlement patterns in the colonial and early national periods. Once established as key agents of growth along the Atlantic hinge with Europe, New York and Philadelphia especially in foundational years and later Baltimore and Washington, DC, linked maritime trade to their hinterlands," solidifying their importance and integral place in the geography of the nation. Ill-defined yet widely used by scholars, the term "Mid-Atlantic" is useful for this study because there is a sense, in the early nineteenth century, of shared legal culture and pace of social change among the states that comprise it. Additionally, the transients at the center of this study circulate primarily through and within this "motley middle," reinforcing the notion of connectivity in this region, at least in the early republic (Randall M. Miller and Beverly Tomek, "Defining the Mid-Atlantic Region," *Pennsylvania History: A Journal of Mid-Atlantic Studies* 82, no. 3 [2015]: 257–59; Howard Gillette Jr., "Defining a Mid-Atlantic Region," *Pennsylvania History: A Journal of Mid-Atlantic Studies* 82, no. 3 [2015]: 373–80; Peter Swirski, *All Roads Lead to the American City* [New York: Columbia University Press, 2007], 100–103; Roger Lane, *Violent Death in the City: Suicide, Accident, and Murder in Nineteenth-Century Philadelphia* [Cambridge: Harvard University Press, 1979], 1–2).

26. Historians of class in the early United States, such as Jacqueline Jones, Seth Rockman, and Billy G. Smith, have constructed a powerful narrative about the unseverable link between capitalism and labor, about the subsistence methods employed by the laboring classes. The work of Marcus Rediker, Peter Linebaugh, and David Montgomery is an exception. Much of their work has been structured from the perspective that because the lower classes themselves could not be constricted and uniformly mapped, neither should studies of these groups (Jacqueline Jones, *American Work: Four Centuries of Black and White Labor* [New York: Norton, 1999]; Rockman, *Scraping By*; B. G. Smith, *The "Lower Sort"*; B. G. Smith, ed., *Down and Out*; Smith and Middleton, *Class Matters*; Merritt, *Masterless Men*; Peter Linebaugh and Marcus Rediker, *The Many-Headed Hydra: Sailors, Slaves, Commoners, and the Hidden History of the Revolutionary Atlantic* [Boston: Beacon, 2000]; Montgomery, *Citizen Worker*).

27. Schmidt, *Free to Work*, 62–65.

28. Cresswell, *The Tramp in America*, 9–10, 12.

29. On the cultural history of indigent transients, vagrants, tramps, and hoboes, see Cresswell, *The Tramp in America*; DePastino, *Citizen Hobo*; Wyman, *Hoboes*; Higbie, *Indispensable Outcasts*; Jeffrey S. Adler, "Vagging the Demons and Scoundrels: Vagrancy and the Growth of St. Louis, 1830–1861," *Journal of Urban History* 13, no. 1 (1986): 3–30; and Todd McCallum, "The Tramp Is Back," *Labor/Le Travail*, 56 (2005): 237–38.

30. These issues have been discussed in Abramovitz, *Regulating the Lives of Women*, 137; Hannon, "Poverty in the Antebellum Northeast"; and Winkle, *The Politics of Community*, 2, 60–61, 175.

31. These groups were feared as economic burdens, interlopers who would degrade local communities, and threats to the physical and physiological well-being of others (Brown, *Foul Bodies*, 284).

32. As Christine Stansell has noted, "the local and migratory poor incorporated relief into their survival patterns; poor relief was, for many, not simply a recourse in a catastrophe but a structural element of subsistence" (Stansell, *City of Women: Sex and Class in New York, 1789–1860* [Chicago: University of Chicago Press, 1986], 33).

33. Rather than viewing migration as a problem in early American life, Samantha Seeley argues, historians should view mobility as ubiquitous and removal as a foundational concept shaping countless legislative, social, and economic processes in this period (Seeley, "Continental Visions and Manumission in Post-Revolutionary Virginia," paper delivered at Society for Historians of the Early American Republic annual meeting, July 22, 2017).

34. Herndon, *Unwelcome Americans;* Dayton and Salinger, *Robert Love's Warnings*.

35. This argument is put forward in Dayton and Salinger, *Robert Love's Warnings*, 15, 65, 166.

36. *Porter Township vs Susquehanna Township*, Supreme Court of Pennsylvania, 1935.

37. Katz, *Undeserving Poor*, Michael B. Katz, *In the Shadow of the Poorhouse: A Social History of Welfare in America* (New York: Basic, 1996), 18–22; David J. Rothman, *The Discovery of the Asylum: Social Order and Disorder in the New Republic* (1971; rev. ed., New Brunswick, NJ: Rutgers University Press, 2009).

38. Katz, *Undeserving Poor*, 2013, 5–6.

39. Ibid.; Clement, *Welfare and the Poor*, 51. An additional note on terms that are used throughout this book: Some of the terms used here are those used by contemporaries, whereas others are anachronistic. Where the former offers a descriptive explanation for twenty-first-century readers, the contemporary term has been used. An example of this is "removal," which had numerous meanings in the eighteenth and nineteenth centuries that ranged from any semi-permanent geographical movement to the technical usage regarding the forced transportation of paupers. Where contemporary terms are insufficiently descriptive or do not adequately convey their meaning, other terms have been used. An example of this is "mobility," which I use interchangeably with "geographical movement" but would not have been employed in the period of this study.

40. SenGupta, *From Slavery to Poverty*, 96, 133; Monique Bourque, "Poor Relief 'Without Violating the Rights of Humanity': Almshouse Administration in the Philadelphia Region, 1790–1860," *Down and Out in Early America*, ed. Billy G. Smith (University Park: Pennsylvania State University Press, 2010), 189.

41. "No clear-cut line between the deserving and undeserving poor existed in reality," though middle and late nineteenth century reformers and legislators spilled much ink laying out the distinctions between the two groups (Hidetaka Hirota, *Expelling the Poor: Atlantic Seaboard States and the 19th-Century Origins of American Immigration Policy* [New York: Oxford University Press, 2017], 137).

42. As Philip Morgan has argued that early American historians should consider that "slaves were the poor" (Morgan, "Slaves and Poverty," in *Down and Out in Early America*, ed. Billy G. Smith [University Park: Pennsylvania State University Press, 2010], 93; Sarah L. H. Gronningsater, "The Arc of Abolition: The Children of Gradual Emancipation and the Origins of National Freedom" [forthcoming, University of Pennsylvania Press]; Edmund S. Morgan, *American Slavery, American Freedom: The Ordeal of Colonial Virginia* [New York, 1975], 341).

43. Hidetaka Hirota echoes this idea, citing Stanley on the expectation that "all free Americans" should "find employment," while "vagrants who placed themselves outside the contract relation were viewed as a menace to the integrity of postslavery American society" (Stanley, *From Bondage to Contract*, 99; Hirota, *Expelling the Poor*, 136).

44. Stanley, *From Bondage*, 132. Jacqueline Jones, too, has noted that, immediately following the end of the Civil War, many plantation owners and overseers prosecuted the formerly enslaved for exercising "liberty of locomotion" by leaving "the plantation without permission" (Jones, *American Work*, 245).

45. Arthur Zilversmit, *The First Emancipation: The Abolition of Slavery in the North* (Chicago: University of Chicago Press, 1967); Dee Andrews, "Reconsidering the First Emancipation: Evidence from the Pennsylvania Abolition Society Correspondence, 1785–1810," *Pennsylvania History: A Journal of Mid-Atlantic Studies* 10 (Summer 1997): 230–49.

46. Paul Finkelman, "Rehearsal for Reconstruction: Antebellum Origins of the Fourteenth Amendment," in *The Facts of Reconstruction: Essays in Honor of John Hope Franklin*, ed. Eric Arnesen (Baton Rouge: Louisiana State University Press, 1991), 8–9.

47. Laura Edwards has argued this regarding southern labor regulation and vagrancy prosecution: Lawmakers, she writes, "did not have to reinvent slavery" to control the labor of the poor: "Existing laws provided ample precedent. In fact, many postwar statutes reiterated long-established legal practice. In both North and South Carolina, the law already held common laborers to the end of their terms, denied them all their wages if they quit without just cause, and limited legal recourse in conflicts with their employers. Even the black codes' notorious vagrancy measures, which seem an obvious throwback to slavery, duplicated laws in South Carolina that applied to free whites" (Edwards, "The Problem of Dependency: African Americans, Labor Relations, and the Law in the Nineteenth-Century South," *Agricultural History* 72, no. 2 [1998]: 331–32; Gronningsater, "Arc of Abolition").

48. Few efforts have been made to interrogate the meanings of the mobilities described in sources created by or centered on vagrants' lives. But it is possible to use the available sources (e.g., vagrancy dockets, settlement interviews, prison and almshouse descriptive registers) to write what Clare Anderson has called a "subaltern prosopography" that documents indigent transients' lives, mobility, and interactions with the state. For some cities and regions, these available sources are rich and can sustain robust enquiry, while others offer significantly less insight to the researcher. As such, the strength of the archives has guided the inquiry and analysis in this project, making the most of the sources that are available and, where possible, constructing links across the gaps in the record. Clare Anderson, *Subaltern Lives: Biographies of Colonialism in the Indian Ocean World, 1790–1920* (Cambridge: Cambridge University Press, 2012), 6–7.

49. "City Police," *PPL*, 2 September 1837; J. Peirsol to Directors of Poor of Bucks County, 11 February 1830, Letter Book, GPP.

50. As Joanne Pope Melish has noted, the "system of transient examination was designed to elicit information from people who knew their personal history and were known in some other community to which they rightfully "belonged" (Melish, *Disowning Slavery: Gradual Emancipation and "Race" in New England, 1780—1860* [Ithaca, NY: Cornell University Press, 2000], 116).

51. As Ruth Wallis Herndon, whose book *Unwelcome Americans* utilizes them extensively, reminds readers: "The information contained in them was coerced, extracted from people who had little control over the interrogation. They are the result of people being forced to remember (or invent) their lives when confronted by the power of the state, when the "wrong answer might result in disaster for themselves and their families (Herndon, *Unwelcome Americans*, 23; Cray, *Paupers and Poor Relief*, 144).

52. Bourque, "Poor Relief 'Without Violating the Rights of Humanity,'" 201.

53. Marxist legal historians and sociologists have long acknowledged these relationships in the context of vagrancy (see William J. Chambliss, "A Sociological Analysis of the Law of Vagrancy," *Social Problems* 12, no. 1 [1964]; Foote, "Vagrancy-Type Law"; and Jerome Skolnick, "Reflections on Caleb Foote on Vagrancy-Type Laws," *Berkeley Journal of Criminal Law* 12, no. 2 [2007]).

54. Several historians of the United States, notably Herndon, Melish, Clement, Cray, and Wilson, have utilized examination records related to the settlement and removal process to interrogate poverty and transiency. Clement's "Transformation of the Wandering Poor," in particular, is the only published account of the narratives of thousands of indigent transients recorded in Philadelphia in the first half of the nineteenth century. Approximately 1,600 examinations are extant, of which Clement's work drew on less than a fifth. Her brief study provides a tantalizing glimpse as to how the poor of Philadelphia fit into the wider scope of the social milieu and experiences of vagrants and other indigent transients in the antebellum United States (Clement, "Transformation"; Lisa Wilson, *Life after Death: Widows in Pennsylvania, 1750–1850* [Philadelphia: Temple University Press, 1992], 86).

55. S. Nicolazzo, "Henry Fielding's *The Female Husband* and the Sexuality of Vagrancy," *Eighteenth Century* 55, no. 4 [2014]: 339.

56. See Manion, *Liberty's Prisoners*, 16, for illustration of the relevance of looking at demographic trends in historical studies of this nature.

Notes to Chapter 1

1. "Editor's Table," *Knickerbocker*, vol. 12 (New York, 1838), 171; "Humors of the Day," *Harper's Weekly*, vol. 11, 26 October 1867, 679; "Visible Means of Support," *The Book of Modern English Anecdotes* (London, 1872), 72. Vagrants were common fodder for riddles and anecdotes in nineteenth-century newspapers, magazines, and other print curiosities, including cigarette cards. For examples, see George Arents Collection, New York Public Library, "Why are balloons in the air like vagrants?," New York Public Library Digital Collections, http://digitalcollections.nypl.org, for an example that appeared as early as the 1860s, and earlier, "A Humorous Vagrant," *Daily Pittsburgh Gazette*, 18 November 1840; "How did you get such a cold, Ben?" *Pittsburgh Gazette*, 10 April 1832.

2. Beier, *Masterless Men;* Schmidt, *Free to Work,* 55–67. As S. Nicolazzo and Markus Dubber have argued, "vagrancy . . . epitomizes the distinctive function of police power which is not interested in its object's criminal responsibility, but its potential for future threat" (Nicolazzo, "Vagrant Figures: Law, Labor, and Refusal in the Eighteenth-Century Atlantic World," Ph.D. diss., University of Pennsylvania, 2014, 348). Jorge Ramos describes vagrancy as the "disturbing flow of misplaced bodies," in reference to Cuba's laws against indigent transients in the early nineteenth century which were particularly tied to epidemiological concerns, both figurative and literal, much like the English and American contexts (Ramos, "A Citizen Body: Cholera in Havana [1833]," *Dispositio: Subaltern Studies in the Americas* 19, no. 46 [1994]: 190).

3. As Lawrence Friedman has described it, this identity was "based on mobility and immigration," and yet "suspicious of immigrants and strangers, especially those who were detached and alone, without community or social circle or family, without fixed setting (Friedman, *Crime and Punishment in American History* [New York: Basic, 2010], 158).

4. Melish, *Disowning Slavery,* 206.

5. Tomlins, *Freedom Bound,* 69–71.

6. This was another vestige of English law, where mobility for the poor was curtailed by law (Parker, *Making Foreigners,* 23; Cresswell, *Tramp in America,* 16–17).

7. Engrossed and corrected copy of the Articles of Confederation, showing amendments adopted, 15 November 1777, Papers of the Continental Congress, 1774–1789; Records of the Continental and Confederation Congresses and the Constitutional Convention, 1774–1789, Record Group 360, National Archives.

8. John D. Cox, *Traveling South: Travel Narratives and the Construction of American Identity* (Athens: University of Georgia Press, 2005), 3.

9. Kathleen Arnold considers this perspective as a holdover from feudalism, when "the poor were not considered citizens" (Arnold, *Homelessness, Citizenship, and Identity: The Uncanniness of Late Modernity* [Albany: State University of New York Press, 2004], 24).

10. "An Act to prevent the increase of pauperism in this Commonwealth," *A Digest of the Laws of Pennsylvania* (Philadelphia, 1837).

11. As John David Cox has noted, "by traveling too freely (and thus subversively), these people," meaning paupers, vagabonds, and fugitives, "had lost the right to travel" (Cox, *Traveling South,* 3).

12. Ramos, "A Citizen Body," 190.

13. As David Rothman has noted, "the most punitive sections" of states' poor laws "were directed more at vagrants and dependent strangers than at the local poor" (Rothman, *The Discovery of the Asylum,* 20).

14. Foote, "Vagrancy-Type Law," 616, 623.

15. Foote referred to removal laws as cities' and states' "banishment polic[ies]" (Foote, "Vagrancy-Type Law," 617).

16. "Act for the relief of the poor within the several counties therein mentioned," *The Laws of Maryland* (Baltimore, 1811); "Act to consolidate and amend the laws for the relief of the poor," *Laws of the State of Delaware* (Wilmington, 1829).

17. "Act for the settlement and relief of the poor," *A Digest of the Laws of New Jersey* (Bridgeton, 1838).

18. *A Digest of the Laws of Pennsylvania* (Philadelphia, 1831); *Laws of the State of New York* (Albany, 1802).

19. *A Digest of the Laws of Pennsylvania* (Philadelphia, 1831), 742; *A manual for the Guardians of the Poor: of the City of Philadelphia, the district of Southwark, and township of the Northern Liberties* (Philadelphia, 1823), LCP.

20. Adams, "Constitutional Law," 715-17.

21. In 1942, Edward W. Adams lamented that the laws regulating management of poor populations in the United States had not changed with the times despite the fact that "the modern indigent is not to be treated as the traditional pauper. . . . [T]he present-day settlement laws and their analogies" were still "derived from the old laws" (Adams, "Constitutional Law: State Control of Interstate Migration of Indigents," *Michigan Law Review* 40, no. 5 [March 1942]: 715-17).

22. This legal definition dates back to at least 1802 and remained in effect into the late nineteenth century. Vagrancy laws, then, essentially defined homelessness, because, as Tim Cresswell has summarized, "vagrancy . . . is nothing if not a construction of the law . . . The legal definition of vagrancy . . . is not free-standing, but linked to the more commonplace definitions based on mobility and work" (*Digest of the Laws of the State of New York* [New York, 1874], 116; Cresswell, *Tramp in America*, 55).

23. Studies of citizenship, identity, and poverty generally look at exclusion of "indigent males, women, and racial minorities" as a denial of "membership in political community," clearly an important factor in not just the rights afforded these groups but in their experience of civic life. But as the above discussion of the Articles of Confederation illustrates, the state frequently "deployed citizenship . . . to restrict individuals'" access to, or presence within, its territory." The concrete nature of territory, and theoretical claims to presence on it, meant that, as Kunal Parker has argued, "a lack of settlement, rather than a lack of citizenship" prohibited many indigents from being able to reside legally within a given district (Parker, "From Poor Law to Immigration Law: Changing Visions of Territorial Community in Antebellum Massachusetts," *Historical Geography* 28 [2000]: 61, 66).

24. The English origins of vagrancy law as applied in the United States are incredibly well established in both American and British historiographies of law and poverty. A. L. Beier's *Masterless Men: The Vagrancy Problem in England 1560-1640* is arguably the definitive study on the topic. For a brief summary of the application of fourteenth-century England's Statute of Labourers and the Old Poor Law in America, see Schmidt, *Free to Work*, 62-65. For a discussion with more emphasis on the English statutes and their eventual adoption in the colonies, see Tomlins, *Freedom Bound*; and Robert B. Morris, *Government and Labor in Early America* (New York: Octagon, 1965).

25. Terry Bouton, "Moneyless in Pennsylvania: Privatization and the Depression of the 1780s," in *The Economy of Early America: Historical Perspectives and New Directions*, ed. Cathy D. Matson (University Park: Pennsylvania State University Press, 2006), 218-35.

26. As Jacqueline Jones has stated, in the Revolutionary era, "one-fifth of all residents of Boston . . . and New York and Philadelphia . . . could be classified as the poor." These cities were filled with "a hodgepodge of vagabonds, unskilled free Negroes and freed servants, "the strolling poor," and the chronically unemployed." This "highly transient group" became "a permanent fixture" on the landscape of the young nation (Jones, *American Work*, 162; Herndon, *Unwelcome Americans*, 11-12; Dayton and

Salinger, *Robert Love's Warnings*, 86-87; Douglas Lamar Jones, "The Strolling Poor: Transiency in Eighteenth-Century Massachusetts," in *Walking to Work: Tramps in America, 1790-1935*, ed. E. Monkkonen [Lincoln: University of Nebraska Press, 1984], 21-22).

27. Cray, *Paupers and Poor Relief*, 115-18; Mohl, *Poverty in New York*, 52-65; John K. Alexander, *Render Them Submissive: Responses to Poverty in Philadelphia, 1760-1800* (Amherst: University of Massachusetts Press, 1980).

28. Mohl, *Poverty in New York*, 54-55.

29. As John Alexander writes, this law was a "powerful weapon to keep vagabonds and other undesirables from flocking to Philadelphia" (Alexander, *Render Them Submissive*, 106-7; "Poor" [1782], *A Digest of the Laws of Pennsylvania* [Philadelphia, 1818]).

30. "Act for the better relief of the poor," *Laws of the State of Delaware* (New Castle, 1797).

31. New Jersey's 1774 law dealing with paupers and vagrants was still in effect as of 1838 ("Act for the settlement and relief of the poor," *A Digest of the Laws of New Jersey* [Bridgeton, 1838]).

32. "Act for the relief of the poor within the several counties therein mentioned," *The Laws of Maryland* (Baltimore, 1811).

33. This effective duty to work system was developed because, as Jen Manion has noted, "poverty and its attendant life circumstances (homelessness, unemployment, living on streets, illness, begging, relying on religious or public charity) . . . threaten[ed] the American experiment" (Manion, *Liberty's Prisoners*, 15).

34. Clement, *Welfare and the Poor*, 36.

35. *The second annual report of the managers of the Society for the Prevention of Pauperism, in the City of New-York* (New York, 1820), 16

36. There, as William Trattner has written, "destitution was widespread; beggars and vagrants stalked the streets" throughout the early decades of the nineteenth century (Trattner, *From Poor Law to Welfare State*, 68).

37. Dire straits drew many to the city, where better economic opportunities were perceived to lie, which meant that Philadelphia, as Gary B. Nash notes, "function[ed] as a catchment for an area stretching from the West Indies to New England" as "new infusions of outsiders continued" in the first decades of the nineteenth century. African Americans were especially vulnerable in these decades of economic distress, and from 1815 through the 1820s, "the proportion of blacks in the almshouse outstripped their share of the population" (Nash, *Forging Freedom: The Formation of Philadelphia's Black Community, 1720-1840* [Cambridge: Harvard University Press, 1988], 214; Gary B. Nash, *First City: Philadelphia and the Forging of Historical Memory* (Philadelphia: University of Pennsylvania Press, 2013), 163. Priscilla Ferguson Clement, "The Philadelphia Welfare Crisis of the 1820s," *Pennsylvania Magazine of History and Biography* 105, no. 2 [1981]: 151).

38. Kenneth A. Scherzer, *The Unbounded Community: Neighborhood Life and Social Structure in New York City, 1830—1875* (Durham: Duke University Press, 1992), 87.

39. Historians discuss this decade as the time when many Americans began to turn "against the poor" (Manion, *Liberty's Prisoners*, 15, 92). Using an average from Clement's data on the vagrant population in the Philadelphia Prison from three sample years: 1823, 1825, and 1826, combined with data from the Philadelphia Almshouse

census counting inhabitants of the vagrant cellars, the overall population figure hovers between 1.25 and 1.7 percent (Clement, "Transformation," 66; Almshouse Weekly Census, Alms House Records, GPP; Clement, "Philadelphia Welfare Crisis"; Alan M. Zachary, "Social Disorder and the Philadelphia Elite before Jackson," *Pennsylvania Magazine of History and Biography* 99, no. 3 [1975]: 288–308).

40. Vagrancy laws were used to respond to social threats posed by "anyone who threatened . . . to move "out of place" socially, culturally, politically, racially, sexually, economically, or spatially," as Risa Goluboff notes (Goluboff, *Vagrant Nation: Police Power, Constitutional Change, and the Making of the 1960s* [New York: Oxford University Press, 2016], 3).

41. *The Revised Statutes of the State Of New-York*, vol. 1 (Albany: Packard and Van Benthuysen, 1829), 632.

42. Conviction of Ann Elmendorff, UCCA.

43. Ibid.; Kann, *Punishment, Prisons, and Patriarchy*, 21, 73.

44. Conviction of Joseph Ruland, UCCA.

45. Commitment of Unis Maria Quin, VAG, 1832–1836.

46. *A digest of the laws in force relating to the police of the city of Philadelphia* (Philadelphia, 1851), LCP.

47. Barker Family Papers McA MSS 023, Box 1 Folder 31, LCP; Address of the Mayor to the High Constables, Police Officers, and Watchmen, 1832, Philadelphia, LCP.

48. "An Act to prevent the increase of pauperism in this Commonwealth," *A Digest of the Laws of Pennsylvania* (Philadelphia, 1837).

49. One state supreme court justice ruled that vagrancy was indeed a status crime, and as such, would be demonstrated not in an instant, but as a "pattern of behavior displayed over time." (*Commonwealth v. Sullivan, Same v. Daniels* [Massachusetts, 1862]).

50. Ranney, *In the Wake of Slavery*, 17; Essah, *House Divided*, 116; Jones, *American Work*, 110–11.

51. A. Simonds, *Boston Common Council—No. 15, 1835, Report on Almshouses and Pauperism* (Boston, 1835), 26; EXPA, 1822–1831; Non-Resident Register, GP, PCA.

52. Maryland Penitentiary Prisoners Record, 1811–1840, S275-1, MSA.

53. *Report of a committee appointed by the guardians for the relief and employment of the poor of Philadelphia, etc. to visit the almshouses of Baltimore, New York, Boston, and Salem* (Philadelphia, 1834), HSP.

54. Delaware introduced such legislation in 1849 (Essah, *House Divided*, 116).

55. New Jersey's 1774 law dealing with paupers and vagrants was still in effect as of 1838 ("Act for the settlement and relief of the poor," *A Digest of the Laws of New Jersey* [Bridgeton, 1838]).

56. Poor Law Commission, "United States: New Jersey," *Report from His Majesty's Commissioners for Inquiring into the Administration and Practical Operation of the Poor-laws*, appendix F (London, 1834).

57. As Caleb Foote has asserted, "vagrancy laws might be unintelligible if we did not regard them as a supplement to the old Poor Laws" (Foote, "Vagrancy-Type Law," 603).

58. Mohl, *Poverty in New York*, 58–64.

59. Ibid., 58.

60. Ibid., 65; Gerald L. Neuman, *Strangers to the Constitution: Immigrants, Borders, and Fundamental Law* (Princeton: Princeton University Press, 2010), 27.
61. "Pauperism," *New York Columbian*, 10 August 1820.
62. Ibid.
63. Marilyn Wood Hill, *Their Sisters' Keepers: Prostitution in New York City, 1830–1870* (Berkeley: University of California Press, 1993), 114.
64. Mohl, *Poverty in New York*, 64.
65. Linda K. Kerber, *No Constitutional Right to Be Ladies* (New York: Hill and Wang, 1998), 51; Max Weber, *The Protestant Ethic and the Spirit of Capitalism*, trans. Talcott Parsons (New York: Penguin, 1958), chap. 5; Richard Stott, "British Immigrants and the American 'Work Ethic' in the Mid-Nineteenth Century," *Labor History* 25 (1984): 86–102, cited in Schmidt, *Free to Work*, 244. Johanna Innes's description of the sixteenth-century English perception of a duty to work appears to be an origin point, as well: "the rationale of bridewell punishment . . . in no way depended on a vision of labor as the source of wealth . . . it was necessary only that a duty to labor should be considered a distinguishing mark of the poor" (Innes, "Prisons for the Poor: English Bridewells 1555–1800," in *Labor, Law and Crime: an Historical Perspective*, ed. Francis G. Snyder and Douglas Hay [London: Tavistock, 1987]).
66. Internationally, Amy Dru Stanley argues that "the sanctions against dependency and the labor compulsions that accompanied the American triumph of freedom were more extreme" than had been experienced by the British as the originators of such policies. Tim Cresswell also emphasizes the unique context of American vagrancy statutes and poor laws, arguing that while tramp scares in the United States "share[d] many features with the moral panics surrounding vagrancy in Europe," there were "some important differences" brought on by the sheer size of the United States and the accessibility of movement across its expanse (Stanley, *From Bondage*, 131; Cresswell, *Tramp in America*, 19; Stanley, *From Bondage*, 137).
67. As David Rothman argues, "safeguards against vagrants, not a fear of all dependents, stimulated harsh and rigid legislation" (Rothman, *Discovery of the Asylum*, 22).
68. As Kenneth Winkle has noted, "election laws . . . disfranchised migrants" because every time an individual "moved across a political boundary he lost his right of suffrage," often for up to a year. Kathleen R. Arnold argues that migrants, vagrants, and the homeless "suffer the most in a wide range of exclusions" from civic life as a result of their lack of rootedness, because "home marks the distinction between access to democratic power and rights and the complete denial of this." Kathryn Hansel claims that because "economic independence is an essential component of citizenship" in the American context, "a lack of economic independence coupled with a total exclusion from political and national identity results in non-citizenship, leaving vagrants "essentially stateless (Winkle, *Politics of Community*, 175; Arnold, *Homelessness, Citizenship, and Identity*, 19; Kathryn Hansel, "Constitutional Othering: Citizenship and the Insufficiency of Negative Rights-Based Challenges to Anti-Homeless Systems," *Northwestern Journal of Law and Social Policy* 6 [2011]: 445).
69. Gerald G. Eggert, "'Two Steps Forward, A Step-and-a-Half Back': Harrisburg's African American Community in the Nineteenth Century, *Pennsylvania History: A Journal of Mid-Atlantic History* 58, no. 1 (1991): 1–36; Eric L. Smith, "The End of Black Voting Rights in Pennsylvania: African Americans and the Pennsylvania

Constitutional Convention of 1837–1838," *Pennsylvania History: A Journal of Mid-Atlantic Studies* 65, no. 3 (1998): 279–99.

70. Hansel describes this process of exclusion from citizenship privileges "constitutional othering" (Hansel, "Constitutional Othering," 468).

71. But James Schmidt argues that, even after the revision, Pennsylvania law's definitions of vagrants retained for the most part their eighteenth-century terms, which were imprecise and could be applied to huge swaths of the population. One early twentieth-century historian claimed that the 1836 poor law was "essentially English in character and not drawn in accordance with American ideals and practices," yet "revision at present seems to be impossible" (W. C. Heffner, *History of Poor Relief Legislation in Pennsylvania, 1682–1913* [Cleona, PA, 1913], 270; Schmidt, *Free to Work*, 63).

72. *Proceedings and Debates of the Convention of the Commonwealth of Pennsylvania*, vol. 2 (Harrisburg, 1838), 519.

73. Smith, "The End," 279–99; Julie Winch, *Philadelphia's Black Elite: Activism, Accommodation, and the Struggle for Autonomy, 1787–1848* (Philadelphia: Temple University Press, 1988).

74. *Proceedings and Debates*, 5:301.

75. Alexander Keyssar, *Out of Work: The First Century of Unemployment in Massachusetts* (Cambridge: Cambridge University Press, 1986).

76. *Proceedings and Debates*, 3:167.

77. Ibid.

78. *Proceedings and Debates*, 5:303; Charles E. Rosenberg, "Social Class and Medical Care in 19th-Century America: The Rise and Fall of the Dispensary," in *Sickness and Health in America: Readings in the History of Medicine and Public Health*, ed. Judith W. Leavitt and Ronald L. Numbers (Madison: University of Wisconsin Press, 1997), 309–22.

79. *Proceedings and Debates*, 3:168; ibid., 5:303.

80. Kathleen M. Brown has described these dominant "suspicions" that African Americans, the Irish, and other poor whites "were inherently dirty" and that with this dirt came disease (Brown, *Foul Bodies*, 284).

81. Jim Downs, *Sick from Freedom: African American Illness and Suffering during the Civil War and Reconstruction* (New York: Oxford University Press, 2012), 100–101.

82. *Proceedings and Debates*, 2:490.

83. "Presentment of the Grand Inquest for the City of Lancaster," *Lancaster (PA) Journal*, 3 September 1819.

84. Commitment of Charlotte Palmer, VAG, 1822–1825.

85. DePastino, *Citizen Hobo*, xix.

86. Commitment of Margaret Caster, VAG, 1822–1827.

87. Examination of Margaret Caster, EXPA, 1822–1825.

88. Examination of Margaret Caster, EXPA, 1826–1831.

89. "City Police," *PPL*, 2 September 1837. News reports like those detailing Gantdron's arrest occasionally provide greater details of vagrants' transiency than do their conviction records.

90. Rockman, "The Unfree Origins of American Capitalism," 353–54.

91. Clement, "Transformation," 56.

92. Society for Promotion of Public Economy report, 1817.

93. Rockman, *Scraping By*, 351.

94. James Rogers, 1832, Watchmen's Returns, NYCM.

95. Though Rogers's crime was part of the legacy of English laws relating to vagabonds, most states had by the second decade of the nineteenth century developed punishments that were less harsh than those that had developed out of the original laws in England, where punishments for food theft by the 1820s were notoriously harsh. There, petit larceny of small quantities of cheese and bread regularly led to convictions of colonial transportation to convict settlements for terms of seven years, whereas the same crime in the northern United States involved usually a short term of incarceration. Early examples are found in Edith M. Ziegler, *Harlots, Hussies, and Poor Unfortunate Women: Crime, Transportation, and the Servitude of Female Convicts, 1718–1783* (Birmingham: University of Alabama Press, 2014), 15.

96. Conviction of John Cox, UCCA.

97. Convictions of John Cox, Lucius Sands, and Benjamin York, UCCA.

98. In eighteenth-century Boston, officials took actions to limit the appeal of the city to the itinerant poor and stave off strolling "strangers" that went beyond warning out policies, and even criminalized fishing in public waters for nonresidents. A hundred years later, in the late nineteenth-century rural South, African Americans found fishing were frequently accused of participating in "vagrancy in acute form" and were prohibited from using the produce or animals of public lands for subsistence. Concerned that natural resources would be enjoyed by vagrants alone, many whites advocated for game and fish laws to stem poor black and whites' access to free food (B. G. Smith, ed., *Down and Out in Early America*, 15–16; Sean E. Giltner, *Hunting and Fishing in the New South: Black Labor and White Leisure after the Civil War* [Baltimore: Johns Hopkins University Press, 2008], 151–61). Marcus Rediker refers to subsistence crimes such as these as the "re-appropriat[ion of] the value of . . . labor through what the legal system called "theft" (Rediker, "Review of *Scraping By: Wage Labor, Slavery, and Survival in Early Baltimore* by Seth Rockman," *William and Mary Quarterly* 67, no. 1 [2010]: 164–65). Policies in antebellum New York prevented hunting, fishing, and seaside squatting by nonresidents (Cray, *Paupers and Poor Relief*, 144–46).

99. Commitment of Thomas Cane, VAG, 1822–1825.

100. "Northern Liberties Police," *PPL*, 26 June 1838.

101. The Guardians of the Poor Letter Book from the Philadelphia Almshouse, held in the Philadelphia City Archives, illustrates the extent this intra-institutional network of poor relief and punishment remarkably. Similar letters are to be found at UCCA, HTCA, MDHS, and presumably elsewhere (Rothman, *Discovery*).

102. Staats Van Deursen, a local poor relief official, slaveholder, and trustee of Queen's College (now Rutgers University), was also instrumental in the illicit movement of people enslaved in New Jersey to Louisiana despite state laws forbidding such actions. He facilitated the sale of land belonging to Jacob Klady, a local slaveholder, so that he could establish a plantation on which Van Deursen's former slaves would labor. Van Deursen then facilitated the purchase of this land for use as a poorhouse farm for Middlesex County paupers, closing a loop of forced labor (White and Fuentes, *Scarlet and Black*, 76–78).

103. The association of cleanliness with nonvagrants and dirtiness with vagrants is a continuously significant factor in the continuity of historical perspective and legal consideration of the category of vagrancy (Foote, "Vagrancy-Type Law," 606).

104. Jeremiah Peirsol to Staats van Deursen, Esq., 11 March 1828, Letter Book, GPP.
105. Ibid.
106. Adler, "Vagging the Demons," 9.

Notes to Chapter 2

1. Examination of Lucy Ann Griffin, EXPA, 1831–1836.
2. Jones, "The Strolling Poor," 26.
3. Marcus Rediker has described such resistance as indigent transients' use of "their fast feet, their autonomous mobility, against the aggregating powers" (Rediker, "Review of *Scraping By*," 164–65).
4. This had the result of effectively establishing the first police forces (Dubber, *Police Power*, 51–59). Tim Cresswell saliently discusses the construction of transients, especially vagrants and tramps, as threatening to established systems of order, a common theme in the historiography on the subject, in *The Tramp in America*, 14.
5. Linda Kerber, *Women of the Republic: Intellect and Ideology in Revolutionary America* (Chapel Hill: University of North Carolina Press, 2000), 142.
6. In eighteenth-century England, Henry Fielding presciently observed that "all laws against vagabonds" might more accurately "in a synonymous phrase, be called laws against wanderers." What was true in Fielding's England remained true in nineteenth-century America, a young nation living with the legacy of colonial poor laws and vagrancy statutes. As Patricia Fumerton has found, the element of mobility in vagrants' lives had essential importance: in order to understand vagrants, she wrote, "we must track them in their own space—a space of itinerancy, fragmentation, disconnection, and multiplicity that produces a very different topographical mapping of societal relations than those determined by place." For Fumerton, individuals who lived in this realm experienced, to some extent, an "unsettled subjectivity" that instigated and perpetuated their geographical mobility, economic instability, and political transiency. The legal landscape constructed citizenship as geographically determined, but it was superimposed over a physical landscape upon which citizens and "aliens" alike traversed.

Studies of travel and physical movements have tended to "subordinate the path to the point." Gilles Deleuze and Felix Guattari have argued that this is because history is generally "written from the sedentary point of view." In order to tell the histories of transients, then, scholars must "prioritize the trajectory and the space between points," as opposed to only the "factual necessity" of fixed points. This chapter aims to do this by considering the directions chosen by indigent transients as they participated in subsistence migration. These individuals—migrants, wanderers, vagrants—who live in-between, what Fumerton refers to as "the interstices," are often elusive in the historical record. Even when the archival sources can be located, the nature of their mobility and realities of their mobile lives are often subverted by narratives that privilege fixity and stability. In the early American republic, this subversion was written into law, as discussed in chapter 1, through prohibitions of ingress and regress for the perpetually mobile, criminal, and indigent. This is because, as Tim Cresswell has argued, the "moral geography of roots and progress [is] marked by a sedentary metaphysics." These meanings of stasis and movement combined with populations' socioeconomic status to create a dichotomy in antebellum travel where class "played the decisive role in determining [individuals'] ability to travel," even, as Sandra Frink notes, for women, over gender (Henry Fielding, *Enquiry into the Causes of the Late Increase of Robbers* [London, 1751], xi, cited in Nicolazzo, "Henry Fielding's *The Female Husband* and the Sexuality of Vagrancy," 349; Patricia Fumerton, *Unsettled: The Culture of Mobility and the Working Poor in Early Modern England* [Chicago: University of Chicago Press, 2006], xiv, xxi; Gilles Deleuze and Felix Guattari, *A Thousand Plateaus: Capitalism and Schizophrenia*, trans. Brian Massumi [Minneapolis: University of Minnesota Press, 1987], 23; P. Mitchell, *Cartographic Strategies of Postmodernity: The Figure of the Map in Contemporary Theory and Fiction* [London: Routledge, 2008], 86–87). For a discussion of different types of migration, especially as followed by the middling and lower classes, see Dayton and Salinger, *Robert Love's Warnings*, 75; Cresswell, *Tramp in America*, 56; and Frink, "Strangers," 161.

7. Examination of Ebenezer Widdington, EXPA, 1831–1839.

8. Examination of John Devar, EXPA, 1822–1825.

9. D. B. Warden, *A Statistical, Political, and Historical Account of the United States of North America* (Philadelphia, 1819).

10. *Journal of Proceedings of the First Branch City Council of Baltimore* (Baltimore, 1833), 122.

11. *Fifth Report of the Society for the Prevention of Pauperism, in the City of New-York* (New York, 1821), LCP, 14.

12. The foreign-born numbered 386/1,600, or 24 percent (EXPA, 1822–1844).

13. "City Police," *PPL*, 8 July 1837.

14. "Pauperism," *New York Columbian*, 10 August 1820.

15. "City Police—John Swift Mayor," *PPL*, 19 December 1837.

16. "Pauperism," *New York Columbian*, 10 August 1820.

17. *The second annual report of the managers of the Society for the Prevention of Pauperism, in the City of New-York* (New York, 1820), LCP, 8.

18. *Report of the Library Committee of the Pennsylvania Society for the Promotion of Public Economy* (Philadelphia, 1817), 20.

19. Rockman, *Scraping By*, 209.

20. "City Police," *PPL*, 2 September 1837.

21. "Mayor's Office," *PPL*, 25 March 1836.

22. These anecdotes call into question Priscilla Ferguson Clement's assumption that, because most early nineteenth-century indigent transients "probably journeyed to the city on foot," "they could not have come too far." Furthermore, she argues, a majority "arrived in [Philadelphia] from destinations one to 100 miles away . . . First, of course, necessity could have contravened any preference of conveyance method, and settlement examinations do not generally contain a record of a mode of travel. And at any rate, as Clement notes, the reason that settlement had such carefully protected currency was that most indigent transiency was intermittent, broken up with varying lengths of stays in certain areas. Indeed, "most persons moved not direct from farm to city, but from farm to small town and then perhaps to a larger city" ("City Police," *PPL*, 2 September 1837; Clement, "Transformation," 76).

23. Examination of Park Cullen, EXPA, 1822–1825.

24. These individuals numbered 421/1,600 (aggregated data from EXPA, 1822–1844).

25. Examinations of William Gore and Samuel Benton, EXPA, 1822–1825.

26. Examination of Joseph Robinson, EXPA, 1822–1825.
27. J. Peirsol to Directors of Poor of Bucks County, 11 February 1830, Letter Book, GPP.
28. Examination of Jeremiah Mahaney, EXPA, 1822–1825.
29. Examination of Theophilus Grew, EXPA, 1826–1831.
30. Examination of Willoughby Newton Howell, EXPA, 1826–1831.
31. Maryland Penitentiary Prisoners Record, 1811–1840, S275-1, MSA. Penitentiary records list a Bazil Tobin, while the almshouse records list Basel Dobbins; the descriptions, testimony, age, and other identifying characteristics match. The same is true for the woman listed as Mary O'Neale in penitentiary records and as Mary O'Neil in almshouse records.
32. Prisoners Record, Bazil Tobin, MSA. Commitment of Basel Tubbins. Examination of Basel Dobbins, EXPA, 1822–1825.
33. Wood Hill, *Their Sisters' Keepers*, 113–16; Patricia Cline Cohen, *The Murder of Helen Jewett* (New York: Knopf, 1999), 65–67; Nicole Hahn Rafter, *Partial Justice: Women, Prisons, and Social Control* (New Brunswick, NJ: Rutgers University Press, 1990), 115–16; Rockman, *Scraping By*, 338.
34. Mary O'Neale, Prisoners Record, MSA; Examination of Mary Oneil, EXPA, 1822–1825.
35. African Americans and women of all races exhibited slightly less dramatic geographical mobility than white men. For the former, this was likely as a result of legal restrictions on their movements, especially among free and unfree blacks. EXPA, 1822–1844.
36. Examination of Samuel Meninger, EXPA, 1826–1831.
37. Examinations of John Devar and John China, EXPA, 1822–1825.
38. Examination of Isaac Wiley, EXPA, 1822–1825.
39. For more on the plight of veterans in the early republic, see John P. Resch, *Suffering Soldiers: Revolutionary War Veterans, Moral Sentiment, and Political Culture in the Early Republic* (Amherst: University of Massachusetts Press, 2010).
40. "Act for the settlement and Relief of the Poor," *Acts of the General Assembly of the Province of New-Jersey* (Woodbridge, NJ, 1761). The ubiquity of such suspicions reflects an American cultural tendency to see profiteering where it may or may not exist (Ann Fabian, *The Unvarnished Truth: Personal Narratives in Nineteenth-Century America* [Oakland: University of California Press, 2002], 10–15).
41. "Real Poverty!!!," *PPL*, 30 September 1839.
42. Ibid.
43. Additionally, with the introduction of police lodgings and boarding houses after the 1850s where individuals could essentially voluntarily incarcerate themselves for a night or more, such practices were much more common in the late nineteenth and early twentieth centuries. For more on these facilities and the people who used them, see Kusmer, *Down and Out, on the Road*; and Cresswell, *The Tramp in America*.
44. "Mayor's Office," *PPL*, 25 March 1836.
45. *PPL*, 19 March 1836. A John Ramsey of similar description appears in almshouse records with a settlement in Lebanon County, in February 1838, but without a given age it is not possible to connect the two.
46. Examination of Charles Hough, EXPA, 1826–1831.
47. Examination of Susan Hall, EXPA, 1822–1825; and Commitment of Susan Hall, VAG, 1822–1827.

48. Examination of Loraina Butler, EXPA, 1826–1831.
49. Examination of Margaret Hempstead, EXPA, 1826–1831.
50. Examination of Evan Richardson, EXPA, 1826–1831.
51. Examination of Hudson Springer, EXPA, 1822–1825.
52. Examination of Richard Mickilravy, EXPA, 1831–1839.
53. Receipt of Paupers, Transportation Book, Pauper and Poorhouse Records and Ulster County Paupers Name Book, UCCA.
54. Examination of Park Cullen, 1821–1825.
55. Examination of Rebecca Benson, EXPA, 1822–1825.
56. Examinations of John Steele, EXPA, 1831–1839 and 1826–1831.
57. Examination of William Stewart, Examinations of Paupers, 1822–1825, PCA.
58. Examination of Edward Campbell, Examinations of Paupers, 1826–1831.
59. *Report of the Library Committee of the Pennsylvania Society for the Promotion of Public Economy*, 16–18.
60. Daniel S. Dupre, "The Panic of 1819 and the Political Economy of Sectionalism," in *The Economy of Early America: Historical Perspectives and New Directions*, ed. C. D. Matson (University Park: Pennsylvania State University Press, 2006), 263–93.
61. *Report of the Library Committee*, 16–18. Aggregated data for 1827 extracted from EXPA, 1827.
62. Hirota, *Expelling the Poor*, 57; Roger Lane, *Violent Death in the City: Suicide, Accident, and Murder in Nineteenth-Century Philadelphia* (Cambridge: Cambridge University Press, 1979), 1; J. Matthew Gallman, *Receiving Erin's Children: Philadelphia, Liverpool, and the Irish Famine Migration, 1845–1855* (Chapel Hill: University of North Carolina Press, 2000).
63. W. J. Bromwell, *History of Immigration to the United States . . . from September 30, 1819 to December 31, 1855* (New York, 1856).
64. Clement, "Transformation," 60. This figure, which appears in Clement's work as eleven vagrants for every one thousand Philadelphians, could be misleading; population figures for antebellum American cities are skewed toward residents and taxpayers—which vagrants, by and large, were not.
65. Samuel Rezneck, "The Depression of 1819–1822, A Social History," *American Historical Review* 39 (1933–34): 28–34.
66. "An act to prevent the increase of pauperism in this commonwealth," *Laws of the Commonwealth of Pennsylvania* (Philadelphia, 1822), 480; "Annals of Pauperism," *Hazard's Register of Pennsylvania*, vol. 2 (Philadelphia, 1829); Clement, "Philadelphia Welfare Crisis," 151; Blanche D. Coll, "The Baltimore Society for the Prevention of Pauperism, 1820–1822," *American Historical Review* 61, no. 1 (1955): 77–87.
67. "Act providing for the establishment of county poorhouses," *Laws of the State of New York* (Albany, 1824); J. Cummings, *Poor-laws of Massachusetts and New York* (New York: 1895), 95–96.
68. Rothman, *Discovery of the Asylum*, 157.
69. William C. Heffner, "History of Poor Relief Legislation in Pennsylvania, 1682–1913," PhD diss., University of Pennsylvania, 1913.
70. See Cresswell, *The Tramp in America*, for an in-depth discussion of the tramp as a cultural category in the United States.
71. Michael B. Katz studied the tramp population of the 1870s, assessing its demographic makeup using surveys sent to almshouses and police departments across New

York State in 1875. He gleaned information that, when compared with the evidence presented in this study, clearly illustrates the changes that took place among the mobile poor in the first three-quarters of the century. The individuals whom Katz refers to as tramps were almost entirely men, about 94 percent of the roughly 5,000 surveyed and even more predominantly white, almost 98 percent. Over half were under the age of thirty, and just over half had been born outside of the United States. And in Philadelphia during this same time period, data from similar institutions—almshouses and prisons—confirm that men comprised over three-quarters of the vagrant population in the prison, among whom over 95 percent were white (Katz, *Poverty and Policy*, 166-71; Clement, "Transformation," 66).

72. "Northern Liberties Police," *PPL*, 9 June 1838.

73. Katz's data come from a larger sample—roughly 5,000 entries derived from police and almshouse records, covering all of New York State, while my data come from a complete set of 668 entries derived from almshouse records but cover only the city of Philadelphia. Clement's article "The Transformation of the Wandering Poor in Philadelphia" uses incomplete selected data (a sample size of 300) from the Philadelphia Prison that largely affirm Katz's figures for the later 1870s, and confirm my figures for the 1820s. (In 1823, 460/966 vagrants, or 48 percent, were women, and 450/966, or 47 percent, were African Americans) (Clement, "Transformation," 66).

74. In 1823 there were 44 percent women and 51 percent people of color; in 1825, 41 percent women and 53 percent people of color, and in 1826, 46 percent women and 46 percent people of color.

75. "Returns received from the Arch Street Prison," *The Register of Pennsylvania*, vol. 1, ed. S. Hazard (Philadelphia, 1828), 240, 244.

76. Clement, "Transformation," 66.

77. These numbered 470/1,156 women and 299/1,156 people of color (EXPA, 1822-1825, 1826-1831, and 1831-1839; Katz, *Poverty and Policy*, 166-69).

78. EXPA, Public Assistance Folders, Town Clerk's Records, HTCA.

79. Monthly Census Data Calverton Almshouse, Baltimore City and County, MDHS.

80. The necessity of using sparse data sets to make these estimates undoubtedly leaves calculations of their import as tenuous at best, especially in using both populations of relieved paupers and punished criminals to estimate the size of a single population of indigent transients.

81. Kusmer, *Down and Out, on the Road*, 24; Clement, "Transformation," 69-70.

82. Bellevue figures appear in "Penitentiary System," *Niles' Weekly Register*, vol. 19 (Baltimore, 1821), 296. New York population figures appear in C. Gibson and K. Jung, "Historical Census Statistics On Population Totals by Race, 1790 to 1990, and by Hispanic Origin, 1970 to 1990, for Large Cities and Other Urban Places in the United States," Working Paper 76, Population Division, United States Census Bureau, 2005.

83. New Castle County Almshouse, Trustees of the Poor, DPA. In addition to this chronological change, Timothy Lockley notes geographical variation of the racial distribution among public poor relief recipients, as fewer African Americans are recorded as having received aid the farther south an institution was situated (Lockley, *Welfare and Charity in the Antebellum South* [Gainesville: University Press of Florida, 2007], 39).

84. EXPA, HTCA.

85. Steven Lubet, *Fugitive Justice: Runaways, Rescuers, and Slavery on Trial* (Cambridge: Harvard University Press, 2010), 2–21; Sarah N. Roth, "The Politics of the Page: Black Disfranchisement and the Image of the Savage Slave," *Pennsylvania Magazine of History and Biography* 134, no. 3 (2010): 209; Thomas P. Slaughter, *Bloody Dawn: The Christiana Riot and Racial Violence in the Antebellum North* (New York: Oxford University Press, 1991), 40–42.

86. Examinations of Catharine Shaw, Martha Erwin, Harriott Davis, and Elizabeth Sammons, EXPA, 1822–1825.

87. The tendency of widows to choose to reside in cities is discussed in Karin A. Wulf, *Not All Wives: Women of Colonial Philadelphia* (Ithaca, NY: Cornell University Press, 2000), 15–16; and the prevalence of female-headed and widow-headed households in early republic Baltimore is discussed in Rockman, *Scraping By*, 165. Jacqueline Jones describes urban widows as ubiquitous: "As the hubs of colonial and new-nation commerce, the seaport cities beckoned to widows and children left homeless by military conflict, to sons lacking an inheritance of land, and to the "wandering poor" warned out of towns" (Jones, *American Work*, 161).

88. In New Orleans between 1823 and 1824, 36 percent (187/491) of all arrests in the city were of vagrants (see Frink, "Strangers," 167). Women comprised a large proportion of those warned out and removed from Rhode Island towns at the turn of the nineteenth century, according to Ruth Wallis Herndon, "Women of 'No Particular Home,'" in *Women and Freedom in Early America*, ed. Larry D. Eldridge (New York: New York University Press, 1996), 269–89.

89. The descriptions of the conduct of Georgia's female vagrants is nearly identical to northern vagrant women in the same period, from "idle" immorality to unemployment to lack of property (Timothy J. Lockley, "Survival Strategies of Poor White Women in Savannah, 1800–1860," *Journal of the Early Republic* 32 [2012], 428–29).

90. Monthly Census Data, Calverton Almshouse, Baltimore City and County, MDHS.

91. Lyons, *Sex among the Rabble*, 339–40.

92. Mark E. Kann, *Taming Passion for the Public Good: Policing Sex in the Early Republic* (New York: New York University Press, 2013), 88.

93. Manion, *Liberty's Prisoners*; Hahn Rafter, *Partial Justice*, 115; Wood Hill, *Their Sisters' Keepers*, 113–16; Cline Cohen, *Murder of Helen Jewett*, 65–67; Estelle B. Freedman, *Their Sisters' Keepers: Women's Prison Reform in America, 1830–1930* (Ann Arbor: University of Michigan Press, 1984), 10; Kann, *Taming Passion*, 21, 156.

94. Kusmer, *Down and Out, on the Road*, 10–11.

95. Manion, *Liberty's Prisoners*, 2; Kerber, *Women of the Republic*; Jan Lewis, "The Republican Wife: Virtue and Seduction in the Early Republic," *William and Mary Quarterly* 3rd ser, 44, no. 4 (1987): 689–721; Monkkonen, *Walking to Work*, 13–4.

96. Clement, *Welfare and the Poor*, 141.

97. Kathleen D. McCarthy, *American Creed: Philanthropy and the Rise of Civil Society, 1700–1865* (Chicago: University of Chicago Press, 2003), 168; Lori D. Ginzberg, *Women and the Work of Benevolence: Morality, Politics, and Class in the Nineteenth-Century United States* (New Haven: Yale University Press, 1992), 5; Anne Boylan, *Sunday School: The Formation of an American Institution, 1790–1880* (New Haven: Yale University Press, 1988); Stansell, *City of Women*.

98. Alexander, *Render Them Submissive*, 140–41.

99. Clement, *Welfare and the Poor*, 145.
100. Jeremiah Peirsol to Directors of the Poor of Bucks County, 23 September 1829.
101. For more context regarding the Panic of 1837, see Jessica M. Lepler, *The Many Panics of 1837: People, Politics, and the Creation of a Transatlantic Financial Crisis* (Cambridge: Cambridge University Press, 2013); and Alasdair Roberts, *America's First Great Depression: Economic Crisis and Political Disorder after the Panic of 1837* (Ithaca, NY: Cornell University Press, 2013).

Notes to Chapter 3

1. The order to whip and remove Turner was signed by justices of the peace but recorded by the overseers of the poor, evidence of the operative link between the two positions (Order for retransporting and whipping Sarah Turner, Records of the Overseers of the Poor, 1807–1815, Adriance Memorial Library, Poughkeepsie, NY).
2. Mohl, *Poverty in New York*, 58.
3. *A Digest of the Laws of Pennsylvania*, (Philadelphia, 1831); *Laws of the State of New York* (Albany, 1802); "Act for the settlement and relief of the poor," *A Digest of the Laws of New Jersey* (Bridgeton, 1838); "Act for the relief of the poor within the several counties therein mentioned," *The Laws of Maryland* (Baltimore, 1811); "Act to consolidate and amend the laws for the relief of the poor," *Laws of the State of Delaware* (Wilmington, 1829).
4. There is very little historiographical coverage of settlement law outside of English and New England contexts. Some scholars have argued that settlement and removal laws, and early New England warning policies, should not be taken literally as laws promoting the banishment of indigent transients but rather as "disclaimers of responsibility." In Robert Cray's detailed study of New York's pauper populations and poor relief system during this period, removal of paupers is cursorily discussed. The longest work to treat it directly is Herndon's *Unwelcome Americans*. See also Cray, *Paupers and Poor Relief*, 54–56, 76; and Dayton and Salinger, *Robert Love's Warnings*, 64.
5. Poor Law Commission, "United States: New Jersey," *Report from His Majesty's Commissioners for Inquiring into the Administration and Practical Operation of the Poor-laws*, appendix F (London, 1834); Mohl, *Poverty in New York*, 58.
6. S. Rapalje and R. L. Lawrence, *A Dictionary of American and English Law*, vol. 2 (Jersey City, NJ, 1888), 974–75.
7. According to Benjamin Klebaner, "by 1770, every colony except Georgia" regulated the settlement of the poor, and most of these laws contained provisions for removal (Klebaner, *Public Poor Relief*, 485–506).
8. Herndon, *Unwelcome Americans*, 4, 23. The role of overseers of the poor and warning in Rhode Island is also discussed in Gabriel Loiacono, "William Larned, Overseer of the Poor: Power and Precariousness in the Early Republic," *New England Quarterly* 88, no. 2 (2015): 223–51.
9. Debates over warning out and pauper removal have been ongoing in the historiography of poverty and welfare in early America. Geography has played a significant role in determining historians' assessments of the subject: transient paupers in eighteenth century Massachusetts, Cornelia H. Dayton and Sharon V. Salinger argue in *Robert Love's Warnings*, were generally offered welfare via provincial funds, and not vulnerable to forced removal. Meanwhile, the Rhode Island paupers Ruth Wallis Herndon considers in *Unwelcome Americans* were governed by poor relief officials

who removed the nonresident poor with "zeal" in the late eighteenth and early nineteenth centuries. More than a half century ago, Benjamin Klebaner attempted to lay out the legal histories of settlement and removal across these states and much of the eastern seaboard in his study of public poor relief, documenting these legal vicissitudes with precision. But the matter has hardly been settled. Some scholars have claimed that these laws and their implementation should not be taken literally as laws promoting the banishment of indigent transients but rather as "disclaimers of responsibility" enabling poor relief officials to restrict funds to those legally settled in their jurisdictions. Dayton and Salinger argue that "the great bulk of warned strangers" in colonial Boston were actually "welcome to stay." They emphasize that physical removal was viewed as too costly by town officials in this period to be used widely, asserting that, "for most, the warning ritual was a fairly benign and inevitable aspect of sojourning" in the region, and did not often result in actual removal (Dayton and Salinger, *Robert Love's Warnings*, 64; Herndon, *Unwelcome Americans*; Klebaner, *Public Poor Relief*).

10. As Raymond Mohl observed, for most northern states in the late eighteenth century "the statewide welfare structure emphasized legal settlement of the poor rather than aid[,] . . . removal rather than relief" (Mohl, *Poverty in New York*, 64; Joan M. Crouse, *The Homeless Transient in the Great Depression: New York State, 1929–1941* [Albany: State University Press of New York, 1986], 29–30).

11. Montgomery, *Citizen Worker*, 63.

12. "Act providing for the establishment of county poorhouses, *Laws of the State of New York* (Albany, 1824); J. Cummings, *Poor-laws of Massachusetts and New York* (New York, 1895), 95–96.

13. According to one 1827 report, "it does not appear that this district [New York] as any arrangements with other states, relating to the removal of paupers. If it is considered most economical to relieve them, it is done; if otherwise, they are removed, or money is given them, to go elsewhere. Strangers without settlement anywhere, are relieved as in other cases, and got rid of as soon as possible; the right of such persons to claim relief, has never been determined by law" (*Report of a committee appointed by the guardians for the relief and employment of the poor of Philadelphia, etc. to visit the almshouses of Baltimore, New York, Boston, and Salem* [Philadelphia, 1827], HSP, 12).

14. "Act for the settlement and relief of the poor," *A Digest of the Laws of New Jersey* (Bridgeton, 1838); "Act for the relief of the poor within the several counties therein mentioned," *The Laws of Maryland* (Baltimore, 1811); "Act to consolidate and amend the laws for the relief of the poor," *Laws of the State of Delaware* (Wilmington, 1829).

15. *Shapiro v. Thompson* 394 U.S. 618 (1969).

16. Cresswell, *Tramp in America*, 51.

17. Hirota, *Expelling the Poor*, 44–45, 54.

18. *New York v. Miln*, 36 U.S. 11 Pet. 102 (1837), 142–43.

19. Ibid., 142.

20. Ibid., 105.

21. Hirota, *Expelling the Poor*, 83.

22. For a discussion of economically driven definitions of community and the moral definitions of poverty and industriousness, see Katz, *Undeserving Poor* (2013), 5–6; Schmidt, *Free to Work*, 53; Steinfeld, *Invention of Free Labor*, 60; William J. Chambliss, "A Sociological Analysis of the Law of Vagrancy," *Social Problems* 12, no. 1

(1964): 67–77; and Seth Rockman, "Class and the History of Working People," *Journal of the Early Republic* 25, no. 4 (2005): 528.

23. Examinations of Paupers (EXPA), 1822–1825; Letter Book, 1824–1829, Guardians of the Poor (GP), PCA. 13/75 or 17 percent, Non-Resident Register, GP, PCA.

24. The frequency of the practice ebbed and flowed throughout this roughly 150-year period, with the greatest discussion of, and possibly recourse to, the practice in the antebellum years. Removal became a greater concern again during the Great Depression (see Crouse, *The Homeless Transient*, 60–62).

25. "Act for the relief of the poor within the several counties therein mentioned," *The Laws of Maryland* (Baltimore, 1811); "Act to consolidate and amend the laws for the relief of the poor," *Laws of the State of Delaware* (Wilmington, 1829); "Act for the settlement and relief of the poor," *A Digest of the Laws of New Jersey* (Bridgeton, 1838); *A Digest of the Laws of Pennsylvania* (Philadelphia, 1831); *Laws of the State of New York* (Albany, 1802). The practice was ubiquitous in New England as well (Herndon, *Unwelcome Americans;* Melish, *Disowning Slavery;* Dayton and Salinger, *Robert Love's Warnings*).

26. Klebaner, *Public Poor Relief*, 504.

27. *Report of a committee appointed by the guardians for the relief and employment of the poor of Philadelphia, etc. to visit the almshouses of Baltimore, New York, Boston, and Salem* (Philadelphia, 1827), HSP.

28. Mohl, *Poverty in New York*, 59.

29. Adler, "Historical Analysis," 214.

30. Commitment of James Gurum, VAG, 1817–1822.

31. The cases examined here include records of removal for both, and any nonresident who entered an almshouse, whether involuntarily or voluntarily, was, according to law, subject to removal ("Poor," *A Digest of the Laws of Pennsylvania* [Philadelphia, 1818], 525–57; *Laws of the State of New York* [Albany, 1802]).

32. Order of Removal of Elizabeth Colley, 10 May 1827, HTCA.

33. Similar paperwork was used in Rhode Island in the early republic period (Herndon, *Unwelcome Americans*, 8–9).

34. *A manual for the Guardians of the Poor of the city of Philadelphia, the district of Southwark, and township of the Northern Liberties* (Philadelphia, 1817), LCP, 1.

35. *Report of the Committee appointed at a town meeting of the citizens of the city and county of Philadelphia on the 23rd of July 1827 to consider the subject of the pauper system of the city and districts and report remedies for its defects* (Philadelphia, 1827), HSP, 20.

36. Jeremiah Peirsol to George Boyer, Esq., 21 April 1830.

37. Act of 29th March 1803, *Abridgment of the Laws of Pennsylvania* (Philadelphia, 1811).

38. Examination of Mary Miller, EXPA, 1826–1861.

39. Jeremiah Peirsol to George Boyer, Esq., 21 April 1830.

40. Order of Removal of Benjamin Pierson, HTCA.

41. Receipt of Paupers, Transportation Book, Pauper and Poorhouse Records, UCCA.

42. Commitment of Benjamin Smith, VAG, 1817–1822.

43. Mohl, *Poverty in New York*, 61.

44. Examination of Edward Armstrong, EXPA, 1822–1825.

45. Examination of Thomas Cochrane, EXPA, 1831–1839.
46. Examination of Ann Sharp, EXPA, 1826–1831 and Almshouse Weekly Census, 1827–1835.
47. Kerber, *Women of the Republic*, 142.
48. The application of coverture law for indigent married female transients is important to Herndon's analysis in *Unwelcome Americans*, 17, 28–47, 127, 143; Marilyn S. Blackwell, "'The Paupers' Removal": The Politics of Clarina Howard Nichols," *Vermont History* 75, no. 1 (2007): 24; Hendrik Hartog, *Man and Wife in America: A History* (Cambridge: Cambridge University Press, 2000), 128–30.
49. Blackwell, "The Paupers," 4.
50. Ibid., 17.
51. Examination of Elizabeth Lee, EXPA, 1826–1831.
52. Jeremiah Peirsol to Directors of Poor of Pittsburgh, 18 January 1830.
53. Examination of Timothy Gribbins, EXPA, 1822–1825.
54. Examination of James Ray, EXPA, 1836–1831.
55. Examinations of John Steele, EXPA, 1831–1839 and 1826–1831.
56. Examination of Henry McCluer, EXPA, 1822–1825.
57. W. Blockton for J. Peirsol to James Bright, Esq., 27 November 1829.
58. *Overseers of the Poor of South Brunswick v. Overseers of the Poor of East Windsor*, November Term, 1824, 8NJL.64.
59. Melish argues that for free African Americans during the years of gradual emancipation, "legal settlement" was "either an empty concept or a threatening one." Herndon also looks at similar cases for early Rhode Island (Melish, *Disowning Slavery*, 117; Herndon, *Unwelcome Americans*, 57).
60. *The Second Annual Report of the Managers of the Society for the Prevention of Pauperism in the City of New-York* (New York, 1820), 60–61; J. A. Dunlap, *The New-York Justice* (New York, 1815), 338–43; *The New-York City-hall Recorder*, ed. D. Rogers (New York, 1819), 44.
61. *Second Annual Report*, 61.
62. Parker, "From Poor Law to Immigration Law," 73.
63. *A New Conductor Generalis* (Albany, 1819). This book served as a manual that elaborated upon applicable laws to provide officials with guidance in carrying out their duties.
64. Ibid., 367–88.
65. T. F. Gordon, *The History of New Jersey* (Trenton, NJ, 1834), 59–60.
66. Receipt of Paupers, Transportation Book, Pauper and Poorhouse Records, UCCA.
67. *Laws of the State of New York*, 1821.
68. Conviction of Cornelius Ylverston, UCCA.
69. Conviction of Joseph Ruland, UCCA.
70. "Report of the Secretary of State in 1824 on the Relief and Settlement of the Poor," *Journal of the Assembly of the State of New-York at their 47th Session* (Albany, 1824), 387–90. For a more detailed discussion of the significance of the Yates report in broader debates about poor relief and welfare provision, see Katz, *In the Shadow of the Poorhouse*, 18–22.
71. "Report of the Secretary of State," 387–90.
72. Ibid., 393–94.

73. Ibid.
74. Ibid., 395.
75. Ibid., 387.
76. Klebaner, *Public Poor Relief*, 502–3; Mohl, *Poverty in New York*, 62–64, 215; Schmidt, *Free to Work*, 69.
77. Sixty-nine out of 275 pauper examinations (or 25 percent) taken between 1822 and 1825 in the Philadelphia Almshouse had a note of "removed" listed below their record (EXPA, 1822–1825; Letter Book, 1824–1829, Guardians of the Poor [GP], PCA). Records are spotty after 1825 until the late 1830s, but when the number of removals began to be tracked again around 1838, the percentage of paupers being removed was only slightly lower, at just shy of one-fifth of nonresident paupers (13/75 or 17 percent, Non-Resident Register, GP, PCA).
78. Jeremiah Peirsol to Directors of the Poor of Bucks County, 23 September, 1829.
79. "City Police—John Swift Mayor," *PPL*, 19 December 1837.
80. *Journal of the Proceedings of the Legislative Council of the State of New-Jersey* (Somerville, NJ, 1836).
81. D. Rogers, *The New-York City-Hall Recorder for the Year 1819* (New York, 1819), 43–44.
82. Ibid., 44–45.
83. Ibid., 45.
84. Ibid., 43–45.
85. Examination of Jacob Merkel, EXPA, 1826–1831.
86. Examinations of Jacob Merkel, EXPA, 1831–1839.
87. Ibid.
88. David P. Delaney, "Laws of Motion and Immobilization: Bodies, Figures and the Politics of Mobility," paper presented at the Mobilities Conference, Gregynog, Newtown, Wales, 1999, p. 3, cited in Cresswell, *On the Move*, 151.
89. EXPA, 1822–1825 and Letter Book, 1824–1829, GPP.
90. Statement of David S. Taylor, Letter Book, GPP.
91. Jeremiah Peirsol to Directors of the Poor for Dauphin County, 25 July 1826, Letter Book, GPP.
92. Ibid.
93. Jeremiah Peirsol to Peter Claason, Esq., 19 June 1828.
94. Jeremiah Peirsol to Overseers of the Poor of Washington Township, 22 September 1831.
95. When Karl Marx defined the lumpenproletariat in 1852, he referred to existing European populations comprised of "vagabonds, discharged soldiers, discharged jailbirds . . . ragpickers, beggars." Many of these terms are obviously derogatory but are apt in light of the contemporary language (Marx, *The Eighteenth Brumaire of Louis Bonaparte* [New York: International, 1987], 75).
96. Katz, *Poverty and Policy*, 163.
97. Bryan Wagner, *Disturbing the Peace: Black Culture and Police Power after Slavery* (Cambridge: Harvard University Press, 2009), Joan Crouse has argued the same for approaching the study of homelessness during the Great Depression, stating that an "almost indiscriminate classification of a diverse aggregate of individuals' were included under the category of vagrancy during that period (see Crouse, *The Homeless Transient*, 12; and Peter Linebaugh and Marcus Rediker, *The Many-Headed Hydra*:

Sailors, Slaves, Commoners, and the Hidden History of the Revolutionary Atlantic [Boston: Basic, 2000], 332, 40).

98. Manion, *Liberty's Prisoners*, 181 and, cited within, "Female Convicts and the Efforts of Females for Their Relief and Reformation," *Pennsylvania Journal of Prison Discipline and Philanthropy* 1, no. 2 (1845): 112.

99. Jeremiah Peirsol to Directors of Poor of Chester Co., 24 December 1829, Letter Book, GPP.

100. Examination of Henrietta Johnston, EXPA, 1826–1831.

101. Jeremiah Peirsol to Overseers of the Poor of Carlisle, Penna., 18 December 1826.

102. Jeremiah Peirsol to Directors of Poor of Carlisle, Penna, 21 December 1826; The Petition of Peter Dougherty, Philadelphia Court of Common Pleas Insolvency Records, PCA.

103. Samuel Fisher to Directors of the Poor of Lancaster County, 21 December 1834, Letter Book, GPP. For definition and context of the Gradual Abolition Act of 1780, see Nash, *Forging Freedom*, 60–63.

104. Melish, *Disowning Slavery*, 117.

105. Ibid., 133. As James Gigantino has documented, "the ejections" of emancipated blacks, usually to districts where they had been held as slaves, via the legal channels of pauper removal have been viewed by scholars of abolition and emancipation as a procedure that "became routine across the North" as a means to "limit [whites'] exposure to abolition's products." While this likely did play a role, it is important to place these efforts within the larger system of settlement and poor relief, which had controlled the residency, welfare provision, and mobility of the poor from the late eighteenth throughout the nineteenth century. Still, former slaves within this system almost certainly experienced a more prejudiced version of poor relief administration. In many cases, welfare distribution restrictions were used to hold free but indigent blacks and their children in bondage. These poor laws functioned as vehicles to maintain the statuses of slavery even into the years of legal abolition (Gigantino, *The Ragged Road to Abolition: Slavery and Freedom in New Jersey, 1775–1865* [Philadelphia: University of Pennsylvania Press, 2014], 135–36).

106. Herndon, *Unwelcome Americans*, 57; Manion, *Liberty's Prisoners*, 15–27.

107. Hirota, *Expelling the Poor*, 44.

Notes to Chapter 4

1. As Ousmane Power-Greene has argued, "Blacks in Philadelphia shared . . . interest in Haitian emigration, and in July 1824, some of them met to consider President Jean-Pierre Boyer's invitation to resettle in the nascent black republic." Many opposed forced migration to Africa but supported the potential of "the Haitian emigration plan" (Power-Greene, *Against Wind and Tide: The African American Struggle Against the Colonization Movement* [New York: New York University Press, 2014], 28; Examination of James Huston, EXPA, 1826–1831). Huston was considered "sick and unable to be removed" (Jer. Peirsol to Directors of the Poor of Delaware Co., Penna, 13 December 1826).

2. Cultural and social historians agree that, as Jean Lee Cole asserts, "the notion of mobility infused the African American consciousness" in the first half of the

nineteenth century (Cole, "Theresa and Blake: Mobility and Resistance in Antebellum African American Serialized Fiction," *Callaloo* 34, no. 1 [2011]: 158–59).

3. Kelly Kennington argues that African American legal culture reflects the importance of "movement for determining personal status" (Kennington, "Law, Geography, and Mobility: Suing for Freedom in Antebellum St. Louis," *Journal of Southern History* 80, no. 3 [2014]: 578, 595, 603).

4. Stephanie M. H. Camp, "The Pleasures of Resistance: Enslaved Women and Body Politics in the Plantation South, 1830–1861," *Journal of Southern History* 68, no. 3 (2002): 534.

5. Cole, "Theresa and Blake," 165. African Americans throughout the nation were immured in "a system of law that held their physical movements through the city as latently criminal and their presence in public spaces intrinsically suspicious." One of the reasons for whites' fears of black mobility lay in uprisings and rumors of uprisings, was because they "crystallized white . . . fears of unregulated black mobility" (Robert Gamble, "African Americans, Mobility, and the Law," *The Junto: A Group Blog in Early American History*, 11 May 2015, https://earlyamericanists.com).

6. Camp, "Pleasures of Resistance," 538.

7. As Edlie Wong notes, under slavery, "mobility and stasis emerge[d] as two powerfully intertwined forces" for African Americans (Wong, *Neither Fugitive nor Free: Atlantic Slavery, Freedom Suits, and the Legal Culture of Travel* [New York: New York University Press, 2009], 10). Stasis was an essential and often elusive goal for many in the antebellum lower classes, especially African Americans, in that it lent itself to greater economic independence. But local laws applied to residents still hindered this activity.

8. Woodson, *A Century*, 120. See also Robert L. Hall, *Making a Living: The Work Experience of African Americans in New England: Selected Readings* (Boston: New England Foundation for the Humanities, 1995), 309; and Wong, *Neither Fugitive*, 10.

9. Hall, *Making a Living*, 309.

10. J. Scattergood, *An antidote to popular frenzy, particularly to the present rage for the abolition of the slave-trade* (London, 1792), 24.

11. Daniel M. Johnson and Rex R. Campbell, *Black Migration in America: A Social Demographic History* (Durham: Duke University Press, 1981).

12. Ellen D. Katz, "African-American Freedom in Antebellum Cumberland County, Virginia—Freedom: Personal Liberty and Private Law," *Chicago-Kent Law Review* 70, no. 3 (1995): 944. In the Deep South, however, vagrancy appears to have been of less concern as a possible outcome for both manumission and migration of former slaves. Laws regulating manumission in the South focused on age (in consideration of a slave's potential remainder of usefulness to the owner) and, in antebellum New Orleans, "honest conduct." A slaveholder could not manumit a slave, nor could an enslaved person purchase their own freedom, if they had attempted to run away or had committed any other crime. While manumission was possible in Louisiana and other southern states, the presence of and migration by free blacks was limited by requirements for free black migrants and recently emancipated slaves to leave the state or face penal punishments (see Judith K. Schafer, *Becoming Free, Remaining Free: Manumission and Enslavement in New Orleans, 1846–1862* [Baton Rouge: Louisiana State University, 2003], 1–6).

13. As Paul Finkelman has noted, this law was the result of "a stereotyped belief that free blacks and fugitive slaves were less capable than whites of supporting themselves" (Finkelman, "Rehearsal for Reconstruction," 8–9). As Sarah Gronningsater explains, lawmakers, particularly in New York, "continued to associate . . . freed slaves with poverty and public expense" (Gronningsater, "Arc of Abolition").

14. Extended definitions of this term and arguments found in Ira Berlin, *The Long Emancipation: The Demise of Slavery in the United States* (Cambridge: Harvard University Press, 2015).

15. Carter G. Woodson, *A Century of Negro Migration* (New York, 1918), 120. His aim was to directly challenge that blacks were somehow inherently migratory, and that mobility, for them, was a product of racial identity.

16. As Stephen Germic has explained: "The black or immigrant is essentially condemned to lower-class status while at the same time class as a social category becomes imperceptible and race obvious. Class difference is reinforced by racial invention" (Germic, *American Green: Class, Crisis, and the Deployment of Nature in Central Park, Yosemite, and Yellowstone* [New York: Lexington, 2001], 35).

17. This is especially clear in Joanne Pope Melish's example from Providence, Rhode Island, where, in the first decades of the nineteenth century, the town council forced to enter into labor contracts "blacks of all descriptions" as well as "transient white people in poor circumstances" against their will (Melish, *Disowning Slavery*, 85–86).

18. The independent, voluntary movement of individuals whose labor is of necessity to the owners of the means of production, in these cases, is seen to have instigated, in response, what Christian DeVito has referred to as the "coerced spatial mobilization of labor" (DeVito, "Labor Flexibility and Labor Precariousness as Conceptual Tools for the Historical Study of the Interactions among Labor Relations," in *On the Road to Global Labor History* [Leiden: Brill, 2016]).

19. This term, loosely defined as a description of or in relation to a particular locality, adroitly illustrates the contextual nature of vagrancy convictions, where the visual characteristics and geographical location of an individual contributed significantly to their status as policed (Nicolazzo, "Vagrant Figures," 94).

20. Ira Berlin, "Southern Free People of Color in the Age of William Johnson," *Southern Quarterly* 43, no. 2 (2006): 10; Emily West, *Family or Freedom: People of Color in the Antebellum South* (Lexington: University Press of Kentucky, 2012), 4–5; Edwards, "The Problem of Dependency," 331–32.

21. Just as historians have been arguing that the study of slavery and of poverty should be conducted in tandem, so should the mobility that was tied up with both—whether as prohibited, utilized, or punished (see Edmund S. Morgan, *American Slavery, American Freedom: The Ordeal of Colonial Virginia* [New York: Norton, 1975], 341; Morgan, "Slaves and Poverty," 93–131; Rockman, *Scraping By*; Hardesty, *Unfreedom*, 52–54; and Merritt, *Masterless Men*). In no way do these commonalities suggest that race was incidental to an individual's status as an indigent transient. Rather, they suggest ways in which the challenges of poverty was exacerbated by racialized laws for African Americans, and that more can be learned about the experiences of both poor African Americans as well as poor white people in this period by considering these populations in tandem.

22. Roberta Ann Johnson, "African Americans and Homelessness: Moving through History," *Journal of Black Studies* 40, no. 4 (2010): 583–605.

23. Ibid., 584.

24. Ibid.; Kim Hopper and N. Milburn, "Homelessness among African Americans: A Historical and Contemporary Perspective," *Homelessness in America*, ed. J. Bauhmohl (Phoenix, AZ: Sage, 1996), 124.

25. Johnson, "African Americans and Homelessness," 584–85.

26. David Roediger, *Seizing Freedom: Slave Emancipation and Liberty for All* (London: Verso, 2014), 44–45.

27. John Hope Franklin and Loren Schweninger, *Runaway Slaves: Rebels on the Plantation* (New York: Oxford University Press, 1999), 282.

28. Examination of Samuel Burton, EXPA, 1826–1831.

29. Jeremiah Peirsol to Directors of the Poor of Lancaster County, 7 October 1829.

30. As Gary B. Nash notes, "of all migrant groups entering the city, blacks were the most vulnerable to arrest for vagrancy because Philadelphia was the destination of many runaway slaves, and dark skin gained one no favors in an era of increasing hostility toward blacks" (Nash, *Forging Freedom*, 157).

31. VAG, 1822–1827; and EXPA, 1822–1831; "Report on Punishments and Prison Discipline," *Register of Pennsylvania*, 19 April 1828, 1, no. 16 (Philadelphia, 1828), 244.

32. Ibid.

33. VAG, 1809–1836.

34. Examination of Samuel Reason, EXPA, 1826–1831.

35. "Law to prevent the increase in pauperism in the Commonwealth," *Laws of the Commonwealth of Pennsylvania* (Philadelphia, 1822), 480.

36. "Presentment of the Grand Inquest for the City of Lancaster," *Lancaster (PA) Journal*, 3 September 1819.

37. Deborah Gray White and Marisa Fuentes, *Scarlet and Black: Slavery and Dispossession in Rutgers History* (New Brunswick, NJ: Rutgers University Press, 2016), 78.

38. Wagner, *Disturbing the Peace*, 37.

39. As Michael C. Cohen notes, Whittier's "vagrant peddler" in his essay "Yankee Gypsies" is "pure 'outside' and as such, "destabilizes the insularity of the home" (Cohen, *The Social Lives of Poems in Nineteenth-Century America* [Philadelphia: University of Pennsylvania Press, 2015], 38, 17–19; Quentin Bailey, *Wordsworth's Vagrants: Police, Prisons, and Poetry in the 1790s* [Farnham: Routledge, 2011], 154–59).

40. Peter Reed, *Rogue Performances: Staging the Underclasses in Early American Theatre Culture* (New York: Palgrave, 2009), 147.

41. Susan M. Schweik, *The Ugly Laws: Disability in Public* (New York: New York University Press, 2010), 185–86.

42. William T. Lahmon Jr., *Jump Jim Crow: Lost Plays, Lyrics, and Street Prose of the First Atlantic Popular Culture* (Cambridge: Harvard University Press, 2003), 16.

43. Wagner, *Disturbing the Peace*, 37.

44. As Jen Manion argues, "vagrancy laws provided the legal justification for the imprisonment of runaways" (Manion, *Liberty's Prisoners*, 25).

45. Ira Berlin, "Southern Free People of Color in the Age of William Johnson," *Southern Quarterly* 43, no. 2 (2006): 10; Edwards, "The Problem of Dependency," 331–32.

46. *Prigg v. Pennsylvania*, 41 U.S. 539 (1842).

47. *The Monthly Law Reporter*, ed. P. W. Chandler, vol. 9, Boston, 1847, 369; John R. Mulkern, *The Know-Nothing Party in Massachusetts: The Rise and Fall of a People's Movement* (Boston: Northeastern University Press, 1990), 103.

48. The assertions made in *Miln* and *Prigg* were upheld again, expressly with reference to removal on the grounds of the prevention of "oppression" by vagabonds and paupers, in relation to fugitive slaves, in *Moore v. People of the State of Illinois* 55 U.S. 13 (1852).

49. I am indebted to Kirsten Wood for raising this important question while offering comment for a panel at the 2015 Society for Historians of the Early American Republic annual meeting.

50. Wagner, *Disturbing the Peace*, 38.

51. Ibid., 75.

52. *Proceedings and Debates of the Convention of the Commonwealth of Pennsylvania*, vol. 2 (Harrisburg, 1838), 519.

53. John Hope Franklin has written extensively about the experiences of fugitive slaves on the road, summing it up as "a harsh and precarious existence, living from day to day, hiding and running, fearful of discovery and capture, always worried about food and shelter" (Franklin and Schweninger, *Runaway Slaves*, 282).

54. Examination of Hannah Thompson, EXPA, 1826–1831.

55. EXPA, 1822–1844.

56. Examination of Venus McClintock, EXPA, 1826–1831.

57. Examination of William Johnson, EXPA, 1822–1825.

58. Examination of Samuel Scott, EXPA, 1826–1831.

59. Examination of Alfred Kennedy, EXPA, 1826–1831.

60. "Items," *PI*, 18 November 1831.

61. These reflect what Teresa Zackodnik has described as the "imagined, material, represented, and philosophical spaces and trajectories" that both groups occupied and employed (Zackodnik, "Indigenous and Black Geographies in Letters to the Editor," *Common-Place: The Journal of American Life* 15, no. 2 [2015]: 5).

62. Examination of Ebenezer Widdington, EXPA, 1831–1839.

63. Spellings of these individuals' names do vary but not beyond recognition; I have chosen to use the spelling to which the younger of the men signed his mark under examination at the Philadelphia Almshouse, though other variations include Whittington and Ebinezar. The Philadelphia Almshouse records for Widdington Jr. bear the "B." that was used to notate that officials viewed the individual in question as Black.

64. Admission and Discharge Records, 1822–1832, New Castle County, Trustees of the Poor, DPA.

65. Examination of Ebenezer Widdington.

66. Examination of John Joseph, Public Assistance Folders, HTCA.

67. Conviction of Isaac Norman, Convictions, UCCA.

68. Regarding distinctions between indentured servitude and apprenticeship, Karin Zipf notes that the two "shared a few characteristics, but otherwise . . . were really quite different." Individuals in both circumstances were unpaid laborers who received temporary physical provisions such as "food, clothing, and shelter." Both involved varying degrees of freedom and unfreedom, depending on the age, class, and race of the laborer. Individuals in both categories often entered contracts voluntarily

and others involuntarily. In general, for both, court-ordered arrangements tended to be involuntary. Both also frequently ended with the laborer absconding from service (Zipf, *Labor of Innocents: Forced Apprenticeship in North Carolina, 1715—1919* [Baton Rouge: Louisiana State University Press, 2005], 10–11).

69. Jen Manion notes that "vagrancy records themselves did not distinguish clearly between servant and slave when recording instances of runaways" and that "the ambiguity of status in the records challenges us to think more carefully not only about the blurred boundaries between the two but also about the limits of freedom more broadly for both groups" (Manion, *Liberty's Prisoners*, 26).

70. The nature of indentured servitude in this period has been called into question by historians, with some debate over its prevalence in the labor market after the late eighteenth century See Abbott E. Smith, *Colonists in Bondage: White Servitude and Convict Labor in America, 1607–1776* (Chapel Hill: University of North Carolina Press, 1947); Jared Ross Hardesty, *Unfreedom: Slavery and Dependence in Eighteenth-Century Boston* (New York: New York University Press, 2016); David W. Galenson, "Labor Market Behavior in Colonial America: Servitude, Slavery, and Free Labor," in *Markets in History: Economic Studies of the Past*, ed. Galenson (Cambridge: Cambridge University Press, 1989), 67, in which Galenson argues that "indentured servitude dwindled to quantitative insignificance in the late eighteenth and early nineteenth centuries."

71. Robert J. Steinfeld notes that while immigrant indentures remained legal in the 1810s, there was an abrupt drop-off in the number of redemptioners arriving in the United States during and after the 1820s (Steinfeld, *The Invention of Free Labor: The Employment Relation in English and American Law and Culture, 1350-1870* [Chapel Hill: University of North Carolina Press, 1991], 164).

72. Kusmer, *Down and Out, on the Road*, 15–16.

73. EXPA, 1822–1831, PCA. These figures are distinct from those who report having been an apprentice, which were recorded separately.

74. Settlement examinations taken from paupers in Huntington, New York (1811–1841), HTCA.

75. Among the 191 documented formerly indentured transients examined in the Philadelphia Almshouse between 1822 and 1831, only eleven were born outside of the United States (EXPA).

76. Examination of Jonathan Smith, EXPA, 1831–1839.

77. Laws allowing for this were in effect at least in New Jersey and Washington, DC, applicable to all vagrants, and in Pennsylvania and New York, applicable at least to vagrants held in almshouses if not also ones held in prisons ("Act providing for the binding out. . . . the children of drunkards, vagrants, and paupers," *Laws of the Corporation of the City of Washington* (Washington, DC, 1833); L. Q. C. Elmer, *Practical Forms of Proceedings Under the Laws of New Jersey* [Bridgeton, 1839], 411).

78. Examination of Robert Caldwell, EXPA, 1826–1831.

79. Examination of James Nixon, EXPA, 1826–1831.

80. For a solid basis on the frequency of the binding out of pauper children in early America, see John E. Murray and Ruth Wallis Herndon, "Markets for Children in Early America: A Political Economy of Pauper Apprenticeship," *Journal of Economic History* 62, no. 2 (2002): 356–82, wherein the authors describe the involuntary bondage of poor children as a "widespread phenomenon in early America" (357); and Farley

Grubb, "Babes in Bondage? Debt Shifting by German Immigrants in Early America," *Journal of Interdisciplinary Studies* 37 (2006): 1–34; Sarah L. H. Gronningsater, "Born Free in the Master's House: Children and Gradual Emancipation in the Early American North," *Child Slavery before and after Emancipation: An Argument for Child-Centered Slavery Studies* (New York: Cambridge University Press, 2017). Thousands of children across the nation were bound out in this fashion, from Massachusetts to South Carolina and beyond.

81. Examination of William Lynch, EXPA, 1826–1831.

82. Examination of Mary Ann Jane McMahon, EXPA, 1826–1831.

83. Examination of William Lytle, EXPA, 1826–1831.

84. Examination of Rebecca Benson, EXPA, 1822–1825; New Castle County Almshouse Admissions and Discharge Register, 1829, DPA.

85. Examination of Phoebe Stull, EXPA, 1822–1825.

86. They lived under, as Linda Kerber describes, strict "constraints about where they lived, what was available for them to eat and wear, and what they might do during their limited leisure time" (Kerber, *No Constitutional Right*, 53).

87. "40 Dollars Reward," *Lancaster (PA) Journal*, 4 July 1817.

88. S. Nicolazzo, "'A Crosscultural Vagabondage': Postcolonial Theories of Diaspora and Colonial Theories of Labor," paper presented at Scenes of Labor and Instruction Panel, Intersections Conference, University of Pennsylvania, 2011, p. 6.

89. Barbara J. Fields, *Slavery and Freedom on the Middle Ground: Maryland during the Nineteenth Century* (New Haven: Yale University Press, 1985), 35; Patience Essah, *A House Divided: Slavery and Emancipation in Delaware, 1638–1865* (Charlottesville: University of Virginia Press, 1996), 111.

90. W. W. Hening, *The New Virginia Justice* (Richmond, 1810), 550.

91. Fields, *Slavery and Freedom*, 63–89; Essah, *House Divided*, 109–11.

92. Jones, *American Work*, 202.

93. Ibid., 110–11.

94. J. R. Brackett, *The Negro in Maryland: A Study of the Institution of Slavery*, vol. 6 (Baltimore, 1889), 219.

95. Joseph A. Ranney, *In the Wake of Slavery: Civil War, Civil Rights, and the Reconstruction of Southern Law* (Westport, CT: Greenwood, 2006), 17.

96. As Linda Kerber explains, "for African Americans . . . the legacy of slavery merged with the legacy of medieval England to create a heightened obligation to appear to be working, a special vulnerability to punishment as vagrants, even when they were working" (Kerber, *No Constitutional Right*, 55).

97. "Reflections on the Census of 1840," *Southern Literary Messenger*, vol. 9 (Richmond, VA, 1843), 346–47.

98. *Journal of the House of Representatives of the Commonwealth of Pennsylvania*, 1836–37, 1:770.

99. Carol E. Hoffecker, *Democracy in Delaware: The Story of the First State's General Assembly* (Wilmington, DE: Cedar Tree, 2004), 102–3.

100. Records of the General Assembly, Legislative Papers, Petition 10383501, 31 January 1825 and Petitions 10384101–10384111, Record Group 1111, DPA.

101. According to Stephen Germic, in the antebellum North, "prosperity and community" were seen as "attributes of whiteness," while "Irishness" and "blackness" were

"only perceived according to images of poverty, including filth and transience" (Germic, *American Green*, 35; DePastino, *Citizen Hobo*, 15).

102. Records of the General Assembly, Legislative Papers, Petition 10383501, 31 January 1825 and Petitions 10384101–10384111, Record Group 1111, DPA.

103. Records of the General Assembly, Legislative Papers, Petition 10384503, 15 February 1845. Record Group 1111, DPA.

104. Roediger, *Seizing Freedom*, 28.

105. Ranney, *In the Wake of Slavery*, 17.

106. For a few examples, see Lubet, *Fugitive Justice*; Roth, "The Politics of the Page"; and Slaughter, *Bloody Dawn*.

107. Thomas Jefferson and James Madison supported gradual manumission via the colonization of African Americans in "free" western territory ("Madison, James, and African Americans," in *Encyclopedia of African American History, 1619–1895: From the Colonial Period to the Age of Frederick Douglass*, ed. Paul Finkelman [New York: Oxford University Press, 2006], 317).

108. Christy Clark-Pujara, *Dark Work: The Business of Slavery in Rhode Island* (New York: New York University Press, 2016), 116–21.

109. Burin, *Peculiar Solution*, 19.

110. Tomek, *Colonization*, 10, 137, 176–78.

111. *Township of Chatham vs. Executors of Samuel Canfield*, Supreme Court of Judicature of New Jersey, September Term, 1824; 8 N.J.L. 52.

112. "An Act Concerning Slaves and Servants," *Laws of the State of New York passed at the Session of the Legislature held in the year 1801* (Albany, 1887).

113. See Gronningsater, "Arc of Abolition."

114. "An act relating to the support and employment of the poor, 1836," *A Digest of the Laws of Pennsylvania* (Philadelphia, 1837), 823–24.

115. Kerber, *No Constitutional Right*, 52.

116. Ibid., 52, citing Steinfeld, *Invention of Free Labor*.

117. Frederick Douglass, "The Work of the Future," *Douglass' Monthly*, November 1862, cited in Melish, *Disowning Slavery*, 86. Regarding connections between manumission and the poor law, see Gronningsater, "Arc of Abolition."

118. James Gigantino has used manumission records in his discussion of free blacks' economic opportunities in antebellum New York and New Jersey, but without explicit reference to the broader poor law origins of legal proceedings like these (see Gigantino, *Ragged Road to Abolition*). In Gloucester County, New Jersey, 39 certificates of slave manumission, filed between 1788 and 1825, are extant. For Hunterdon County, New Jersey, extant records indicate that more than 500 slaves were manumitted via such certificates from the years between 1787 and 1856. For the town of Warwick in Orange County, New York, the records of 103 slave manumissions through the overseers of the poor are extant, covering the years between 1799 and 1827 (Certificates of Manumission, Clerk's Office of Gloucester County, New Jersey. Manumissions of Slaves, 1788–1826, Clerk's Office Records, Hunterdon County, 1977.013, 2005.008, New Jersey State Archives. Slave Births and Manumissions, Town of Warwick, Historical Society of the Town of Warwick, NY).

119. Certificate of Manumission of Beth Seigers and Jim Hall, 1824, Certificates of Manumission, Clerk's Office of Gloucester County, New Jersey.

120. New Jersey Society for Promoting the Abolition of Slavery, *The Constitution of the New Jersey Society, for Promoting the Abolition of Slavery* (Burlington, NJ, 1793), 10-11; H. S. Cooley, *A Study of Slavery in New Jersey* (Baltimore, 1896), 457.

121. Certificate of Manumission of Phillis Wheeler, 1825, Slave Births and Manumissions, Historical Society of the Town of Warwick, NY.

122. "An Act Concerning Slaves and Servants," *Laws of the State of New York* (1801).

123. Gigantino, *Ragged Road to Abolition*, 136.

124. Overseers of the Poor of Upper Freehold v. Overseers of the Poor of Hillsborough, *Reports of Cases Determined in the Supreme Court of Judicature of the State of New Jersey*, vol. 13 (Jersey City, 1833), 90; 13 N.J.L. 289.

125. Overseers of the Poor of Upper Freehold; 13 N.J.L. 289

126. Examination of Thomas Tredwell, HTCA.

127. Alan J. Northrup, *Slavery in New York: A Historical Sketch* (New York, 1900), 291.

128. Petition of Benjamin Morgan to Manumit a Female Slave, 24 May 1809, Court of General Sessions, WCA.

129. Examinations for Settlement, Public Assistance Folders, HTCA.

130. Downs, *Sick from Freedom*, 168-69.

131. In colonial Zanzibar at the turn of the twentieth century, historians have noted the significance of the effect upon the process of emancipation of the inclusion in the "abolition decree" of a requirement "that any slave freed under its provisions "shall be bound on pain of being declared a vagrant, to show that he possesses a regular domicile and means of subsistence" (see Frederick Cooper, "Contracts, Crime, and Agrarian Conflict: From Slave to Wage Labor on the East African Coast," in *Labor, Law, and Crime: An Historical Perspective*, ed. Francis Snyder and Douglas Hay [London: Tavistock, 1987], 236).

132. West, *Family or Freedom*, 60-61.

Notes to Chapter 5

1. Cassey Newman, Habeas 1841 F009, LCHS.

2. Edwards has recorded this in North and South Carolina (Edwards, "The Problem of Dependency," 328).

3. Sarah Thomas, Habeas 1841 F007, LCHS; Elizabeth Thomas, Habeas 1841 F008, LCHS.

4. Ibid.

5. This was a result of what some scholars, including James Schmidt, have argued, from an increasingly "contractual vision of free labor" (Schmidt, *Free to Work*, 53).

6. For similar usage of vagrancy laws in southern states, see Edwards, "The Problem of Dependency," 313-40. See also Steinfeld, *Invention of Free Labor*, 60. Schmidt argues that this communal policing was carried out via "class-based, paternalist" efforts at "reformation" of the lower classes, whose disorderliness was legally and visually connected with their poverty. The result, then, for vagrants, was that they were rendered "legal children, stripped of their full rights as members of the Jacksonian polity" (Schmidt, *Free to Work*, 67).

7. Nayan Shah has emphasized "strangerhood" as "a crucial ingredient" for considering how transients and vagrants were perceived in public spaces, noting that "vagrancy policing ratcheted up the vulnerability of the poorest and most transient

members of society and thwarted their ability to use public space without police harassment and interference" (Shah, *Stranger Intimacy: Contesting Race, Sexuality and the Law in the North American West* [Oakland: University of California Press, 2012], e-book, chap. 2; Rothman, *Discovery of the Asylum*, 20).

8. Manion, *Liberty's Prisoners*, 66.

9. Rao, "Posse Comitatus," 1.

10. "Laws of the District of Columbia," *Congressional Series of United States Public Documents*, vol. 231 (Washington, DC, 1832), 283.

11. Essah, *House Divided*, 116.

12. VAG, 1823, 1832.

13. Steinberg, *Transformation*, 276.

14. Suzanne M. Spencer-Wood, "Feminist Theoretical Perspectives on the Archaeology of Poverty: Gendering Institutional Lifeways in the Northeastern United States from the Eighteenth Century through the Nineteenth Century," *Historical Archaeology* 44, no. 4 (2010): 115–16. For detailed discussion of the relationship between prostitution and vagrancy, see Wood Hill, *Their Sisters' Keepers*; Cline Cohen, *The Murder of Helen Jewett*; and Hahn Rafter, *Partial Justice*.

15. Jane Dabel, *A Respectable Woman: The Public Roles of African American Women in 19th-Century New York* (New York: New York University Press, 2008), 99.

16. "City Police," *PPL*, 19 December 1837.

17. "The County Prison," *PPL*, 21 August 1838.

18. Occasionally it was guardians of the poor who reported indigent transients to the watchmen, as opposed to the other way around. When George Shealds was arrested for vagrancy on 6 November 1819, he was "convicted on oath of William Brook—one of the Overseers of the Poor" of Blockley for being a disorderly person and vagrant, with "no business to support himself." Some misjudgment may have occurred in determining Shealds's neediness or appropriateness for sentencing to the prison rather than the almshouse, as he must have been ill: he died in prison the next day (Commitment of George Shealds, VAG, 1817–1822).

19. *First Annual Report of the New York Association for the Improvement of the Condition of the Poor: Nos. 1–10, 1845–1853)*, 13–17. Some scholars, including Steinberg, have taken the position that vagrancy law in both theory and practice served as a safety net for the homeless and that "cases of common vagrancy reflected the main utility and original intent of the law as a device for providing temporary shelter." Vagrants did, on occasion, request imprisonment as a means of obtaining food and shelter, a practice that became more common in the later nineteenth century as police shelters proliferated. As early as the 1820s, watchmen's records from New York City note individuals who apparently told watchmen that they "wish[ed] to be sent to the penitentiary," like John Ward, arrested on 8 November 1825 as a vagrant, "sick, no means of support," asking "to be sent to the penitentiary"; he was given six months. William Hurley, too, just a few days before Christmas that year, was booked as a vagrant with "no means of support" and "a sore leg," because he "wish[ed] to be sent to the penitentiary." But in the wider archive of vagrancy for the early nineteenth century, Steinberg's assertion that humanitarian efforts were dominant prompts and factors in the implementation of these laws is not supported. See Steinberg, *Transformation*, 123–25; Cresswell, *Tramp in America*; and Kusmer, *Down and Out, On the Road* for more detailed discussion of later nineteenth-century police station housing

for vagrants and tramps. John Ward and William Hurley, 1825, Watchmen's Returns, NYCM.

20. Michael Meranze, *Laboratories of Virtue: Punishment, Revolution, and Authority in Philadelphia, 1760–1835* (Chapel Hill: University of North Carolina Press, 1996), 8.

21. Schmidt, *Free to Work*, 67.

22. Steinberg, *Transformation*, 124.

23. Julia Freeman, 1825, Watchmen's Returns, NYCM.

24. Adler, "Analysis of the Law of Vagrancy," 221.

25. Herndon, "Women of 'No Particular Home,'" 269–89; Kann, *Taming Passion*, 119; Herndon, *Unwelcome Americans*, 17–18.

26. "Overseers of Trenton Appellants against Overseers of Maidenhead," *Reports of Cases Argued and determined in the Supreme Court of New Jersey* (Trenton, 1816).

27. Mark E. Kann, *Punishment, Prisons, and Patriarchy: Liberty and Power in the Early American Republic* (New York: New York University Press, 2005), 80.

28. Ibid. See also "Crime and Punishment," *Women in Early America: Struggle, Survival, and Freedom in a New World*, ed. Dorothy A. Mays (Santa Barbara, CA: ABC-Clio, 2004), 92–94; and Marylynn Salmon, *Women and the Law of Property in Early America* (Chapel Hill: University of North Carolina Press, 1986).

29. Susan Branson, *Dangerous to Know: Women, Crime, and Notoriety in the Early Republic* (Philadelphia: University of Pennsylvania Press, 2013), 61.

30. Kann, *Punishment, Prisons, and Patriarchy*, 208–9.

31. As Michelle Lise Tarter acknowledges, "the names of the same men and women often stud[ded] the intake records of almshouses and jails" (Tarter, *Buried Lives*, 9–11).

32. Meranze, *Laboratories of Virtue*; Manion, *Liberty's Prisoners*, Nicolazzo, "Vagrant Figures."

33. Michel Foucault, *Discipline and Punish: The Birth of the Prison*, trans. A. Sheridan (New York: Vintage, 1977, 1995), 136.

34. Vagrant and black inmates shared the distinction of being housed in cellars, though separately, in the Philadelphia Almshouse, where one prominent physician reported hearing some of the basest "broad slang and low vulgar tales" of his life ("Miscellaneous Intelligence," *Western Journal of the Medical and Physical Sciences*, vol. 7 [Cincinnati, OH, 1834]: 636).

35. Keri Leigh Merritt, "A Vile, Immoral, and Profligate Course of Life: Poor Whites and the Enforcement of Vagrancy Laws in Antebellum Georgia," in *Southern Society and its Transformations, 1790–1860*, ed. S. Delfino (Columbia: University of Missouri Press, 2011), 29.

36. James McCoy and Adrian Allen, 1825, Watchmen's Returns, NYCM.

37. Samuel Hazard, ed., *The Register of Pennsylvania* (Philadelphia, 1831), 100; S. Hazard, *Hazard's Register of Pennsylvania* (Philadelphia, 1836), 160; John F. Watson, *Annals of Philadelphia and Pennsylvania, in the Olden Time* (Philadelphia, 1879), 181–82; For more on how Arch Street's function fits into the larger carceral system in Philadelphia in the early nineteenth century, see Negley K. Teeters, *The Cradle of the Penitentiary: The Walnut Street Jail at Philadelphia, 1773–1835* (Philadelphia: Pennsylvania Prison Society, 1955), 104–8, 113–14.

38. "Sale of Walnut Street Prison," *Hazard's Register of Pennsylvania*, vol. 7 (Philadelphia, 1831), 99.

39. Ibid.

40. Minutes of the Board of Inspectors, 1812–1821.

41. Ibid.

42. Minutes of the Board of Inspectors of the County Prison, 1821–1827, GPP, PCA.

43. Ibid., "Sale of Walnut Street Prison," 99; H. E. Barnes, *Evolution of Penology in Pennsylvania: A Study in American Social History* (Indianapolis: Bobbs-Merrill, 1927), 137; VAG.

44. *Annual Report of the Board of Managers of the Prison Discipline Society*, vol. 1 (Boston, 1830), 362.

45. Ibid., 1:362–63. The infamy of New York City's bridewell has been discussed in Cray, *Paupers and Poor Relief*; and Julie Miller, *Abandoned: Foundlings in Nineteenth-Century New York City* (New York: New York University Press, 2008).

46. H. Niles, "Sept. 29, 1832—Cholera in Arch Street Prison," *Niles' Weekly Register* (Baltimore, 1833), 71.

47. *A Tale of Horror! Giving an Authentic Account of the Dreadful Scenes that took place in the Arch Street Prison* (Philadelphia, 1832), LCP.

48. *Annual Report of the Board of Managers of the Prison Discipline Society*, vol. 5 (Boston, 1830), 363.

49. Ibid.

50. *PI*, 9 November 1832.

51. "On the apartment for Criminals and untried Prisoners in the Arch Street Jail," *Annual Report of the Board of Managers of the Prison Discipline Society* (Boston, 1826), 200.

52. Manion, *Liberty's Prisoners*, 181–82.

53. Peter J. Coleman, *Debtors and Creditors in America: Insolvency, Imprisonment for Debt, and Bankruptcy, 1607–1900* (Madison: State Historical Society of Wisconsin, 1974), xii, 286–87. For more on the history of debt imprisonment in the United States, see Bruce H. Mann, *Republic of Debtors: Bankruptcy in the Age of American Independence* (Cambridge: Harvard University Press, 2009).

54. According to Coleman, this was especially common in Delaware after 1827 (Coleman, *Debtors and Creditors*, 210).

55. This was most likely New York, where she would have gained a legal settlement through her husband, via coverture law, as a result of his property ownership or employment. Examination of Catharine Morrison, 1822, EXPA, 1822–1825. There appears to have been a localized yellow fever epidemic in New York City in the summer of 1820, on the Lower East Side (*Report of the committee of the Medical Society of the City and County of New-York: explanatory of the causes and character of the epidemic fever, which prevailed in Bancker-Street and its vicinity, in the summer and autumn of 1820* [New York, 1820]; Commitment of Catharine Morrison, 1823, VAG, 1822–1827).

56. Almshouse Weekly Admissions and Census, 1827–1833, GPP. The summer of 1832 was not recorded, likely as a result of the cholera epidemic that raged along the East Coast throughout that season. By September, as anxiety over the disease began to abate, it appears that only the bare minimum of vagrants were accepted into the almshouse: twenty-six women and one child, but no men. Vagrants were seen as disease carriers, and newspapers were crediting a vagrant with introducing the epidemic to the city.

57. Robert H. Bremner, *Children and Youth in America: 1600–1865* (Cambridge: Harvard University Press, 1970), 64; Murray and Herndon, "Markets for Children in Early America"; Grubb, "Babes in Bondage?"
58. Clement, *Welfare and the Poor*, 110–11.
59. Commitment of Isaiah White, VAG, 1827–1833.
60. Commitments of Isaiah White and Alexander Bishop, VAG, 1827–1833.
61. Examinations of Isaiah White, EXPA, 1831–1839.
62. Examinations of Mary Porter, EXPA, 1822–1827.
63. Jeremiah Peirsol to Directors of the Poor of Lancaster, 10 January 1827, Letter Book, GPP. Commitments of Mary Porter, VAG, 1822–1827.
64. *New Conductor Generalis*, 367–68.
65. Commitments of Henrietta Blake, VAG, 1822–1827.
66. The court records from these cases are particularly valuable for social historians because their nature necessitates inclusion of the testimony of the convicted petty criminal that is so often silent in the historical record (Habeas Corpus Papers, County Papers, LCHS).
67. John Harkins, Habeas 1836 F003, Habeas Corpus Papers, LCHS.
459. John Purdon, ed., *A digest of the laws of Pennsylvania* (Philadelphia, 1837), 823–24.
68. John Harkins, Habeas 1836 F003, LCHS.
69. As William Novak has explained, "the adjective 'common,'" as used to describe Harkins, was frequently listed on commitment records prior to vagrant, prostitute, or drunkard, and "implied that one need not commit specific illegal acts to be guilty." Allen Steinberg, in his study of criminal justice and police power in nineteenth-century Philadelphia, discovered that "each year the number of vagrancy commitments easily exceeded the number of arrests," possibly suggesting what he describes as "an aldermanic penchant for committing people arrested on other charges as vagrants." It's possible that what Steinberg describes for Philadelphia was happening in Lancaster as well, in Harkins's case. Debt imprisonment was still practiced in some states in the 1830s, despite having been federally banned in 1833. Many debtors would request declarations of insolvency from a city court in lieu of incarceration (see Insolvent Debtors Petitions, PCA; William J. Novak, *The People's Welfare: Law and Regulation in Nineteenth-Century America* (Chapel Hill: University of North Carolina Press, 1996), 168; and Steinberg, *Transformation*, 123). A legislative committee report from 1832 suggested that "the temptation of the costs, it is to be feared, is too frequently the incentive both of the imprisonment and of the release." The committee suggested removing fees and rewards from magistrates' roles in order to prevent improper sentencing, conviction, and especially release practices by magistrates and jail keepers (*Report of the Committee Appointed to Investigate the Local Causes of Cholera in the Arch Street Prison in the City of Philadelphia, 1833* [Philadelphia, 1833], 14–15, HSP).
70. Martha Ann Ramsey, Habeas 1837 F013, LCHS.
71. Ibid. Similar cases are found in New Orleans, where in 1855, a woman named Mary Ann Norman "successfully refuted a charge of vagrancy" by proving "that she had a place to live and, moreover, that she could support herself by honest means" (*Norman, praying for a writ of habeas corpus*, no. 10,498, First District Court of New Orleans, 25 July 1855, cited in Judith K. Schafer, *Brothels, Depravity, and Abandoned*

Women: Illegal Sex in Antebellum New Orleans [Baton Rouge: Louisiana State University Press, 2011], e-book).

72. Steinberg, *Transformation*, 128; Wood Hill, *Their Sisters' Keepers*. As Novak notes, "in addition to open-ended definitions and proofs of criminality, vagrancy statutes also advocated summary judicial procedures patterned after the latitude granted English justices of the peace over the poor" (Novak, *The People's Welfare*, 168).

73. Eliza Henry, Martha Loney, Mary Brown, Habeas 1837 F009, LCHS.

74. Elizabeth Fasnacht, Habeas 1837 F001, LCHS.

75. The connections between vagrancy and illicit sexual activity have been documented extensively by historians such as Christine Stansell, Patricia Cline Cohen, Nicole Hahn Rafter, and Marilyn Wood Hill, especially concerning New York City, where vagrancy laws were designed to cover "five classes of people—prostitutes, habitual drunkards, beggars, "loafers," and the diseased" (Wood Hill, *Their Sisters' Keepers*, 118; Cline Cohen, *Murder of Helen Jewett*; Hahn Rafter, *Partial Justice*).

76. Spencer-Wood, "Feminist Theoretical Perspectives," 115–16.

77. Stansell, *City of Women*, 100.

78. Sarah Cooper, Habeas 1837 F008, LCHS.

79. Steinberg, *Transformation*, 125.

80. Having covered a distance of twelve miles, this amounts to a rate of approximately six cents per mile.

81. Cassey Newman, Habeas 1841 F009. The motivation for such manipulation is clear, with the average daily wage for unskilled male laborers and artisans estimated to have remained well under one dollar around 1850 (the year for which extensive data are available).

82. Commitment of John Kennedy, VAG, 1817–1822. See also the case of Henry Davis, forced into servitude under the 1793 Maryland law allowing for the involuntary indenture of the children of vagrants. In his defense, he asserted his parents' industrious employment to combat their assignation as vagrants. His case was successful and he was released in 1848. Petition of Henry Davis, Register of Wills, 1820–1851 (Petitions and Orders), MSA.

83. Purdon, *Digest*, 823–24.

84. Herndon, *Unwelcome Americans*, 57. And in New York, vagrants' rights to defend themselves were eroded over time, as it was ruled in an 1855 Court of Common Pleas case that the document committing an individual as a vagrant served as the proof that the individual was a vagrant, so long as the convicting magistrate was acting within his jurisdiction when he carried out the arrest (*A Digest of New York Statutes and Reports* [New York, 1884], 567–68; A. Abbott and B. V. Abbott, *Reports of Practice Cases, Determined in the Courts of the State of New York* [New York, 1855], 210–13).

85. Laura F. Edwards has found that the language and legal culture that built and upheld vagrancy laws invited the public to engage with the law intimately in a similar fashion in South Carolina as had occurred in Pennsylvania. This is evident in her discussion of an 1834 South Carolina vagrancy case in which a man was suspected of idleness by men with whom he only occasionally engaged in business. When one neighbor issued a formal complaint against Woodruff, the court handling the case investigated, asking community members about the level of Woodruff's industry. According to the testimony of nearby housewives, the claims against Woodruff were true: he must have

been providing insufficiently for his family, as his wife had recently petitioned neighbors for food so that she and their children would not starve. Woodruff was convicted of vagrancy based on this testimony that he lacked the industrious character to follow through on his duties as husband and father. Edwards's analysis of Woodruff's case demonstrates that, even when comparing communities as starkly different as antebellum Spartanburg County, South Carolina, and Lancaster County, Pennsylvania, the power of the legal culture surrounding concepts of vagrancy transcended geographical and cultural borders. Keri Leigh Merritt asserts that "class functioned as the only universal among southern vagrants," and this argument is clearly applicable across the Mid-Atlantic states. Vagrancy prosecution carried out the systematic designation of pauperism as a criminal status. As Merritt argues, vagrancy laws were used "to lock away anyone who posed a threat" to what she describes as "the southern system." Arguably, it was not a southern value system that vagrancy laws upheld but, rather, a long-standing Anglo-American tradition of legally reinforcing class distinctions and the punitive management of the lower orders. Imprisonment for vagrancy, both in the South and in the North, was a "type of subjective incarceration" that "depriv[ed]" the poor of "personal freedom and bodily liberty" as though it were "a second degree of slavery," in which "class—not race—dictated who could be enslaved." This analogy exaggerates the restraints placed on the personal liberty of criminal paupers and draws a false equivalency between the incarceration of vagrants for periods of time from days (throughout most of the North) up to a few years (in some southern states) with permanent lifetime chattel status (Laura F. Edwards, *The People and Their Peace: Legal Culture and the Transformation of Inequality in the Post-revolutionary South* [Chapel Hill: University of North Carolina Press, 2009]; Merritt, "Vile, Immoral, and Profligate," 28–29).

Notes to Chapter 6

1. *A Tale of Horror!*, 1.
2. Rosenberg, *Cholera Years*, 29; Alan Kraut, *Silent Travelers: Germs, Genes, and the Immigrant Menace* (Baltimore: Johns Hopkins University Press, 1995).
3. Commitments of Jane Welsh and John Welsh, VAG, 1832–1836.
4. John Snow, *On Continuous Molecular Changes, More Particularly in their Relation to Epidemic Diseases* (London, 1853), 28.
5. John Snow, *On the Mode and Communication of Cholera* (London, 1855), 10–11.
6. Ibid., 18.
7. Charles Rosenberg claimed that "there was no doubt in the minds of most observers; the Irish and Negroes seemed its foreordained victims." Despite this, few believed that "the Negro had any racial affinity for the disease" (Rosenberg, *Cholera Years*, 59).
8. Ibid., 103; Catherine McNeur, *Taming Manhattan: Environmental Battles in the Antebellum City* (Cambridge: Harvard University Press, 2014), 267.
9. J. Noble Wilford, "How Epidemics Helped Shape the Modern Metropolis," *New York Times*, 15 April 2008.
10. Philadelphia suffered through cholera epidemics in 1823, 1832, 1849, and 1866. I have chosen to focus on the 1832 epidemic for the rhetorical clarity that records related to it provide on the pathologization of vagrancy, and the intensity of the impact it had on the vagrant prison at Arch Street.

11. Klepp, "Seasoning and Society," 473–506. Singular indicators also arise from time to time, as noted in Julie Miller's study of New York City's foundling children which investigated the naming patterns of such infants that often acted as descriptors of their recent origins: one infant discovered out of doors in the harsh winter of 1838 was given the name Frost (Miller, *Abandoned*, 59).

12. Matthew Carey, *Letters on the Condition of the Poor*, 3rd ed. (Philadelphia, 1836), 5, 7, cited in Clement, *Welfare and the Poor*, 9.

13. In the New Castle County Almshouse, admissions records generally listed information about resident and nonresident admittants separately, but in the following order: name, illness/disease/cause for admission, age, nationality, and length of time spent in the almshouse or else information about release or death.

14. Admission and Discharge Records, 1822–1832, New Castle County, Trustees of the Poor, DPA.

15. Downs, *Sick from Freedom*, 122.

16. This conclusion was drawn from a comparison of the admissions entries for the various hundreds in Delaware's counties, compared to each county's designated sections of entries for "non-residenters" in the admissions ledgers from the 1820s through 1840s, DPA.

17. James Fitzgerald and James Criser, Non-Residenter Admissions, Admissions and Discharge Records, 1833–1850, Paupers' Records, New Castle County Almshouse, DPA.

18. Baltimore's Calverton Almshouse designated origins and residency status in its ledgers, as did Philadelphia and New Jersey's almshouses.

19. Inmates' Property at Death, 1844–1849, GPP.

20. "From the *York Gazette*, July 15," *Lancaster (PA) Journal*, 20 July 1819.

21. James Corsey, Prison Receiving Description Register, Philadelphia Prison System.

22. Commitment of James Coarsey, VAG, 1822–1827; James Corsey, Prison Docket Descriptive Register.

23. *Report of the Committee Appointed to Investigate the Local Causes of Cholera in the Arch Street Prison* (Philadelphia, 1833), 9.

24. Joseph Deyo to Overseers of the Poor of Shawanagunk, June 2, 1824, UCCA.

25. MCR.

26. Examination of Patrick O'Flaherty, EXPA; Patrick O'Flaherty, MCR.

27. Ibid.

28. Examination of Catharine Shearer, EXPA; Catharine Shearer, MCR.

29. Hugh Thompson and William Cane, MCR.

30. Robert Martin, John McGuire, and Catherine Riggins, MCR.

31. Rockman, *Scraping By*, 158; Medical Case Records in the Clinical Ward of the Philadelphia Almshouse, 1824–1825, GPP. For several of the individuals whose case histories are included in this volume, settlement examinations are also extant, making it possible to paint a clearer picture of their lives prior to entering the almshouse.

32. Susan French, "Inmates, Black Women's Cellar," GPP.

33. "City Police," *PPL*, 25 January 1837. As Kathleen Canning has succinctly argued, "people's identities form at the intersection of discourses that define various social roles and the bodily 'experiences of desire and deprivation'" (Canning, *Gender*

History in Practice: Historical Perspectives on Bodies, Class and Citizenship [Ithaca, NY: Cornell University Press, 2006], 87, cited in Higbie, *Indispensable Outcasts*, 19).

34. Brown, *Foul Bodies*, 284.

35. Cresswell, *Tramp in America*, 22–26.

36. Melish, *Disowning Slavery*, 131–32.

37. Also seen in other times and locations, as Frank M. Snowden's study of cholera in late nineteenth-century Italy demonstrates, with "heavy mortality from cholera among the "wandering tribes" of vagrants, huxters, showmen and wayfarers" (Snowden, *Naples in the Time of Cholera, 1884–1911* [Cambridge: Cambridge University Press, 2002], 22).

38. Lawrence C. Feldman, *Citizens without Shelter: Homelessness, Democracy, and Political Exclusion* (Ithaca, NY: Cornell University Press, 2006), 32.

39. Alan Bewell, "'Cholera Cured Before Hand': Coleridge, Abjection, and the "Dirty Business of Laudanum," in *Romanticism and History*, vol. 2 of *Romanticism: Critical Concepts in Literary and Cultural Studies*, ed. M. O'Neill (London: Routledge, 2006), 351–52. As has been discussed previously, and as Sharon Pickering and Leanne Weber explain, "the perceived danger of [vagrants'] uncontrolled mobility was met with measures aimed to prevent free movement, justified "by the belief that poverty, vagrancy, the spread of plague, idleness, immorality, irreligion, and crime were linked together" (Philip Rawlings, *Policing: A Short History* [New York: Willan, 2012], 45, cited in *Borders, Mobility, and Technologies of Control*, ed. Sharon Pickering and Leanne Weber [Dordrecht: Springer, 2006], 5).

40. Alan Bewell, *Romanticism and Colonial Disease* (Baltimore: Johns Hopkins University Press, 2003), 262.

41. Bewell, "Cholera Cured Before Hand," 351–52.

42. Rosenberg, *Cholera Years*, 103; McNeur, *Taming Manhattan*, 267.

43. "North Shields, Dec. 25. 1831," *Guardian* (Manchester), 31 December 1831.

44. According to David Barrie, "prior to 1832 there is little evidence to suggest that the public health risks vagrants posed were an overriding concern . . . despite recurring epidemics" (Barrie, *Police in the Age of Improvement: Police Development and the Civic Tradition in Scotland, 1775–1865* [New York: Routledge, 2008], 194).

45. "From the European Journals," *Philadelphia National Gazette*, 17 March 1832.

46. "Cholera," *Philadelphia National Gazette*, 29 March 1832.

47. *PI*, 6 July 1832.

48. Charles R. Williams, "The Cholera at Quebec," in *Tales: National and Revolutionary* (Providence, RI, 1835), 258.

49. Ibid., 258.

50. Rosenberg, *Cholera Years*, 25.

51. William Baly, *Reports on Epidemic Cholera* (London, 1854), 228.

52. T. H. Buckler, *A History of the Epidemic Cholera at the Baltimore City and County Almshouse, 1849* (Baltimore, 1851), 10, 15.

53. John B. Osborne, "Preparing for the Pandemic: City Boards of Health and the Arrival of Cholera in Montreal, New York, and Philadelphia in 1832," *Urban History Review/Revue d'histoire urbaine* 36, no. 2 (2008): 37. The death tolls for major northeastern cities were as follows: Montreal: 1 in 14 persons, New York: 1 in 47 persons, Philadelphia: 1 in 173 persons, Philadelphia Almshouse: 1 in 13 persons (C. Reynolds,

Albany Chronicles [Albany, 1906]; and Buckler, *A History of Epidemic Cholera at the Baltimore City and County Almshouse*, 5).

54. The official report delivered to the legislature after their requested investigation of the mortality in the prison was carried out concluded that around 75 persons died of cholera in Arch Street between 30 July and 10 August 1832 out of 210 prisoners, a mortality rate of one in three. Other data record 298 prisoners incarcerated in this period, so the rate may be lower, closer to one in four. Other reports, possibly exaggerated, suggest as many as almost one hundred died in one day, "that ever memorable Sunday" (see *A Tale of Horror!*).

55. Rosenberg, *Cholera Years*, 133; Brown, *Foul Bodies*, 284.

56. A few years after the epidemic, an illustrated historical encyclopedia of Philadelphia published by Daniel Bowen in 1839, not even a decade after the crisis, places vagrants' experience with the epidemic at the center of its entry on the disease, emphasizing the significance of the crisis at Arch Street in the public mind (D. Bowen, A *History of Philadelphia* [Philadelphia, 1839], 135–37).

57. Minutes of the Board of Inspectors, November 21, 1798, PCA.

58. Seven percent to be exact ("American Intelligence," in *The Philadelphia Journal of the Medical and Physical Sciences* [Philadelphia, 1824], 245; Manion, *Liberty's Prisoners*, 182).

59. "American Intelligence," 245.

60. The disproportionate loss of life in the Arch Street Jail during the cholera epidemic was not mentioned by Rosenberg in his seminal study *The Cholera Years*, though the assistance rendered by prisoners there during the crisis was noted (Rosenberg, *Cholera Years*, 95).

61. "On the apartment for Criminals and untried Prisoners, in the Arch Street Jail," *Hazard's Register of Pennsylvania* (Philadelphia, 1833), 177.

62. Minutes of the Board of Prison Inspectors of the County Prison, 1827–1835.

63. "On the apartment," 177.

64. Minutes of the Board of Inspectors of the County Prison, 1827–1835.

65. Ibid.

66. *A Tale of Horror!*, 5.

67. "On the apartment," 177–78.

68. A Tale of Horror!, 5.

69. Richard Harlan to John James Audubon, August 1832, cited in Richard Rhodes, *John James Audubon: The Making of an American* (New York: Knopf Doubleday, 2004), 368–70.

70. Jeremiah Peirsol to Directors of Poor of Lancaster County, 18 October 1832, GPP.

71. Though imprisonment for small fines began to be legally phased out around 1800, the incarceration of those owing significant debts was still a common feature on the landscape of the early nineteenth-century United States and was not banned federally until 1833. For further information about early nineteenth-century debt imprisonment and its abolition, see Mann, *Republic of Debtors*.

72. Examination of Patrick Cane, EXPA, 1822–1825.

73. Commitment of Patrick Cane, VAG, 1827–1833.

74. Commitments of Susan Hunter, VAG, 1827–1833.

75. "On the apartment," 177.

76. "For the *National Gazette*," *Philadelphia National Gazette*, 25 October 1832.

77. William E. Watson et al., *The Ghosts of Duffy's Cut: The Irish Who Died Building America's Most Dangerous Stretch of Railroad* (Westport, CT: Greenwood, 2006), 91.

78. Ibid. This anecdote is similar to that related to the sensational deaths of along the railroad at Duffy's Cut, where one man supposedly carrying cholera contagion walked "up to the Valley Creek, near the line of East Bradford and East Caln, where he died" (Samuel Hazard, "The Cholera," *Hazard's Register of Pennsylvania*, vol. 10 [Philadelphia, 1832], 299).

79. Marta Deyrup and M. G. Harrington, eds., *The Irish-American Experience in New Jersey and Metropolitan New York: Cultural Identity, Hybridity, and Commemoration* (Lanham, MD: Rowman and Littlefield, 2013), 177.

80. As Christopher Muller notes, "So tight was the perceived connection between Irishness and disorder that "rowdy, undisciplined behavior in the 1830s was sometimes called "acting Irish" (Muller, "Northward Migration and the Rise of Racial Disparity in American Incarceration, 1880–1950," *American Journal of Sociology* 118, no. 2 [2012]: 293–94).

81. "Progress of the Cholera," *Niles' Weekly Register*, 29 September 1832; Rosenberg, *Cholera Years*, 59.

82. "Progress of the Cholera," *Niles' Weekly Register*, 29 September 1832.

83. As Julio Ramos has noted in discussing the importance of state conceptions of vagrancy in understanding the 1833 epidemic of cholera in Cuba, citizenship was the "category in which the juridical intersects with the medical and cultural technologies intervening in the construction of subjectivity" (Ramos, "A Citizen Body," 188–89).

84. *PI*, 9 November 1832.

85. *Report of the Committee Appointed to Investigate the Local Causes of Cholera in the Arch Street Prison in the City of Philadelphia* (Philadelphia, 1833), LCP.

86. Roberts Vaux, *Notices of the Original, and successive efforts, to improve the discipline of the prison at Philadelphia, and to reform the criminal code of Pennsylvania* (Philadelphia, 1826), 40–41.

87. Vaux, *Notices of the Original, and successive efforts, to improve the discipline of the prison at Philadelphia*, 37.

88. Ibid.

89. Minutes of the Board of County Prison Inspectors, 1827–1835.

90. *Report of the Committee Appointed to Investigate the Local Causes of Cholera* (Philadelphia, 1833), LCP.

91. "On the apartment," 182–83.

92. Pennsylvania's reluctance to abolish imprisonment for debt has at least two potential causes: outright abolition may have seemed inconsequential in light of period adjustments and exemptions introduced to the law in the preceding decades (one of which, for example, banned the imprisonment of women for debts owed), and abolition may have smacked of fraud to mercantilist Pennsylvanians who particularly feared abuse of insolvency declarations by the undeserving (see S. Laurence Shaiman, "The History of Imprisonment for Debt and Insolvency Laws in Pennsylvania as They Evolved from the Common Law," *American Journal of Legal History* 4, no. 3 [1960]: 205–25).

93. *Third Annual Report of the Board of Inspectors of the Philadelphia County Prison* (Harrisburg, 1850), 441.

94. Ibid., 441–70. Philadelphia did not open a house of industry until 1846 (see Clement, *Welfare and the Poor*).

95. "Fourth Annual Report of the Board of Inspectors of the Philadelphia County Prison," *Journal of the Senate of Pennsylvania*, vol. 2 (1851), 421.

96. *Third Annual Report of the Board of Inspectors of the Philadelphia County Prison*, 440.

97. According to Burden, "in 1848 . . . the influence of the vagrant male apartment operated on the convict apartment; and in the female prison, where convicts and vagrants are under the same roof, the mortality was the greatest" ("Fourth Annual Report of the Board of Inspectors of the Philadelphia County Prison," *Journal of the Senate of Pennsylvania*, vol. 2 [1851], 421).

98. Nicolazzo, "Vagrant Figures," 94.

99. *Report of the Committee Appointed to Investigate the Local Causes of Cholera*, 17.

100. Ibid., 19.

101. A lot of these debates have been recurring in recent decades, as incarceration for non-payment of court fees and fines reaches new heights. As law professor Alan White described this process, "If, in effect, people are being incarcerated until they pay bail, and bail is being used to pay their debts, then they're being incarcerated to pay their debts" (Kevin Drum, "Debtors' Prison is Back!, *Mother Jones*, 14 December 2011; Scott Forsyth, "Not Paying a Fine Should not Mean Jail Time," *New York Daily Record*, 31 March 2015).

Notes to Conclusion

1. "Fourth Annual Report of the Board of Inspectors of the Philadelphia County Prison, 1850," *Journal of the Sixty First House of Representatives of the Commonwealth of Pennsylvania*, vol. 2 (Harrisburg, 1851), 389.

2. Schmidt, *Free to Work*, 65–66, 86–88.

3. Yet discussions of poverty in eighteenth- and nineteenth-century America still hinge on the dichotomy between the deserving and undeserving poor (David Graeber, *Debt: The First 5,000 Years* [New York: Melville House, 2011], 388–89).

4. These statements are derived from a helpful comment offered by Richard Kent Evans at the Barnes Club Conference at Temple University in 2016.

5. This suggestion has been made previously by Ira Berlin in "Southern Free People of Color," 10; and in Khalil Gibran Muhammad, *The Condemnation of Blackness: Race, Crime, and the Making of Modern Urban America* (Cambridge: Harvard University Press, 2011), 1–14, 35–87. For continuity of laws regulating the movement of the poor and people of color, see Gamble, "African Americans, Mobility, and the Law," 2; Goluboff, *Vagrant Nation*, 209, 11; DePastino, *Citizen Hobo;* and Cresswell, *Tramp in America*.

6. Hirota, *Expelling the Poor*, 43–45. Even Hirota argues, however, that pauper removal was a "dead letter . . . by the early nineteenth century," which was clearly not the case in Pennsylvania. "Trump administration circulates more draft immigration restrictions," *Washington Post*, January 31, 2017. See also Emma Green, "First, They Excluded the Irish," *Atlantic*, February 2, 2017.

Index

Abolition, 9, 85, 91, 105–6, 109, 200n105, 208n131
Abolitionists, 92, 102–5
African Americans, 9, 25–27, 41, 56, 93–95, 109–11, 141, 159, 184n37, 187n80, 188n98, 191n35, 193n73, 198n59, 200n105, 201nn5, 7, 12, 202nn13, 15, 17, 21, 203n30, 206n96, 207n107; in almshouses, 53, 70, 81, 93, 100, 184n37; citizenship, 27–29, 101; in jail and prison populations, 53; and mobility, 9, 26, 41, 53–54, 81, 85–90, 93–94, 102–9, 159
Almshouses, 8–12, 18–20, 22, 25, 33, 73–82, 192–93n71, 197n31, 205n77, 210n31; Calverton Almshouse (Baltimore), 53, 55, 63, 215n18; inmates within, 29, 34, 43–44, 48–49, 65–69, 80–81, 84, 88, 93–94, 96, 99, 124, 126–27, 140–41, 149, 167, 171, 184–85n39, 204n63, 205n75; Lancaster, Pennsylvania Almshouse, 70, 93, 126–27; New Castle, Delaware Almshouse, 49, 53, 95, 100, 138, 215n13; New York City Almshouses, 69, 119; Philadelphia Almshouse, 40, 43, 52, 75, 93, 97–98, 120, 122, 124, 133, 140, 148, 167, 171, 184–85n39, 188n101, 199n77, 205n75; populations within, 52–53, 89, 95–100; and transients, 37–45, 47–50, 52–53, 55–56, 59–71, 115, 137–42, 149; Ulster County, New York Almshouse, 66, 73, 77, 96; vagrants within, 19, 73, 120–27, 135, 171, 185n39, 210n34
Articles of Confederation, 7, 14–15, 25, 158, 183n23

Baltimore, MD, 22, 39, 41–45, 53, 55, 63, 145–46, 150
Beggars, 2, 9, 17, 20, 25, 36, 45, 90, 104, 130, 144, 184n36, 199n95, 213n75
Begging, 22, 29–32, 96, 106–7, 114, 117–18, 130, 184n33
Black Codes, 9, 85–86, 159–60

Canadian provinces, 38, 40, 43, 76, 144
Capitalism, 3–4, 6–7, 25, 42, 83, 129, 175nn15, 16, 178n26
Caribbean, 45, 104, 182n2, 218n83
Children, 18, 28, 55, 61, 67, 74, 97–99, 102, 117, 119–21, 124–26
Cholera, 12, 134–55, 159, 211n56, 214n10, 216n37, 217nn54, 60, 218n78, 85
Citizenship, 6, 11, 14–17, 25–29, 37, 150, 158–59, 177n22, 182n9, 183n23, 186n68, 187n70, 189–90n6, 218n83
Civil War, 7, 9, 86, 102, 104, 180n44
Cleanliness, 34, 134, 150–51, 188n103
Clothing, 1, 13, 28, 30, 32, 47, 49, 52, 80–81, 94–95, 101, 118, 130, 132, 139–41, 145, 151, 153, 167, 204n68
Colonial laws, 9, 16–18, 20, 23, 46, 62, 119, 137, 159

Colonization, 7, 104–5
Community, 3–4, 6, 12, 56, 61, 82, 87, 158, 183n23, 213n85; entitlement to labor of the poor, 106, 114
Constables, 31, 63–67, 102, 127–28, 130, 132, 177n23; duties of, 21–23, 46, 64, 71–78, 112–19
Criminal justice, 80, 114, 212n69
Cuba, 182n2, 218n83

Debt imprisonment, 89, 101, 115, 148, 152
Debtors, 81, 121–24, 129, 154
Disease, 12, 134–47, 149–54, 159, 187n80, 211n56, 214n7, 215n13, 217n56

Economic depression, 3, 16, 19, 51, 57, 60, 77, 197n24, 199n97
Emancipation, 9, 11, 69, 81, 84–111, 158
Emma Sands vs. The People, 131
Employment, 3, 6, 9, 19–21, 30, 41–50, 53–54, 75, 98–99, 129, 132, 141, 175n16, 213n82; lack of employment, 3, 19–21, 27, 85, 112, 127–29, 175, 184n33, 194n89
Enslaved people, 2, 6–7, 9, 11–12, 14–15, 36, 54, 69–71, 81, 84–86
Examinations of paupers (settlement examinations), 24–25, 47–48, 64, 181n54, 190n22, 199n77; population data available within, 52–53, 93; as sources, 10–11, 43, 88, 148–49
Exposure (environmental), 12, 135, 137–38, 140–42

Food, 13, 17, 22–23, 30–32, 41, 61, 63, 79, 204n68, 209n19, 214–15n85
Forced migration, 4, 7, 9, 11, 45, 58–83, 104–5, 160
Fugitive slave laws, 7, 53–54, 91–92
Fugitive slaves, 2, 7, 9, 11, 86–97, 100–103, 182n11, 202n13, 203nn30, 44, 204nn48, 53, 205n69

Gender: in population data, 50, 54–55; as relates to coverture law, 59, 62, 68, 82; as relates to policing, 117; 189–90n6. *See also* Women
Gradual abolition, 9, 22, 69, 81, 85–86, 93, 105
Guardians of the Poor, 21, 78–79, 81, 88, 122, 209n18; duties of, 10, 33–35, 39, 61–65, 99, 105–9. *See also* Overseers of the Poor

Habeas corpus, 113, 115, 127–33
Haiti, 84, 200n1
Health, 12, 28, 67, 74, 79, 107, 123, 135, 139–55
Hoboes, 6, 8, 25, 159
Homelessness, 17–18, 29–31, 46, 55, 86–88, 97, 130–32, 183n22, 186n68, 199n97, 209n19
Huntington, NY, 53, 64, 66, 96–97, 108–9

Idleness, 18, 28, 30, 42, 56, 90, 105, 116, 123, 128–30, 152, 157
Immigration, 40, 51, 60–61, 72; Irish immigrants, 44–45, 49, 51, 54, 61, 69–70, 98, 126, 144, 149, 150, 187n80, 206n101, 214n7, 218n80
Indentured servants, 29, 48, 84–87, 92, 95–100, 167
Indentured servitude, 16, 18–19, 29, 44, 62, 67, 95–100, 116, 124–25, 167
Ireland, 38, 43, 45, 51, 54, 68–69, 72, 126, 140

Jails, 8, 10, 20, 66, 115, 126, 139, 152; Arch Street Jail/Arch Street Prison, 12, 80, 89, 115, 120–24, 133, 134, 136–37, 139, 143–54, 168, 169, 210nn31, 37, 214n10, 212n69, 217nn54, 56, 60; bridewells, 122, 151; conditions within, 80, 120–24, 136–39, 146–56; inmates within, 20, 25, 32, 52, 73, 104, 115, 118–26, 128–33, 147; Walnut Street Jail, 121, 123, 146
Jim Crow (character), 90–91
Justices of the Peace, 31–33, 58, 60, 64, 69–71, 105–9, 124, 127–29, 167; duties of, 10, 20–23, 72–76, 112–18

Kingston, NY, 20, 32, 73, 139, 167

Labor, 2–6, 8–11, 18–19, 22–23, 25, 27, 30–31, 37, 40–46, 71, 75, 133, 175nn14, 16, 176n16, 78n26, 186nn 65,66, 188n98, 202n18, 213n81; as community resource, 106, 114, 129–32; labor contracts, 9, 99–100, 102–4, 112–13, 202n17; labor market, 3, 42, 83, 86, 124–25, 205n70; labor status, 38, 62, 84–88, 93, 95, 97, 100, 110–11, 114, 158, 180n47, 188n102, 202n17, 204–5nn68, 70
Larceny, 22, 31–32, 167, 188n95
Lumpenproletariat, vagrants as, 80, 91, 110, 199n95

Magistrates, 13, 21, 25, 33–34, 64, 116, 127, 144, 212n69, 213n84
Manumission, 22, 84–87, 93, 105–11
Medical care, 47, 49, 50, 63–64, 67, 77, 124, 135, 137, 139–40
Migration, 16, 35, 36–38, 40–41, 48, 51, 84–85
Mobility, 2–10, 14–16, 27–34, 189–90n6; and African Americans, 84–111; laws governing, 17–25; patterns of movement among mobile poor, 38–45, 50–56, 122; physical impact of mobility for the poor, 134–45; restrictions on, 15, 29–30, 58–62, 78
Morality, 4, 8, 17, 116, 118–19, 126, 131, 137, 142, 154

New England, 7, 59–60, 178n25, 195n4
New York Association for Improving the Condition of the Poor, 117–18
New York City, 19, 24, 38, 42, 55, 63, 76 77, 82, 119, 122, 132, 134, 146–47; poverty in, 19–20, 24, 32, 53, 117
New York v. Miln, 60–61, 92, 204n48

Orders of removal (warrants for removal of paupers), 64–66, 69–72, 78, 126, 140
Overseers of the Poor, 60, 71–72, 74–75, 88–90, 99, 195n8, 207n118; duties of, 23, 33, 39–40, 63–64, 81; and manumission, 105–9. *See also* Guardians of the Poor
Overseers of the Poor of South Brunswick v. Overseers of the Poor of East Windsor, 70–71
Overseers of the Poor of Upper Freehold v. Overseers of the Poor of Hillsborough, 107–8

Panic of 1819, 3, 18–19, 51
Panic of 1837, 3, 19, 57, 117
Pauperism, 8, 15, 45, 51–52, 73, 89
Paupers, 167, 170–71. *See also* Almshouses; Mobility; Pauperism; Poor laws; Poor relief; Poverty; Vagrants; Removal of paupers; Subsistence
Peirsol, Jeremiah, 34, 70
Pennsylvania Abolition Society, 105
Pennsylvania Constitutional Convention, 26–29, 92
Pennsylvania Society for the Promotion of Public Economy, 31, 41, 50

Personal industry, 30, 106, 128, 159
Philadelphia, 38, 42, 51–54, 75, 89, 113, 119, 121, 123, 146; policing in, 21, 212n69; poverty in, 19, 22, 31, 51–54. *See also* Almshouses; Arch Street Jail; Eastern State Penitentiary; Vagrants
Police, 2, 17, 30–33, 40, 47, 55, 94, 182n2, 189n4, 191n43, 192–93n71, 193n73, 209nn7, 19, 212n69; discretion in policing, 5, 12, 20, 23, 25, 31–33, 67, 69, 73, 89, 101, 112–15, 119–20, 122, 125, 127, 142, 151, 160; police power, 21, 60, 90–92, 116–18, 145; policing, 4–5, 8, 11–12, 15, 18, 46, 61–62, 82–83, 86–87, 101–2, 104, 125, 127, 130, 133, 142, 154, 157–60, 202n19, 208n6; of vagrants, 2, 21, 114
Poor laws, 3, 14–18, 26, 31–32, 55, 58–62, 69, 73–74, 77, 86, 91, 107–10, 159; English origins of poor laws, 4, 9, 114, 174n8; in Delaware, 16, 18, 22, 42–43, 53, 62, 101–4, 116, 138, 150, 215n16; in Maryland, 16, 18, 22, 41, 43–45, 62–63, 90, 101–4; in New Jersey, 16, 46, 59, 62, 73, 90, 105, 107, 109–10, 150, 159; in New York, 16, 18, 24–25, 49, 51, 58–69, 71–77, 124, 131; in Pennsylvania, 15–16, 18, 21, 26–29, 52, 89, 124, 130
Poor relief, 16, 30–31, 41–44, 49, 60, 74–83, 160, 175nn14, 16, 177n25, 179n32, 193nn83, 195, 196, 4, 9, 10, 13, 198n70, 200n105; administration, 18–19, 24–27, 33–37, 39, 50–52, 62–66, 72, 133; origins of American, 3, 5–9, 137; recipients of, 19, 54–56, 59, 72, 97–98, 105–7, 125
Poorhouses. *See* Almshouses
Posse comitatus, 116–18
Poverty, 2–4, 7–9, 13–17, 36–38, 45–57, 61–62; criminalization of, 4, 32, 56, 110, 128, 159, 177n20; deserving and undeserving poor, 7–8, 56, 117, 179n41, 219n3. *See also* Almshouses; Mobility; Pauperism; Poor laws; Poor relief; Removal of paupers; Subsistence; Vagrancy; Vagrants
Prigg v. Pennsylvania, 86–87, 91, 110, 204n48
Prisons, 127, 157, 168, 169, 177nn20, 23, 184–85n39, 193nn71, 73, 205n77, 209nn18, 19, 214n10, 217n54, 219nn97, 101; Bellevue Penitentiary, 53; conditions, 80, 134–37, 139–40, 142, 145–54;

Prisons (continued): Eastern State Penitentiary, 123, 146, 150–52; management, 66, 90, 117, 136, 139, 147–48; Maryland Penitentiary, 22, 44–45; populations within, 52–54, 59–60, 82, 89, 104, 120–27, 168–69; prisoners, 2, 11, 40, 46–47, 115–16

Prostitution, 55–56, 117–18, 130–32

Punishment, 31, 33, 42, 73, 89, 91, 130, 154, 157–59; corporal punishment, 22–24, 58–59; of vagrancy, 6, 11–13, 15, 17–25, 30, 52, 98, 102, 116

Racial issues, 5, 9, 19–20, 26–27, 84–111, 118, 138, 159, 191n35, 202nn16, 21, 204n68, 213n85

Reform, 7, 28, 33, 51, 73–75, 120, 123, 153–54, 160

Removal of paupers, 2, 4, 7–8, 16–17, 19, 23–25, 41, 49, 52, 57, 86, 179n39, 195–96nn4, 9, 196nn10, 13, 197n24, 199n77, 200n105, 219n6; experiences of, 58, 64–71, 78–81; and fugitive slave law, 90–92; process and practice of, 58–78, 119; and slavery, 108–9

Resistance, 63, 65, 66, 88, 99, 127, 133, 189n3

Runaway servants, 2, 14, 86, 97, 100–101, 121, 158

Sailors, 1–2, 46, 69, 84, 119, 141, 173n4

Settlement (legal settlement), 42–45, 48–53, 70, 81–82, 119, 157, 175n16, 183nn21, 23, 195n4, 196nn9, 10, 13; definitions of, 2–3; and former slaves and servants, 85–86, 91, 98, 102, 108–10; laws relating to, 6–11, 16, 13–35, 47, 68, 119; and pauper removal, 58–65, 68, 71–79

Sexual behaviors, 55–56, 131–32, 185n40, 213n75

Slavery, 86, 88, 91, 93–94, 102–3, 106, 108–9, 133, 180n47, 200n105, 201n7, 202n21, 206n96, 213–14n85

Slaves. See Enslaved people

Society for the Prevention of Pauperism in New York, 3, 19, 39, 71

Subsistence, 4, 6, 29–31, 38, 41–43, 82–83, 86, 89, 103–4, 107, 141, 167, 178n26, 179n32, 188nn95, 98; achieved through illegal activity, 30–33, 108, 114; achieved through poor relief, 15; achieved through wage labor, 43, 45–46, 83; migration, 38, 42, 52, 56, 82, 92. See also Visible means of support

Suffrage, 26–29

Taxes, 16, 18–19, 25, 42–43, 58, 61–63, 68, 105, 175n16, 192n64

Tramps, 6, 8, 25, 50, 52, 55, 159

Transiency. See Mobility

Vagabonds, 6, 15, 17, 20–21, 28, 46, 60, 84–85, 91, 110

Vagrancy: defined, 2–10, 13–26, 80, 157–59; in art and culture, 90–91, 144, 181n1; and emancipation, 86, 91, 92, 104–11; and gender, 54–55, 68; and mobility, 13–15, 37, 82; and pauper removal, 71–78, 127; and public policing, 116–20; and race, 85–95, 100–120; and slavery, 85, 92, 97, 104; as strolling, 29, 46, 49, 119, 122, 124, 183n26, 188n98; as wandering, 7, 13, 17, 20, 21, 26, 31, 36, 44–45, 49, 55–56, 82, 108, 122, 139, 145, 194n87, 216n37

Vagrancy laws, 4–6, 9, 11, 13, 17, 13–35, 106, 114, 177nn20, 23, 183nn22, 24, 185nn40, 57, 208n6, 209n19, 213n75, 213–14n85; English origins of vagrancy laws, 137, 142; in Delaware, 22, 102, 116; in Maryland, 22, 101–2; in New Jersey, 23, 46, 119; in New York, 19–20, 25, 119, 131–32; in Pennsylvania, 19–21, 112, 116, 119, 152

Vagrants: in almshouses, 25, 120–27; associations with disease, 12, 134–37, 142–55; overlap with pauper population, 11–35, 64, 100, 148; punishment and incarceration of, 20–25, 44, 46–47, 52, 54–55, 98, 149; resistance to policing and punishment, 127–33; runaway slaves as, 86–95, 97; as wanderers, 2, 14, 30, 87, 92, 138, 189n6

Veterans, 44, 46, 54, 69–70, 125, 140, 191n39

Virginia, 85, 101, 104

Visible means of support (visible means of subsistence), 13, 20, 30–32, 102–4, 112, 116 117, 130, 142, 208n131. See also Subsistence

Warning (out) of paupers, 7, 59, 119, 188n98, 195n9

Washington, DC, 116, 178n25, 205n77,

Watchmen, 21, 31–34, 46–48, 64, 67, 113–19, 121–24, 128, 142, 177n23, 209n18 and 19,

Welfare. *See* Poor relief
Whites: poor, 19, 25, 52, 56, 86–88, 91–92, 95, 102–4, 109, 138, 180n47, 187n80, 188n98, 200n105, 201n5, 202n13; and racial antipathy, 22, 53, 87, 150
Women, 31, 74, 167–69, 190n6, 191n35, 193nn73, 74, 77, 194n88, 194n89, 202nn17, 21, 211n56, 218n92; as paupers, 24, 52–53, 55–56, 58; as relates to coverture law, 68–69, 82, 120; as relates to gendered policing, 55–56, 117, 119, 130–32; as vagrants, 11, 28, 52, 54, 119–20, 122–25, 147–48. *See also* Gender
Workhouses, 8, 73–74

Yates, John Van Ness, 74–75
Yellow fever, 124, 142, 146, 211n55

About the Author

Kristin O'Brassill-Kulfan is an instructor of history at Rutgers University.

www.ingramcontent.com/pod-product-compliance
Lightning Source LLC
Chambersburg PA
CBHW021845090426
42811CB00033B/2147/J